Thrive

10 Commandments for 20-Somethings to Live the Best-Life-Possible

Jeffrey J. Froh

HUMAN TOUCH PRESS

New York

HUMAN TOUCH PRESS

New York

thrive10commandments.com

Dedication

To my adjoining puzzle piece, Cara,
for still loving me even after my long bike ride.
To my "Golden Retriever," James,
for waking me at 5 am.
To my genetic clone, Julianne,
for signing "low-platformed people" like me.
To my future rebel, _____,
for making doubters believe.

To my pen pal, Professor William Thieben,
for keeping the human touch alive.
3/28/1935-4/15/2021

PERMISSIONS

* Deacon Jean Cantave and Deacon Allan Longo, thank you for giving me permission to use your photograph.

* Brian Cirillo and New York 360 Tours & Digital Media, thank you for taking and giving me permission to use your photographs of my tattoos.

* Stephen Gorchov, Associate Director of Athletics for Communications at Hofstra University, thank you for giving me permission to use the Hofstra alumnus photograph of William Thieben.

* Excerpt(s) from HOW THE GRINCH STOLE CHRISTMAS! by Dr. Seuss, TM & copyright © Dr. Seuss Enterprises, L.P. 1957, renewed 1985. Used by permission of Random House Children's Books, a division of Penguin Random House LLC. All rights reserved.

* Gianna Caponera, Joseph Corrado, Ashleigh Garretson, and Mairead Ryan, thank you for giving me permission to use your interviews and photographs. Gianna, thank you also for giving me permission to reprint your poem, *Reclaiming Freedom*, and your letter to me.

* Brian Stieglitz and the East Meadow Herald, thank you for giving me permission to reprint the article, *Strong is Beautiful: A Woman Reclaims Her Health with E.M. Trainer.* Copyright © 2019 Richner Communications, Inc.

* Capitol Christian Music Group, thank you for giving me permission to reprint lyrics from NF's song *Green Lights*.

* Mario Anzuoni and Reuters News & Media INC, thank you for giving me permission to use the photograph of NF.

* Frederick Soviero, Director of Grounds at Hofstra University, thank you for giving me permission to use the photograph of the tulips.

* Thank you to the National Park Service for giving me permission to use the photograph of the bird and fog.

* Kate Hennessy, thank you for giving me permission to use the photograph of Dorothy Day.

* Hal Leonard LLC, thank you for letting me reprint the lyrics for *The Rainbow Connection*. Words and music by Paul Williams and Kenneth L. Ascher © 1979 Fuzzy Muppet Songs. All rights reserved. Used by permission.

* Thank you, St. Catherine University Archives, for giving me permission to use Ade Bethune's artwork of St. Joseph.

* Professor William Thieben, thank you for giving me permission to use your photographs and for reprinting your letter to me, your essay, *A Philosophical Dilemma*, and your lyrics, *High Tech Blues*.

* Keara Durand, thank you for giving me permission to reprint your letter to me and use your photograph.

TABLE OF CONTENTS

Dear Reader,

Many people meander through life. They avoid asking the hard questions and shy from the mirror of truth, unknowingly trading meaning for ignorance. Eventually, something festers inside. An unease about who they are—and who they can be. They struggle bridging these discrepant selves. Despair grows. Pain deepens. Suffering compounds. I've seen this turmoil with the thousands of emerging adults I've taught and counseled. They have good hearts. They're trying. They want to thrive. But, they're confused.

Like many 20-somethings, I was, too. Growing up, I was severely abused and often bullied and single. I covered my insecurities with anger and perfectionism. Eventually, I developed panic attacks, became depressed, and met my Mr. Hyde: bipolar II disorder. During this darkness, I tried numbing my pain with "cultural Kool-Aid." I thought pleasure was the answer; it wasn't. I thought approval was the answer; it wasn't. I thought success was the answer; it wasn't. Thriving, thus, remained elusive. Like mastering chess, I first had to learn the rules of the game. I then had to learn how to defend, how to attack—and how to think like the Enemy. After almost 25 years and with God's grace, I finally know when—and where—to move my pieces. Checkmate.

In this book, I'll teach you how to thrive. While other approaches to thriving exist, this one has worked for countless others and me. I hope it works for you, too. Rejoice. Today starts anew. No more coasting. No more drifting. No more snoozing. Lift the shade, open the window, and welcome the light.

Best,

Jeffrey J. Froh

PROLOGUE

"...A sower went out to sow. And as he sowed, some seed fell on the path, and birds came and ate it up. Some fell on rocky ground, where it had little soil. It sprang up at once because the soil was not deep, and when the sun rose it was scorched, and it withered for lack of roots. Some seed fell among thorns, and the thorns grew up and choked it. But some seed fell on rich soil, and produced fruit, a hundred or sixty or thirtyfold." — Matthew, 13:3-8

One Sunday Mass, Deacon Jean, a clergyman at my church, stressed keeping God's 10 Commandments. "Keeping the Commandments sets us free," he concluded. Something in me stirred. I pondered it for days. Rules, I thought, suffocate and restrict us. Set us free? It seemed paradoxical. The following week, I asked Deacon Jean about his counterintuitive message. In his cool, charming Haitian accent, and with a warm, radiant smile, he said, "Keeping God's Commandments protects us from sin. And, when we're free from sin, we can be all God created us to be." Wow. That hit hard. I got it. Violating God's Commandments creates pain and chaos; it's imprisoning. Keeping God's Commandments, however, creates joy and order; it's liberating. Following rules, therefore, provides freedom—and helps us thrive.

With His 10 Commandments, God created the original and author-itative guide for living the best-life-possible. The 10 commandments to thrive map onto His; modeling the master planner and divine architect made sense. God's Commandments and the commandments to thrive, however, are ordered differently. I'm sure God had His reasons. I have mine (see *The Skeleton* on the next page).[1] Keeping earlier command-ments to thrive facilitates keeping later commandments to thrive. So, ini-tially grind. Dig deep. Figure it out. I can't promise you admittance into Heaven. But, following the commandments to thrive will set you free to realize your potential, fostering a love for living. As a seed planted in rich soil, with time, nourishment, and the Son you'll later bear psychologi-cal fruit—a hundred or sixty or thirtyfold. I'll now explain how God's 10 Commandments and the 10 commandments to thrive connect, present-ing them in my prescribed order for living your best-life-possible.

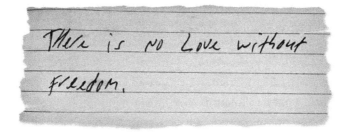

This is an excerpt from my Mass journal.
I've sprinkled them throughout this book.

1 This was first the "Theoretical Framework." But, that's too academic. Then, it was "The Heart." This would be appealing, catchy, and cute. Something, however, seemed wrong. Also, my original model for thriving had three tiers. The 10 commandments to thrive comprised the first tier. The three domains to thrive (i.e., personal, social, and spiritual) comprised the second tier. Finally, overall thriving comprised the third tier. Again, I knew something was wrong. My conceptualization of thriving was more nuanced; however, I couldn't articulate the problem. As stated in this prologue, I theorized that keeping earlier commandments to thrive facilitates keeping later commandments to thrive. Yet, I couldn't visualize it. My then 12-year-old son, James, and I discussed this one day at the bus stop. He said, "Daddy, calling it 'The Heart' doesn't really make sense. The heart gives us life. But, it doesn't provide structure to our body. The skeleton does. Also, I know you think everything leads up to mastering our mission and that spiritual stuff is the most important. So, wouldn't it make sense for your model to be vertical, with each commandment linked to its own area of thriving? Then, everything could build up to mastering mission and then that would finally lead to *overall* thriving." James, you're a gentleman and a scholar. I'll follow you anywhere, sir.

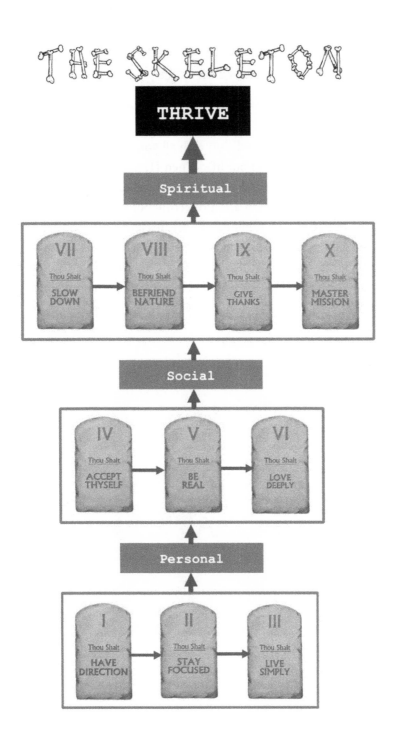

I am the Lord your God:
You shall not have strange gods before me.

The Pharisees tested Jesus, asking Him which Commandment in the law is greatest. Jesus said, "You shall love the Lord, your God, with all your heart, with all your soul, and with all your mind" (Matthew, 22:37). God desires center stage of our life. When He is center stage, we act holy. When He isn't, we act sinfully. Giving God the starring role, however, is tough. It requires nurturing and protecting our faith while rejecting opposition. The same with fulfilling our dreams and mastering our mission. After surrendering to God and waiting to discover His mission for us, we must protect our priorities and dismiss trivial demands. If not, our dreams will remain dreams—and our mission will remain unknown and incomplete.

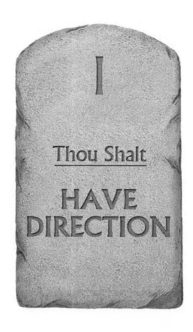

You shall not kill.

God forbids murder. Most people, however, are killers. We get distracted. We forget what matters. We then kill our time and widgets, wasting them on frivolous activities and pleasing others.[2] Like many murderers, we experience first blood with small game. Exercising dies. Sleeping dies. Praying dies. Bloodthirsty, we then kill the biggest game: relationships. Unless stopped, we keep killing. Creating lives filled with exhaustion, chaos, despair, and loneliness. God warned against this. "Beloved, I urge you as aliens and sojourners to keep away from worldly desires that wage war against the soul" (1 Peter, 2:11). Stop killing your most precious resources. Start guarding them.

---

2 A joule is the standard unit of work or energy. A widget is a small gadget or mechanical device with an unknown name. Therefore, while "joule" is a more accurate term for "energy," I use "widget(s)" because it makes my friend, Matt, laugh.

You shall not covet your neighbor's goods.

Envy and avarice are covetous desires. They drive immorality, create pain, and impede discipleship. Envy especially should be banished from our hearts because through it death entered the world. God tries protecting us from these sins by providing everything we need. "Can any of you by worrying add a single moment to your life-span? Why are you anxious about clothes? Learn from the way the wild flowers grow. They do not work or spin. But I tell you that not even Solomon in all his splendor was clothed like one of them" (Matthew, 6:27-29). Stop emulating models, musicians, and movie stars. Start emulating Jesus. Stick to the basics. Less is more.

You shall not take the name of the Lord your God in vain.

Jesus' name "is above every name" (Philippians, 2:9). Whatever His disciples asked in His name was done—including expelling demons, curing the sick, and raising the dead. Thus, we must honor God's name. We must also, however, honor our name. Sadly, we don't. We routinely call ourselves "stupid," "loser," or "moron" for mishaps. We're even nastier when we don't get things that define our worth. Especially when that "thing" is others' approval. When God created us, He created a masterpiece. "I praise you, so wonderfully you made me; wonderful are your works!" (Psalm 139:14). Therefore, acknowledge your worth. Replace criticism with compassion. Hate with love. Judgment with acceptance.

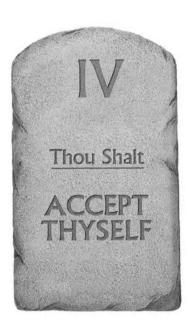

You shall not bear false witness
against your neighbor.

This Commandment forbids lying to deceive or speaking unjustly against our neighbor. If we were honest, though, we'd admit we often lie. We lie to our family. We lie to our friends. We lie to our colleagues. We even lie to ourselves. Yet, God commands us to be truthful. "Lying lips are an abomination to the Lord, but those who are truthful are his delight" (Proverbs, 12:22). We're petrified of exposing our true selves because vulnerability makes us feel insecure and weak. Longing to belong, we then wear our costumes, play our character, and deliver our performance. We want connection. Yet, we're disconnected from the person most responsible for our connection: ourselves.

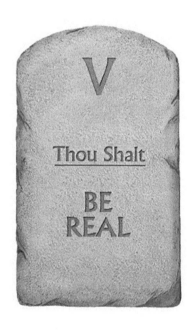

You shall not commit adultery.

Adultery is an injustice. It breaks the commitment between spouses, violates the victim's rights, and undermines the marital contract. Our sex-obsessed culture—in which naked bodies abound—might be straining our commitment to each other and weakening our fidelity. Ignore pop culture. Ignore marketers. Get your sex ed from God. "Love is patient, love is kind. It is not jealous, [love] is not pompous, it is not inflated, it is not rude, it does not seek its own interests, it is not quick-tempered, it does not brood over injury, it does not rejoice over wrongdoing but rejoices with the truth. It bears all things, believes all things, hopes all things, endures all things" (1 Corinthians, 13:4-7). Be honest. Be faithful. Be loving.

Remember to keep holy the Lord's Day.

God created the heavens and Earth in six days and rested on the seventh day. God doesn't need rest—He's God! He created the Sabbath for us. To pause. To recharge. To sit with Him in silence. "Come to me, all you who labor and are burdened, and I will give you rest" (Matthew, 11:28). When we stop, unplug, and listen to God, we discover our mission. When we don't, we become drained, indecisive, and withdrawn. Ultimately remaining confused and burning out. This isn't what God meant by a "burnt offering." Resist the cultural ADHD. Sleep deprivation doesn't signify success—it signifies masochism. Rest your mind. Rest your soul. Rest in God.

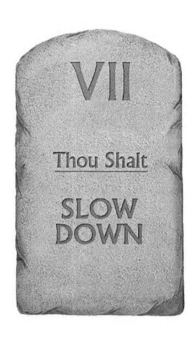

Honor your father and your mother.

God commands that we honor and respect our parents. That we always care for them. Similarly, we should honor, respect, and care for our communal omnipresent parent: nature. "For everything created by God is good, and nothing is to be rejected when received with thanksgiving" (1 Timothy, 4:4). Like any loving mother, nature rests between the divine and human. She's kind, generous, supportive, and nurturing. A good son or daughter, we should sit with her. Silently. Holding her hand, appreciating her beauty, listening to her stories, and internalizing her wisdom. Time with nature is restorative. We think clearer. We feel peaceful. We hear God whispering to us our mission.

You shall not covet your neighbor's wife.

God believes sexual desire for someone besides your spouse is immoral. It injures the marriage bond and, when taken too far, can become an idolatrous sin. Sex helps forge a spiritual union between spouses. Sex, therefore, is sacred. It's a divine gift—like life. "For in him were created all things in heaven and on earth, the visible and the invisible...all things were created through him and for him" (2 Colossians, 1:16). Life becomes more cherished, significant, and holy when considered a gift. Gratitude for life fuels our passion for helping others, doing God's work, and fulfilling our destiny. Therefore, don't covet your neighbor's wife. Don't covet your neighbor's life. Be grateful for yours.

You shall not steal.

This Commandment condemns theft. Most people are law-abiding citizens. Yet, many are also thieves. Unlike typical thieves, though, the stolen good isn't material. It's far more valuable, important, and meaningful. What is it? We try stealing people's mission. Like fingerprints, however, everyone's mission is different. Not knowing yours is scary and intimidating. But, be brave. Ask God. Listen to Him. "Trust in the Lord with all your heart, on your own intelligence rely not; In all your ways be mindful of Him, and He will make straight your paths" (Proverbs, 3:5-6). The world doesn't need another C. S. Lewis, Gautama Buddha, or Pope John Paul II. The world needs you.

Keeping God's 10 Commandments saves us from spiritual sin and helps us live virtuously. Keeping the 10 commandments to thrive saves us from "psychological sin" and helps us live our best-life-possible. Thus, keeping both sets of commandments is critical for developing our whole being. Unlike Moses atop Mount Sinai, God didn't give me two stone tablets written with His finger. Instead, He gave me 10 stone tablets written with His heart. Come to confession. Let's absolve your "sins." For penance, read this book. And, pray to God. Often. Sincerely. Humbly. You'll need Him to thrive.[3]

We have to have a passion to follow the commandments of God.

---

3 I'm quoting Scripture when I reference God writing the 10 Commandments "with His finger." "When the Lord had finished speaking to Moses on Mount Sinai, He gave him the two tablets of the commandments, the stone tablets inscribed by God's own finger" (Exodus, 31:18). And as Moses says in Deuteronomy, 9:9-10, "Meanwhile I stayed on the mountain forty days and forty nights without eating or drinking, till the Lord gave me the two tablets of stone inscribed by God's own finger." Of course, God also wrote the 10 Commandments with His heart. But, I state that He wrote the 10 commandments to thrive "with His heart," and not also with His finger, as a literary device to emphasize how much I felt His love while creating my approach to thrive.

Personal Thriving

Personal thriving provides the bedrock for social thriving. Initially, you must *have direction*. Unfortunately, our world reveres speed over direction. Speed conveys competence. It draws attention. It yields status. But, going fast in the wrong direction only helps you reach the wrong destination quicker. After heeding your heart's counsel—not the world's counsel—you'll pinpoint your priorities. This will help you *stay focused* and avoid needless distraction and empty goals, giving you more time and widgets for pursuing your potential. Dying embers will become a blaze. *Living simply* will fan the flames by providing the resources for social thriving.

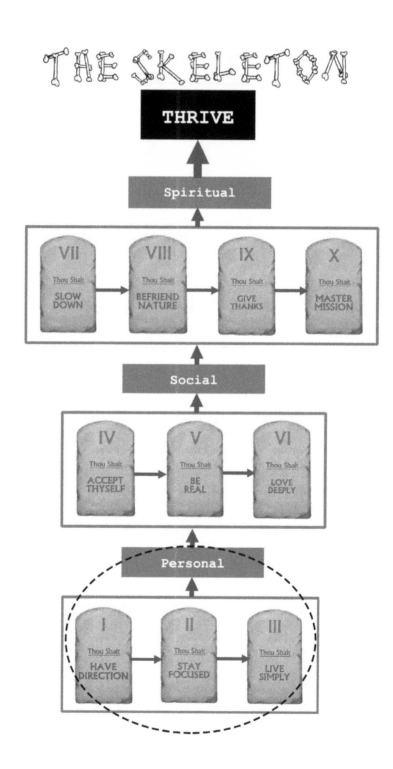

I

Thou Shalt

HAVE
DIRECTION

Scott, 22, like many emerging adults I've taught before, was adrift. He sat afar in my positive psychology class. Occasionally, our eyes would meet. He'd smile, seemingly engaged with our discussion. I usually, however, saw the top of his hood as he stared blankly at his desk, trying to cover his pain. The Scotts of the world eventually fall behind; he was no exception. Mid-semester with failing grades, I hoped he'd rally for the upcoming exam. But, I had doubt. Unfortunately, my hunch was right. Scott got a 68. **"WHUMPH!"** Panicked, Scott looked around to see what made the noise. Everything seemed fine. He then finally looked up. This time, he pushed it. Scott triggered an avalanche.[4]

Scott was used to snowdrifts. After plodding along, he'd eventually reach packed snow, occasionally slipping. Snowdrifts, however, are manageable—avalanches are deadly. Scott tried avoiding his imminent fate. He asked about extra credit. "You're in college, Scott," I said. "I don't give extra credit. Focus on the remaining assignments and tests. We can also meet to review everything." Although I followed up with him several times, he never scheduled an appointment. Scott got a 63 on the final and a C- in the course. Now, the avalanche was going faster. It was growing.

---

4 I refer to Scott and other people around 18-29 years-old as "emerging adults," not "young adults," because it's the term used by developmental psychologists.

It was accumulating debris. Cedar, spruce, and pine trees were snapping like dry twigs. Scott then realized while avalanches are beautiful from a distance, they're terrifying when you're in their wake.

Scott tried outrunning the avalanche. He requested an appointment about the grade I "gave" him. Scott began our meeting by saying, "I know we've discussed me not paying attention in class. But, I really loved your lectures. I always left feeling happy and like I was learning something. I don't want you thinking I wasn't taking class seriously. I was. It's just…." Scott paused at the correct beats to convey a "profound emotion." "I've been dealing with a lot of stuff," he revealed. "I'm all over the place and totally stressed. I really don't know what the hell I'm doing with my life."

This has happened with other students. Therefore, being cynical of Scott's motivation, I wasn't caving to his kind, scripted words. So, I probed. "I'm sorry to hear that, Scott. Is everything okay?" Sighing, he said, "I recently I got a DUI. I've been going to court a lot trying to figure this out. That's why I've been late to class and looking spacey." Scott continued, "I really screwed up. If I get a C- in your class, I'll have to move out of the dorms and back home." Then it happened. Trying to escape the avalanche, Scott said, "I was thinking you could round my grade up to a B so I can keep my room." I was shocked. My posture straightened. "I can't assign a grade you didn't earn, Scott," I said. "That would be unethical. You can choose your behaviors. But, you can't choose your consequences." Scott got buried in snow.

Having direction orients our life—and saves us from avalanches.

THE HARD QUESTIONS

Alice: Would you tell me, please, which way I ought to go from here?
The Cheshire Cat: That depends a good deal on where you want to get to.
Alice: I don't much care where.
The Cheshire Cat: Then it doesn't much matter which way you go.

Where are you going? Who do you want to become? How close are you to living your dream? If you're like me when I was in my 20s, you're probably thinking, "Living my dream? Is this guy nuts? I feel like I'm lost in a dream!" A recent survey of 1,700 Americans found that only 36% of emerging adults think life has meaning.[5] Amazing. Sad. How can so many young people—supposedly bursting with spirit, ambition, and passion—be in existential despair? Maybe they need more sacrifices. Maybe they need more scars. Maybe they need more faith. Regardless, many emerging adults are struggling. They need help. They need guidance. They need direction.

Big Rocks

Knowing your priorities helps you have direction and thrive. It guides your choices and creates your habits, thus building your character and helping you fulfill your destiny. Imagine there's a large empty container. If you placed medium-sized rocks in the container, could you add more stuff? Sure. You could add small rocks. What else can you add? Sand. Good. After the sand fills the gaps, is it full? No. You can add water. Now, imagine I then gave you several big rocks. How could you get them into the packed container? Put the book down. Ponder this. I'll wait.

The answer? Put the big rocks first! The big rocks represent your priorities (e.g., personal growth, relationships, and faith). Everything else represents life's busyness (e.g., chores, texts, and social media). If you don't identify those big rocks and make them happen, nobody else will. As the creator of the "big rocks" metaphor, Stephen Covey, says, "The main thing is for the main thing to remain the main thing." Neglect your priorities, and instead of a house party with joy, hope, and meaning you'll invite despair, gloom, and nihilism. The former are great guests; the latter are messy monsters. No blanket or stuffed animal will protect

---

5 Major differences existed among religious groups. Fifty-five percent of Protestants and 51% of Catholics think their life has meaning, whereas only 29% of atheists or agnostics think their life has meaning. These data will have more significance when you read about my spiritual struggles while I was in my 20s.

you from the torture and horror of a life wasted. Your best armor is having direction.

I've asked hundreds of people about their priorities. Ninety percent are clueless. Most people reply, "I don't know. You're the first person to ask me that." Before each semester, I say to my students, "Why do you attend my class? Don't tell me you need the credits. Don't tell me your friend is taking it. And don't tell me it fits your schedule." Crickets. You can say mastering your craft is important. But, when did you last get up early instead of stay out late? You can say loving others is important. But, when did you last take someone out and not take your phone out? You can say knowing God is important. But, when did you last treat Him to coffee? Show me your calendar, show me your credit card statement, and show me your grades and performance reviews. I'll know your priorities. I'll know your direction. I'll know the life you're creating.

Behaviors bellow. Words whisper.

Lost & Found

Mid-20s

Like Scott and many others, I spent much of my life drifting. This became clear when I was 24. One night driving home from grad school, alone with my thoughts, I analyzed my life and asked myself the hard questions. *"What are my priorities? Where am I going? Am I pursuing my potential?"* Actions speak louder than words. The silence was deafening. Anxiety, grief, and sadness encroached. I pulled over and cried. After a ruthless self-examination, I realized I was squandering my life. I neglected my dreams. I lost my direction. And, it was my fault. Ouch. Why did I self-sabotage? Was it unconsciously deliberate? Did I really hate myself, as several therapists suggested? Was potential failure paralyzing me? This was a defining moment. At exit 48 on Sunrise Highway, I started turning around. I made myself several promises. I promised to honor my priorities (see Commandment II). I promised to find my mission. I promised to have direction.

Twenty years later, I'm still (generally) keeping my promises. How? I spent considerable time in silence. I sat on the deck outside my apartment and emptied my mind while watching the world go round. I walked the beach. I shot hoops. Instead of avoiding the discomfort, I faced it. Though arduous and terrifying, I embraced self-doubt. I also prayed and opened my heart to God. Finally, I started listening to Him, trusting Him, and surrendering to Him. Eventually, I began finding my way—and learning how to thrive.

After countless hours alone, I created the value system I follow today: *faith, family, fitness, work,* and *friends.* These values inform my
dreams, crystallize my mission, and give me direction (see Commandment X). Do I have everything figured out? No. Does my ship still drift,
sometimes even capsize? Yes. Frequently. Thankfully, God always throws
me a lifejacket. If I caved to fear in my earlier years (and I wanted to), if
silence and solitude remained strangers, I'd still be lost. "Listen in silence
because if your heart is full of other things you cannot hear the voice of
God," said St. Mother Teresa. Heed her advice. The outcome? Your heart
and soul will forever point you in the right direction—Heaven.

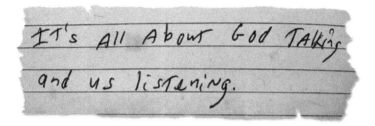

It's All About God Talking and us listening.

Mid-30s

Even with a heart-driven value system, as an "official" adult, I continued struggling with having direction.[6] In 2011, my colleagues and I secured a $1.1 million grant from the John Templeton Foundation to study
gratitude in children and adolescents. It was a lifetime accomplishment.
There were, however, surprising consequences. This was my first grant,
and I was unaware of the workload and the foundation's expectations of
me. Almost immediately, I learned I wasn't in Kansas anymore. Clicking my red ruby slippers was futile. Ask anyone who knows me now, and
they'd say I'm a "family man." During this grant, though, I was a "company man."

---

6 I'm now in my 40s, and I still occasionally meander and must find shelter in caves, deadfalls, and
quinzhees. Yes, creating this value system in my 20s has limited my bushwhacking and helped me
stay on my path. Nonetheless, I still travel with several maps, lots of water, and a personal locator
beacon for when I get lost and need help. Thankfully, God always knows my coordinates. He knows
yours, too.

Over time, I burnt out. I was emotionally exhausted and avoided work. My head was spinning, and my body ached. Work became dreadful. God reminds us, "Let your eyes look directly forward, and your gaze be straight before you" (Proverbs, 4:25). I revisited the hard questions I asked myself 10 years ago. I knew the answers. Guilt brought me to my knees. Good. That's a great prayer position. And, pray I did. I vowed to God that I'd honor my vocations of husband and father. Family would now come first—always. Work would get done—eventually. This intense period of self-reflection and prayer taught me an important lesson: pausing promotes progress.

Once professors board the grant treadmill, they usually keep running—until collapsing. So, when this grant ended, my colleagues surged ahead, trying to secure the next major grant. Now, a $3.6 million grant was in their crosshairs. They were expert snipers. I knew where we were going, and I didn't like the direction. Securing this grant would've likely guaranteed me an early promotion to full professor before 40 (most only attain associate professor by 39). I also would've earned another $100,000. Tempting. Having worked with hundreds of distressed families, however, I knew my wife and children benefited more from my presence than my presents. Therefore, I decided to honor my vow to God.

While walking to the bus stop to get my son, I told my colleague I was abandoning this "dream" for another dream. Family time now mattered more than overtime. "You should get a nanny for your kids. We just got one," he said. "She does their homework and cooks for us. My wife and I can finally work more. It's awesome!" He wasn't getting it. "It's 2:30," I said. "I'm waiting for my son at the bus stop. This is where I want to be. This is where James needs me to be." Man, that felt good.[7]

Saying "peace out" often creates peace within.

---

7 Recall how James helped me create *The Skeleton* one morning while waiting for his bus. Imagine if he had a nanny seeing him off.

OPIUM OF THE MASSES

"Doubt your doubts before you doubt your faith." — Dieter F. Uchtdorf

People struggle with direction in many domains. Sometimes, it's personal. Sometimes, it's professional. Other times, it's spiritual. If you're like me, you probably struggle in all areas. In my 20s, however, I really struggled spiritually. I was adrift. More than losing my life, however, I risked losing my afterlife. Thankfully, though God doesn't always come when He's called, He's always on time.

Growing up, my family acknowledged God. We attended church on Easter and Christmas, said "Thank God" to blessings, and received the sacraments. My father even wore a Jesus charm on his necklace. In my young, naïve mind that was religious. During my teens, however, our superficial commitment to Jesus bothered me. If God was a supreme being, why was our devotion to Him lukewarm? Shouldn't we be on fire? Existential philosopher, Søren Kierkegaard, believed doubt strengthened faith. But, for me, doubt weakened faith.

As an undergraduate, I was insecure, impressionable, and drawn to brilliance. I listened intently to my professor preach the sociology of religion like it was the gospel. Seven words changed my life. "Religion is the opium of the masses," said Dr. Bengston, quoting German philosopher, Karl Marx. "The masses?" I thought. "Forget the masses. I'm no sheep! I won't be controlled by antiquated church dogma. I'm too smart for that. And I sure as hell don't want something numbing my mind!" I was instantly directed away from God—and toward atheism.[8]

---

8 According to a recent Pew Research Center survey, 70% of emerging adults are atheist. A drastic spike from < 1% of emerging adults years earlier, and a stark contrast to the < 1% of Generation X, Baby Boomers, the Silent Generation, and the Greatest Generation. Furthermore, among atheist emerging adults, 98% "seldom/never" pray, 95% completely don't believe in God, and 48% "seldom/never" experience spiritual peace and well-being. Emerging adults are also suffering from historically unprecedented levels of nihilism, anxiety, and depression. For example, per the American Freshman Survey, between 2011 and 2016, their anxiety increased 51% and their depression increased 95%. Exacerbating matters, emerging adults are also considered the *"Loneliest Generation"* (see ~~Deleted~~ Scenes). I'm not saying atheism is causing these difficulties; however, it's likely worsening them. It did for me.

My newfound academic tribe gave me an identity and a sense of belonging. Embraced by intellectuals, I felt worthy, important. Forever battling insecurity, I took it. I pledged allegiance to science. I thought it answered everything. If something was unmeasurable or escaped detection in a laboratory, it must be imaginary. Talk about oblivious. I maintained my arrogance for about 10 years. God had enough. With gentle whispers, loving nudges, and many breadcrumbs, God made His sheep return using the same thing making him flee: science.

Several years later, everything changed. My friend, Sal, knowing my love for learning and my awkwardness with atheism, suggested I read Lee Strobel's, *The Case for Christ*. With meticulous detective work, Strobel proved Jesus existed. More importantly, he proved Jesus wasn't just a friendly neighbor or a sage—He was God's son. That stimulated my appetite for truth and further directed me back to God. Officially free from the ivory towers of atheism, and with space to ponder my faith, I went deeper down the rabbit hole. I wondered if science supported or refuted God's existence. I read everything possible on the interface of science and religion. I read about evolution, cosmology, physics, astronomy, biochemistry, biology, and consciousness. Many hours of pondering and praying led me to conclude that *it takes more faith to be an atheist than a theist* (find the *Easter eggs* in this book ☺).[9] If you think faith and science are mutually exclusive, I understand. I did, too. I encourage you, however, to study this independently. Draw your own conclusions. Your direction—and your life—depends on it.

When the disciples saw Jesus walking on water, they became terrified and thought He was a ghost. Commanded by Jesus, Peter also walked on the water. But, when he shifted his attention from Jesus to the strong wind, he began sinking. Jesus reassured Peter. "Take courage, it is I, do not be afraid!" (Mark, 6:50). Eventually, Jesus had to save him. Like Peter, when we look away from Jesus, we suffer—sometimes even sink. If you

---

9 Here's a jelly bean: *If the constants of nature—unchanging numbers like the strength of gravity, the charge of an electron, and the mass of a proton—were even the tiniest bit different, then atoms wouldn't bond, stars wouldn't burn, and life wouldn't exist.*

struggle having direction, especially spiritually, look toward Jesus. He'll calm the storm. He'll calm the sea. He'll help you thrive.

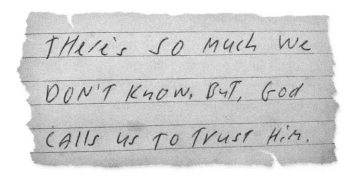

There's so much we don't know, but, God calls us to trust Him.

"WEIRD"

"When you look for me, you will find me. Yes, when you seek me with all your heart, you will find me with you...." — Jeremiah, 29:13-14

After learning that science and faith coexisted, my faith deepened and I gained more spiritual direction. I relaxed. I felt more comfortable trusting God. Yet, I still struggled. An atheist for many years, I remained hesitant. I couldn't take the leap. Not yet. When Thomas learned the other disciples saw Jesus resurrected, he said to them, "Unless I see the mark of the nails in his hands and put my finger into the nail marks and put my hand into his side, I will not believe" (John, 20:25). I, too, was a Doubting Thomas. I, too, needed to see Him to believe. A staunch scientist, I kept challenging God. "Show me the data," I begged. Ask, and you shall receive.

Mysterious Moving Moments

Dawn

My wife and I are mushy. Our children call us "lovebirds." But, in the hospital waiting room dealing with our second miscarriage, we remained withdrawn, processing our pain. Outwardly, we seemed fine; inwardly, we were hurting. After leaving the hospital, walking toward our car in the parking lot, we heard from behind, **"BOOM!"** We turned. A woman busted through the doors and was running toward us. "My name is Dawn," she said. "You don't know me, and I don't know what you're going through. But, God wanted me to tell you that everything will be fine and that He loves you." We sobbed, hugging our divine messenger.

During this pregnancy, we joked about my next tattoo because my two sleeves were already complete and filled with portraits of my family. Thus, another child would force me to extend my canvas. Weeks after the hospital visit, we realized I already had a tattoo of a beautiful angel, praying over candles, with wings wrapped around my children who are running, holding hands.

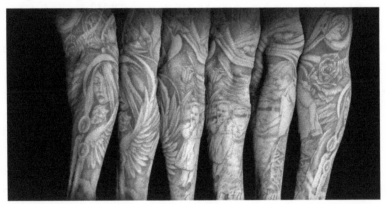

Our angel remains forever etched in our hearts—and on my forearm.[10]

Q&A

Prayer was instrumental in me stepping down from that $3.6 million grant. Upon receiving Communion the Sunday after making the deci-

---

10 Per Dr. Robert Emmons, the world authority on gratitude, two main obstacles to being grateful are *forgetfulness* and *lack of mindful awareness*. Visual reminders, thus, help us remember and recognize our good fortune. Therefore, still acknowledging our blessings despite our pain, below this image is "Grateful" written in my then 5-year-old son's handwriting. Post-its work. Pictures work. I prefer tattoos.

sion, I thanked God for guiding me and reorienting my direction. I then did something new. Now having more time and widgets, I asked God *the* question: *"What do you want me to do?"* Minutes later, leaving Mass, I shook Father Peter's hand. He pulled me in close and whispered, "Think diaconate." I froze. Goosebumps. Eerie. Only my family knew I felt called to become a deacon. Father Peter never whispered in my ear before—and he never has since.

My Girl

From birth, my daughter, Julianne, was a momma's girl. Though we're incredibly close now, I initially struggled and felt insecure. One morning, when she was around 3, we were listening to *My Girl* by the Temptations. I thought, "I love Julez like crazy. I know she has something special with Cara. I just hope I'm being the best father possible." Immediately after having this thought, Julianne did something for the first time. She ran over, squeezed my leg, and said, "I walloo, Daddy. Soooooo much!" Daddy's little girl then became—and will now forever remain—"my girl."

Gospel with a Beat

I bought Cypress Hill's debut album in 9th grade. The rap bug bit. I loved the rhyming and heavy bass lines. But, as an adult, I stopped listening to hardcore rap. One day, waiting for my dentist, I saw a random, hidden magazine featuring a story about Christian rap. Intrigued, I read it. I learned about trailblazing Christian hip-hop artist, Lecrae, and how he evangelized with music. After my appointment, I bought his album, *Anomaly.* I was hooked. Preaching the gospel and giving sermons with lyrical genius, captivating bars, and soul-stirring beats, Lecrae brought me closer to God than any bible study, book, or clergyman (except for the deacon you'll read about next).

One morning, two sins plagued my mind. Trying to distract myself from the pain, I played Lecrae's station on Pandora. First, I heard Ivan B.'s, *Forgive me for my Honesty.* Then, Lecrae's, *Just Like You.* Followed by Tedashii's, *Chase.* Now, I was listening. God had my attention. He was speaking to me through music. I welled with tears. Hammering home His message, the final song was Lecrae's, *Prayin' for You*. I wept. Knowing my history and specific struggles, you'd agree the song selection and order was perfect. So much for distraction.

Seven

The number seven is biblically significant. It portrays fullness or perfection. God created Earth in six days and rested on the seventh. The number seven symbolizes the unity of the four corners of Earth with the Holy Trinity and is featured in the Book of Revelation with the seven churches, seven angels, seven seals, seven trumpets, and seven stars. Learning I was raised Lutheran, yet an active member in our parish, my friend, Deacon Allan (below), asked if I wanted to become a Catholic. "How about you take our *R.C.I.A.* program?", he asked.[11] I did. In 2010, I received the Eucharist, made my Confirmation, and was received into the Catholic Church (see Commandment X). Seven is the foundation of God's word. Seven words made me reject God and lose direction. Seven words also made me love God and have direction.

"Weird."

---

11 R.C.I.A. stands for the *Rights of Christian Initiation of Adults*.

DIVINE DIRECTION

"No trial has come to you but what is human. God is faithful and will not let you be tried beyond your strength; but with the trial he will also provide a way out, so that you may be able to bear it." — 1 Corinthians, 10:13

Everything changes when we have direction. Especially when God is our North Star. We then brim with joy, gratitude, hope, and love. Our life becomes more fulfilling, meaningful. Surrendering to God, however, is scary. It requires change, something we avoid. Therefore, like me, we commit to Him…just enough. We cherry pick His Commandments. We occasionally follow His lessons. We only pray when we need Him. Our halfhearted commitment works—until it doesn't. A void remains. The solution? Sacrificing our life to God. Most of us, however, struggle sacrificing sweets for Lent! For inspiration, consider Jesus. No one sacrificed more than Him.

After John the Baptist baptized Jesus, the spirit led Him to the desert. Jesus fasted for 40 days and 40 nights. He was starving, exhausted. Human, Jesus was vulnerable to persuasion. So, the Devil tempted Him several times. Jesus rejected every temptation. Seeing that Jesus' will was stronger than anticipated, the Devil tempted Him once more. This time, he made Jesus an offer He couldn't refuse—or so he thought. Bringing Jesus to the top of a towering mountain, the Devil showed Him all of the world's magnificent kingdoms. The Devil said to Him, "All these I shall give you, if you will prostrate yourself and worship me" (Matthew, 4:9). Jesus replied, "Get away, Satan! It is written: 'The Lord, your God, shall you worship and Him alone shall you serve'" (Matthew, 4:10). Satan fled, and angels arrived. Jesus then returned to Galilee and began His ministry. Jesus trusted God. He followed Him. He made completing God's mission for Him not a big rock—but a boulder!

Our culture promises far less than world dominion if we ignore our mission. Approval, pleasure, and success are some of the "prized" outcomes. This, we're told, is worth meandering and sacrificing our dreams and destiny. Sadly, many of us believe the serpent. We forget what happened in the Garden of Eden. We forget how one bad apple spoils the bunch. So, we sign with Satan. Here's what we've agreed to:

Το συμβόλαιο του Σατανά

Henceforth you relinquish all joy, fulfillment, and meaning. You accept a life filled with despair, emptiness, and chaos. You understand shallow pursuits and abandoning your destiny will make you weep, scream, and gnash your teeth. You accept Me taking pleasure in your pain. You will watch Me laugh while you struggle, helplessly trying to escape, begging for release. You give Me eternal ownership of your freedom and dreams. You accept responsibility for your careless decision. You accept responsibility for wasting your life. You will worship Me Forever.

_____
YOUR NAME

Thankfully, Jesus read the fine print. You should, too.

The Devil is in the details.

We should all imitate Jesus.

Thou Shalt
Have Direction

1. Ask yourself the hard questions:

What are my priorities?
Where am I going?
Am I pursuing my potential?

To help answer these questions, spend considerable time in silence. Hike in the woods. Walk along the beach. Sit under a shady tree. Watch a sunrise or sunset. Stargaze. Relax in an empty church. Expect angst, confusion, and tears. Stop existing. Start becoming. Replace drifting with direction.

2. Identify what matters to you. Having deep connection? Getting a new job? Finishing school? Starting a family? Launching a ministry? Write it down. Make it your lock screen or your screensaver. Use these reminders to help you honor your priorities and have direction. When you start wandering, remember what matters most. Remember what gives your life meaning. Then, recommit to your priorities. Put the big rocks first!

3. Create a life map. Make your ultimate end the destination. Then, plan your adventure. How will you get there? What's the most direct route? Where are the potential detours? How long might it take? Who are the best and worst travel companions? What must you pack? What should you leave behind? What will

be the weather conditions? Where will you sleep? Before starting your trip, check your destination again. Ensure it's correct. If so, begin. Bring a bible for when you get lost.

4. If you question God's existence and think faith and science are mutually exclusive, review the *Easter eggs* in this book. Study the "weird" science. Ponder it. Try dismantling the logic, and question the facts. Then, to learn more about the interface of science and religion, select one (or more) of the books from *God's Library* and create a book club with atheists, agnostics, and theists. Challenge each other. Debate each other. Push each other (figuratively). Be flexible and open-minded. Perhaps you'll get closer to God. Perhaps not. But, if you keep analyzing the data, you'll likely have to make room in your heart for another friend.

5. Become more committed to following God. Start small. Talk with Him, listen to Him, and feel Him. Then, act like Him. Forgive someone. Donate more to charity. Help someone struggling. With time, try trusting God to be your North Star. Like Jesus, don't sign with Satan. The Devil is in the details.

II

Thou Shalt

STAY FOCUSED

Erin, 20, is a typical emerging adult. She loves chilling with her friends. Together, they enjoy mountain biking, trail running, and attending concerts. She's been with her boyfriend, Bill, for 3 years. Their long distance relationship can be stressful. Yet, they remain committed. Because of a teenage obsession, she still watches an occasional *Full House* or *Buffy the Vampire Slayer* episode. Though otherwise "normal," one quality makes Erin exceptional: her ability to stay focused.

At 8, Erin became fascinated with the violin. Unlike many instruments, being adept at playing the violin requires understanding linear systems theory. Therefore, beyond raw talent, mastering the violin demands much time and widgets. In his book, *Outliers*, Malcom Gladwell writes, "10,000 hours is the magic number of greatness." Erin exceeded this by 19. As a young girl, she began practicing 1 hour daily. Then, 2 hours daily. Then, 3 hours daily. Now, in college, she practices 4-5 hours daily. I asked Erin, "What did you forgo to practice so much?" "I never really watch TV," she said. "I also never get caught up in nonsense. Especially with social media. Rather than using social media to communicate with friends, I use it as a tool to be plugged into the music world." Unlike many, Erin knew that setting limits fosters transcending limits.

Erin got many rewards for staying focused. At 17, she earned a fellowship at an elite classical musical festival. By 18, having won a national competition, she was appointed Concertmaster of the national symphony ensemble. Ten violinists challenged her for the position—and lost. This win also earned Erin $1,000 and a performance of a full concerto with a professional orchestra. Later, she was awarded a 4-year full-tuition scholarship to a famous conservatory. Forever searching for fun, many are forever searching for a life. Wisely, Erin rejected passivity for passion.

Erin lives nearby. During family walks, we'd always hear her practicing. The notes were like enchanting cardinal songs. I'd often say to my children, "That's focus, guys. Someday, Erin will be a world-class violinist." I love being right.

We create dreams off task. We fulfill dreams on task.

REACTING vs. RESPONDING

"Between stimulus and response there is a space. In that space is our power to choose our response. In our response lies our growth and our freedom." — *Viktor E. Frankl*

People often react—instead of respond—to life's demands. But, reacting is visceral; responding is deliberate. While we may have scheduled time for our priorities, we often let others hijack our plans. We then spend our time and widgets on what's urgent—not on what's important. The important things, however, are rarely urgent. Must you go swimming today? No. Must you have lunch with your friend tomorrow? No. Must you look for jobs tonight? No. But, are these important? Yes. I, too, was often a ping-pong ball. Until being hit by enough paddles.

Eventually, I made staying focused a strength. Every morning, I now wake thinking, "I'm starting today with 100 widgets. How can I best use them to thrive?" All day, I monitor my widget levels. Like in a video game, I picture my widget bar rising and falling with each behavior, activity, and interaction. Took a polar bear plunge with my friend, Anthony? Twenty widgets gained. Sat in traffic for 30 minutes? Ten widgets lost. I even strategically plan my months and years for the best time and widget use (more on this later). Many judge, saying, "Jeff, you're crazy. Do you ever just relax?" "Just relax" is code for "do nothing." No thanks. Doing "nothing" is doing nothing.[12]

My strategy to stay focused is theoretically simple. Yet, psychologically challenging. Beware. Everyone stumbles at each step. Need evidence? Almost 80% of New Year's resolutions fail. Worse, 77% of people keep their pledge for only 1 week. How many succeed? Eight percent. Staying focused is arduous. Master the steps below, however, and you'll play harder, work smarter, and love greater.

Time matters. Energy matters. Focus matters.

Step 1: Pinpoint Your Priorities

In Commandment I, I discussed how pinpointing priorities helps us have direction. Being thorough, I briefly mention it again because it's required for staying focused. Avoiding redundancy, I share another story hoping you learn from my mistakes.

A new assistant professor in my late 20s, I dove into work. While adjusting to this position, I didn't identify my professional goals and priorities. Thus, I lacked focus and overcommitted. Creating projects was exhilarating. The initial buzz, however, faded. Pain ensued. Once, my colleagues and I almost secured a major grant (not the $3.6 million one mentioned in Commandment I). Professors and scientists dream of such grants. Yet, as principal investigator, I withdrew our project. I told the team I was dealing with "health issues." I was. But, not like most think. Anxiety consumed me. Stress paralyzed me. Panic attacks plagued me. My chest tightened, and my head pounded. I was a mess. Partly from overwork. But, also because work chaos was creating home chaos, and living value-incongruent was harming my health and well-being (which

---

12 Winnie the Pooh disagrees (see Commandment VII). We're both right. Excuse the confusion.

happens when we ignore our values). If there's one thing I'm not, it's a quitter. This time, however, I tapped. My colleagues worked tirelessly trying to get the grant. I felt terrible terminating it. I still do.

A husband and father with a mortgage and endless bills, I appreciate grinding. But, when I was younger, I wish I paused sooner to pinpoint my priorities. Thankfully, I eventually did. Sadly, many never do. Their ultimate concerns then remain unknown and neglected. Despair encroaches. Addiction lurks. Demise looms. Ignorance isn't bliss—it's misery.

Step 2: Prioritize Your Priorities

People often blame others for losing focus. Perpetuating agony and frailty, they point to their circumstances. Call them on it, and they snap, "There's nothing I can do. Everyone and everything keeps pulling at me. Take. Take. Take." The problem, however, isn't "out there." It's you. Ask yourself, "How can I stay focused on my priorities?" The answer? Schedule your priorities first. Then, work your other commitments around them. So, if you've scheduled a study session from 3 pm - 8 pm, and your friend invites you to dinner at 7 pm, you can say, "Thank you for the invitation. I'd love to see you, but I'll be studying then. Can I meet up with you a little after 8?" Some will respect this, others won't. Be prepared.

Foes encourage distraction. Friends encourage focus.

How do you know if you made the right decision? If you grew. If you accomplished your goals. If you have haters. Also, listen to your body. If you experience order, clarity, and focus, you succeeded. If you experience chaos, confusion, and distraction, you goofed. Be strong. Be willing to sleep in the doghouse. Don't worry. Snoopy will keep you warm.

Teach us to Number our days Aright, that We May gain Wisdom of heart.

Step 3: Protect Your Priorities

Guarding your time and widgets is tough. People push. People pull. People demand. You don't, however, *need* their approval (see Commandment IV). Start saying, "No!" Begin small. Delete the ridiculous YouTube video your friend sent you. Decline an invitation to stay out late. Agree to see your parents once—not twice—a week for dinner. Then, go big. Tell your colleague to start doing her share—or you'll file a complaint. Tell your boyfriend to stop grunting and start communicating—or it's over. Tell your roommate to hang her own damn clothes—or they'll be curbside. You'll gain confidence. You'll gain respect. You'll gain widgets to thrive.

Before becoming a professor, I worked as a school psychologist. Every knock or call was a potential emergency. This is a nightmare for love slobs like me who reflexively said, "Yes." Eventually, though, I had enough. One day, I was leaving my office to spend time with students. We were celebrating Caitlyn's birthday. This was important. En route, a parent cornered me. "Dr. Froh, I'm Stacie's mother. I have to speak with you," she said. I wanted her to like me. I wanted to appease her and maintain my reputation. Something in me, however, stirred. Slightly stammering, I said, "I care about Stacie's welfare. I want to speak with you, but other students are expecting me now. I can call you in about 45 minutes." Silence. She stared at me. I stared back. I rode the wave of anxiety.

Though I expected an agitated mother, she seemed to respect me. "Okay," she said. "I look forward to speaking with you."

Every time you say, "No," you say, "Yes."

Staying focused takes guts. You must pinpoint your priorities. You must prioritize your priorities. And, toughest of all, you must protect your priorities. When you get weak and start surrendering (we all do), seek God. Pray. Ask Him for the strength to say, "No!" "For God has not given us a spirit of timidity, but of power and love and discipline" (2 Timothy, 1:7). If you need encouragement, remember Jesus. He only surrendered to God.

WINDOWS OF TIME

"Most of what we say and do is not essential. If you can eliminate it, you'll have more time, and more tranquility. Ask yourself at every moment, 'Is this necessary?'" — Marcus Aurelius

Spontaneity keeps life exciting. I love impromptu city trips for dinner and a show. Unlike many, however, I don't romanticize spontaneity. I plan—a lot. Every Saturday since my mid-20s, I've spent about 1 hour alone in silence planning my next week. My current schedule (below) is simple, streamlined, and effective. Keeping it gives me peace, vitality, and meaning. Why? Because it makes my value system—*faith, family, fitness, work,* and *friends*—guide my behaviors. American philosopher and psychologist, Dr. William James, said it best: "That which holds the attention, determines the action."

Life is about choices. Choose wisely.

Thrive	Sun.	Mon.	Tues.	Wed.	Thur.	Fri.	Sat.
12am							
1am							
2am							
3am							
4am							
5am							
6am							
7am							
8am							
9am							
10am							
11am							
12pm							
1pm							
2pm							
3pm							
4pm							
5pm							
6pm							
7pm							
8pm							
9pm							
10pm							
11pm							

With few exceptions, this is my schedule. Week. After week. After week. Routine? Sure. Boring? Maybe. Contrast this to scrolling social media daily (true for 90% of emerging adults; the average time spent is 3 hours), gaming 2-12 hours weekly (true for 52% of emerging adults), and binge-watching shows at least several times monthly (true for 85%

of emerging adults). Yes, I veg. Sometimes. But, it's planned. Challenging our mind and body builds new brain cells and strengthens connections between them, whereas excessive screen time fosters depression and impedes the growth of new brain cells.[13] If Netflix, Candy Crush, and Snapchat are your thing, fine. I'm not judging you. Before judging me, however, answer this question: *What will likely add more years to your life and more life to your years? My "ho-hum" schedule? Or, adorning selfies with cartoon whiskers?* You decide.

We do a lot when we do a little.

As another example, consider Benjamin Franklin's daily schedule. Note the similarities with mine. Shortly after rising, we read, study, connect with God, and create our aim for the day.[14] Then, we only work during scheduled windows of time. After work, we invest in our relationships and pursue our hobbies. Following Franklin's wisdom, "Early to bed and early to rise, makes a man healthy, wealthy, and wise," we then go to sleep. It worked for Franklin. It works for me. It changed my life. Maybe it could change yours, too. As Benjamin Franklin said, "If you fail to plan, you are planning to fail."

---

13 Neurogenesis occurs when new brain cells develop in the hippocampus (the brain region that regulates motivation, emotion, memory, and learning) or the olfactory bulb (the neural structure that aids odor selectivity and, thus, memory and emotion). Exercise, sex, and creative and novel pursuits foster hippocampal neurogenesis, whereas binge-watching shows and excessive swiping and gaming impede hippocampal neurogenesis (even shrinking the hippocampus by 10% if there's accompanying depression, which is likely). Resist your couch. Resist your controller. Resist your computer. Instead, pursue growth.

14 Franklin's name for God was *"Powerful Goodness."*

The morning question, What good shall I do this day?	5	Rise, wash, and address *Powerful Goodness;* contrive day's business and take the resolution of the day; prosecute the present study; and breakfast.
	6	
	7	
	8	
	9	Work.
	10	
	11	
	12	Read or overlook my accounts, and dine.
	1	
	2	
	3	Work.
	4	
	5	
	6	
	7	Put things in their places, supper, music, or diversion, or conversation; examination of the day.
	8	
	9	
Evening question, What good have I done today?	10	
	11	
	12	
	1	Sleep.
	2	
	3	
	4	

I also spend considerable time and widgets planning special events months—even years—away. For example, after summer, my wife and I grab our family calendar to "big rock" holiday traditions: apple picking, pumpkin picking, cutting down our Christmas tree at Shamrock farms, attending the tree lighting in Northport village, seeing the tree at Rockefeller Center, and visiting St. Patrick's Cathedral. We also schedule a holiday musical and "family movie nights" for *The Polar Express, Elf,* and *The*

Grinch. Everything makes the calendar. Imagine how many traditions we'd lose if we over-embraced spontaneity. Imagine how many memories we'd miss if we weren't calendar-conscious. Make your big rocks find their way into your calendar. Make your pebbles fight their way into your calendar.

Nothing happens when we let things "just" happen.

The Matrix

The distraction we allow into our lives is historically unparalleled. We're drowning in voicemails, requests, messages, notifications, posts, updates, alerts, reminders, texts, and—the tsunami of all distractions—emails.[15] The time and widget matrix below will help you stay focused. Unlike Neo in *The Matrix*, you won't see the world in green code. But, it will save you from lampreys, vampire bats, and other life-suckers. Study it. Internalize it. Follow it. Protect your time and widgets like your life depends on it—because it does.[16]

---

15 Task-switching, like responding to a text while working, increases our stress and impedes our planning, problem-solving, and attention. Even if we're only distracted for several tenths of a second (e.g., glancing at our phone when it buzzes), the constant change of ideas, conversations, and transactions wastes almost 40% of our brain's widgets. Splitting attention, thus, creates splitting headaches—and makes us lose focus.

16 The time and widget matrix is adapted from Stephen Covey, the time and widget management master. For a deeper analysis of how to stay focused, read his classic book, *The 7 Habits of Highly Effective People*. It's worth the time and widgets.

Thrive	Urgent	Not Urgent
Important	**I** *EXPECT* 📖 Deadlines 📖 Health Concerns 📖 Fulfilling Basic Needs 📖 Self/Other Safety	**II** *PLAN* 📖 Values Clarification 📖 Nurturing Relationships 📖 Exercise 📖 Play
	CRISIS	**THRIVE**
Not Important	**III** *BEWARE* 📖 Many Emails 📖 Most Texts 📖 Some Meetings 📖 All Gossiping	**IV** *AVOID* 📖 Internet Surfing 📖 Binge-Watching Shows 📖 Needless Shopping 📖 Excessive Social Media
	DISTRACTION	**WASTE**

We spend our time and widgets in one of these four quadrants. It took years for me to understand this. It took even longer for me to embrace it. Throughout the day, I'm constantly wondering, "What quadrant am I in now? Am I moving toward thriving? Or, am I moving toward languishing?" If someone asks me to repeat myself one too many times I think, "There goes a widget!" When people needlessly "reply all" to emails I "reply all" with, "Please only respond to the person interested. I find it distracting and draining. Thank you." (My internal response is evil.) And, God help you if you add chaos to my life from shoddy work. You'll pay—with more than money.

Admittedly, I'm sometimes too obsessed with staying focused. Thoreau's words loop in my mind. "Time is but the stream I go a-fishing in. I drink at it; but while I drink I see the sandy bottom and detect how shallow it is." Ironically, protecting my time and widgets sometimes wastes my time and widgets. There's diminishing returns. Experiment. Find the balance. Saving you widgets, here are CliffsNotes for creating healthy, useful windows of time with the time and widget matrix.

Important/Urgent
Quadrant I: *Expect* crises. Deal. Quickly.

Important/Not Urgent
Quadrant II: *Plan* for thriving. Make it a big rock.

Not Important/Urgent
Quadrant III: *Beware* of distractions. Use the *3 Ds to Stay Focused*: **delay, delegate,** and **delete.**

Not Important/Not Urgent
Quadrant IV: *Avoid* wasting time and widgets. Live your best-life-possible.

If you're overwhelmed by this level of time and widget management, I understand. It's intimidating. It's tough. But, it helps you stay focused. As inspiration, here's the schedule my daughter created for a father-daughter day.

She was then 9. You got this.

Start planning. Start thriving.

GROW WITH THE FLOW

"Life is growth. If we stop growing, technically and spiritually, we are as good as dead." — Morihei Ueshiba

Our culture promotes hedonism. It encourages eating till dullness, drinking till numbness, and resting till weakness. We only grow, however, when we confront the mysterious. When we explore. When we pursue our dreams. Neuroscientists recently learned that new genes in our brain and spinal cord activate when we're in novel situations. These genes code for new proteins, helping to build new brain structures. Thus, much of you remains latent and undeveloped. To thrive, you must test your limits.

If not, as clinical psychologist, Dr. Jordan Peterson, said, "you remain in-complete, and life is too hard for anyone incomplete." It's also wasted.[17]

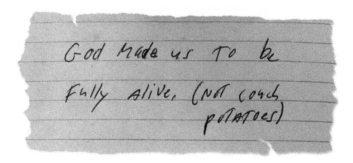

God made us to be fully alive, (not couch potatoes)

Has time ever seemed to stop? Maybe this happened kayaking. May-be this happened sketching. Maybe this happened gardening. If so, you experienced what psychologist, Dr. Mihaly Csikszentmihalyi, called "flow." Staying in flow requires a 1:1 ratio between your skills and the challenge. When your skills are high and the challenge is low, you're bored. When your skills are low and the challenge is high, you're anx-ious. But, when your skills match the challenge (especially when both are high), you're in flow. Experiencing flow, therefore, expands your being because it requires greater challenges. It also requires staying focused on your priorities. That's when you'll push yourself to exhaustion, tran-scending mediocrity and approaching excellence. So, plan your escape from pleasure's prison. Get your hacksaw. Study the ventilation system. Bribe some guards. Freedom awaits—so does your potential.

Recall Erin the violinist? Nearing international stardom, she's now hyper-focused. And, she keeps raising the bar. Practice sessions become grueling when she believes she mastered a piece. Hiding in darkness amidst monsters are her enemies: fatigue, frustration, and failure. There-fore, she rolls up her sleeves. She wipes her brow. She takes a breath. "Let's do this," she thinks, gripping her violin like a battle-axe. I asked

17 Genetic coding is also discussed in Dr. Jordan Peterson's book, *12 Rules for Life: An Antidote to Chaos*. Few people have influenced me like Dr. Peterson. Read his book. Approach your potential.

Erin, "Why do you keep sacrificing so much? Why do you keep grinding?" She said:

God created everyone to have their own special gifts and talents, no matter how big or small. I believe God put us on Earth to nurture these gifts to minister to others and spread His love. Waking up at 5am to practice gives my life meaning. It's a joyful sacrifice of time for me to strive closer and closer toward this "unattainable musical perfection" aiming to transcend an audience to a heavenly realm. The countless hours I spend in the practice room is not merely time spent with myself and the violin—it's time spent with God. To me, practicing is prayer. It helps me show God how thankful I am that He is steering my life according to His will and gracing me with the motivation to keep going. It's occasionally tough to stay on track, and the process of mastering a technique or passage can be tedious and difficult. Sometimes, it's very tempting to throw in the towel. But, what has made me get over the rough patches is my relationship with God, and how I trust that He's with me during the dark times. I experience peace knowing He has an awesome plan for my life. I believe He will take care of me during my entire career journey. Wherever I end up in life is where God wants me to be. What better motivation is there to maximize your full potential than to give it all up to God?

Erin's response perfectly captures Dr. Csikszentmihalyi's view on staying focused and its critical role in thriving. As Dr. Csikszentmihalyi said, "The best moments in our lives are not the passive, receptive, relaxing times...The best moments usually occur when a person's body or mind is stretched to its limits in a voluntary effort to accomplish something difficult and worthwhile...It is not enough to have an excellent life. The point is to be happy while doing things that stretch our skills, that help us grow and fulfill our potential." It seems our culture got it wrong— again. Shocker.

Benjamin Franklin thought similarly to Dr. Csikszentmihalyi. During wartime, Franklin's men built forts for protection. Torrential rain prohibited this for one week. He then observed:

> ...when men are employ'd, they are best content'd; for on the days they worked they were good-natur'd and cheerful, and, with the consciousness of having done a good day's work, they spent the evening jollily; but on our idle days they were mutinous and quarrelsome, finding fault with their pork, the bread, etc., and in continual ill-humor, which put me in mind of a sea-captain, whose rule it was to keep his men constantly at work; and, when his mate once told him that they had done everything, and there was nothing further to employ them about, "Oh," says he, "Make them scour the anchor."

God put Adam and Eve in the Garden of Eden to cultivate it. Thus, God made us to create sustenance for others and ourselves. He made us to approach life, not to avoid it. Therefore, put your phone away—before your life slips away.

Weariness, despair, and agony are Satan's weapons. He brandishes his sword hoping you remain lazy, lethargic, and low-spirited. Why? Because we experience the most intense flow staying focused doing God's work and pursuing our mission. Satan, therefore, wants us dreary and dumb so we sit on the sidelines. God, however, wants us wakeful and wise so we get in the game. Glorify God with your actions. Keep pushing Satan back down into the netherworld. He'll resist. Fight hard. Pitchforks hurt temporarily. Sloth hurts eternally.

Idleness makes us easy prey for the Devil. Stay safe. Stay alive. Stay focused.

ONE SHOT

"How we spend our days is, of course, how we spend our lives." — Annie Dillard

Staying focused is harder than ever. Yet, it's more important than ever. Adam Merrill, co-author of the book, *The 5 Choices of Extraordinary Productivity*, reminds us, "In today's environment, the key to true productivity is not to get more things done, but to get the right things done." Imagine if Albert Einstein, Marie Curie, Ludwig van Beethoven, Benjamin Franklin, and Isaac Newton got distracted. Broken bones might be undetected. Catheters might be metal tubes. Gravity might be unfounded. Even worse, imagine if Jesus got distracted. We'd have to try paying for our sins. Thankfully, He's a paragon of focus.

Being human, Jesus was scared of His impending fate. The night before His crucifixion, He went to the Garden of Gethsemane to pray to God. Becoming distressed, He said to His disciples sitting nearby, "My soul is sorrowful even to death. Remain here and keep watch" (Mark, 14:34). Falling to the ground, Jesus then prayed. "Abba, Father, all things are possible to you. Take this cup away from me, but not what I will but what you will" (Mark, 14:36).[18] When He returned, the disciples were snoozing. Imagine your friends falling asleep while you spoke to God about your imminent torturous death. Imagine your Father forsaking you. Imagine knowing that tomorrow you'd be crucified to establish a new covenant between God and humanity. Walk in Jesus' sandals. Feel the agony. Feel the rejection. Feel the betrayal. Might we, too, have sweat blood?[19] Might we, too, have become distracted—even from fulfilling

---

18 When reading Commandment X, remember that Jesus asked God to, *"Take this cup away from me...."* Even Jesus struggled mastering His mission.

19 Hematidrosis can occur under extreme physical or emotional stress. It's when the capillary blood vessels feeding the sweat glands rupture and ooze blood. Therefore, Jesus sweating blood isn't hyperbole or legend. Like God, it's the truth. And it happened because Jesus loved us—to death.

God's divine plan for us? God, however, didn't ask us to save the world. Jesus got that mission.

You have one shot to live your best-life-possible. Take it. The next time you're about to waste your time and widgets, neglecting your priorities, ask yourself, "What would Jesus do?" The answer? He'd pray. He'd remember what mattered most. He'd stay focused. Do likewise.

Don't watch time fly by. Grab its wings. You'll soar to Heaven.

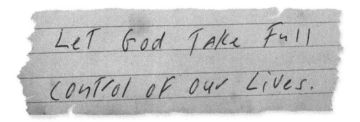

Commandment II Tips

Thou Shalt
Stay Focused

1. Every morning, remember you only have 100 widgets for the day. Spend them wisely. Notice your widget bar rising and falling with every behavior, activity, and interaction. If you feel fatigued, rest. Do something energizing. Exercise. Read. Nap. Pray. After recharging, you can then refocus on thriving.

2. Spend about 30 minutes planning your next week. Consider your roles (e.g., spouse, parent, student, employee, and parishioner). What's the most *important* thing you can do in each one? After pinpointing your priorities, prioritize and protect them. Make your big rocks find their way into your calendar. Make your pebbles fight their way into your calendar.

3. Study the time and widget matrix. Ask yourself throughout the day, "What quadrant am I in now? Am I moving toward thriving? Or, am I moving toward languishing?" Then, ask yourself, "How did I get here? Did I schedule my priorities first? Or, was I a love slob?" Use the CliffsNotes for creating meaningful windows of time with the time and widget matrix:

Important/Urgent
Quadrant I: *Expect* crises. Deal. Quickly.

Important/Not Urgent
Quadrant II: *Plan* for thriving. Make it a big rock.

Not Important/Urgent

Quadrant III: *Beware* of distractions. Use the *3 Ds to Stay Fo-cused:* **delay, delegate,** and **delete.**

Not Important/Not Urgent

Quadrant IV: *Avoid* wasting time and widgets. Live your best-life-possible.

4. Restrict your screen time to 1 hour daily. Then, disconnect. Turn off your phone, computer, radio, television, and video game. Use the time and widgets for engaging hobbies, creative pursuits, intellectual stimulation, meaningful work, and spiritu-al formation. Challenge yourself. Celebrate your growth. Then, raise the bar. Keep testing your limits. Keep experiencing flow. Keep pursuing your potential.

5. Look at a picture of Jesus crucified on the cross. Study it. No-tice His anguish. Notice the wounds. Notice the blood. Then, consider knowing that sacrificing yourself (literally) to save hu-manity was your mission and still staying focused to complete it. The next time you become distracted and neglect your priorities, remember Jesus—a paragon of focus. Be inspired by Him. Pray to Him. Then, try emulating Him.

III

Thou Shalt

LIVE
SIMPLY

After completing his education at Hofstra University, William Thieben played in the NBA. To many, he was living the dream. But, after 2 years, he left the court for the classroom. Though 6'7", William thought being a teacher was his mission. After teaching for 3 years, he was an assistant principal for another 10. Then, a principal for 23 more. After retiring from the public schools, William returned to the classroom as an adjunct professor at St. Joseph's College. Few would abandon layups for lesson plans. Few would leave adoring fans for adoring students. Few would forgo money for meaning. Thankfully, William did. An excerpt from an alumni association's letter confirms he made the right decision.

Mr. Thieben's positive influence on the students of Bay Shore was recognized in July of 2000. Almost three decades after leaving Bay Shore, students of the sixties honored Mr. Thieben by establishing a permanent memorial plaque at the High School in his name. It states: William B. Thieben - "The voice that launched a thousand school days remains forever in our hearts." A William B. Thieben Scholarship Fund was also created. An annual award is given to a senior graduate who needs a helping hand. Mr. Thieben was always there to lend a helping hand.

William mastered his mission. He followed his heart. May we all be so brave.

Jesus aside, Professor Thieben most influenced my life. We met when I was 20 and an undergrad student at St. Joseph's College. Before then, the only book I read for pleasure was *Boyz in the Hood*. Professor Thieben, however, was a voracious reader. He read three newspapers every Sunday. He finished *Time* magazine the day it arrived. And he averaged two books weekly. "People who don't read are no better off than people who can't read," he preached. Thanks to Professor Thieben, I replaced drowning in self-hatred with swimming in books. As the saying goes, "When the student is ready, the teacher appears."

Most importantly, Professor Thieben taught me how to live simply. When buying us lunch, he never took my order. Instead, holding a sandwich in each hand, he'd ask, "Turkey or roast beef?" Professor Thieben traveled simply, too. Though then in his 60s, he still rode his bike to work and the library. Because his heart was even bigger than his hugs, every day he took his phone off the hook between 5 pm - 7 pm to connect with his wife—uninterrupted. On Sunday morning, he had coffee with Manvik, the local gas station attendant. His hobbies were even simple. A Luddite, Professor Thieben preferred sailboats to motor boats. Sharing his love for sailing with me, when I was 27, he gave me his 14-foot Sunfish. I named it *Eudaimonia* (Aristotle's term for "thriving").

Being my surrogate father, Professor Thieben did a reading at our wedding. When he reached me at the receiving line, tears brimmed in his piercing blue eyes. Wearing a warm, gentle smile, he placed a chunk of used yellow chalk in my hand and squeezed. We shared a moment. Professor Thieben left me with his final lesson: to teach is to touch a soul.

Live simply. Live purposely. Live fully.

CULTURAL KOOL-AID

"It is the mark of an educated mind to be able to entertain a thought without accepting it." — Aristotle

Osmosis is the gradual or unconscious assimilation of ideas and knowledge. Thanks to osmosis, we unknowingly internalize toxic materialistic values. In the 1970s, people saw about 500 ads daily. Now, we see about 4,000-10,000 ads daily. That's 4-10 ads per minute—all day! Unfortunately, many people drink the "cultural Kool-Aid." Jesus warned us. "Watch out, guard against the leaven of the Pharisees and the leaven of Herod" (Mark, 8:15). Metaphorically, leaven represents the malignant, encroaching influences on our lives. Leaven permeates a whole batch of dough. Likewise, cultural values permeate our whole being.[20]

---

20 Our culture even influences eating disorder prevalence. See ~~Deleted~~ Scenes for how it facilitated my struggle with body dysmorphic disorder.

We become what we consume.

When house shopping, my wife and I prioritized a stellar school district over a stellar kitchen. Many top districts are in wealthy neighborhoods. Higher taxes provide higher teacher salaries, thus generally attracting and retaining better teachers. Higher taxes also fund professional development, enriching academic programs, educational field trips, extensive mental health services, and competitive athletic, music, and art departments. The downside, however, is having neighbors who typically embrace materialistic values.[21] Initially, my wife wanted to move into the same school district, coincidentally, as the rapper 50 Cent. It was then ranked 73rd in New York State among nearly 1,000 school districts. Enticing. But, my wife knows that our neighbors shape our values—and thus our lives. So, the search continued.

We settled in a beautiful hamlet, a hidden gem. It's Rockwellian, Whoville-ish. I connected with our children's bus driver, Derrick. He was dedicated, friendly, and loving. Each morning at the bus stop, we discussed politics and local happenings. We even shared CDs. Given our bromance, we frequently hugged good-bye. Not seeing him all summer, when the school year began, I always asked what he did over the past 2 months. Ironically, one time, Derrick mentioned how he drove a bus in 50 Cent's town. "How was that?", I asked. "The people wouldn't look at me when I got their kids. They gave me their backs. No one even waved to me," he replied. Touching his fist to his heart, Derrick continued, "But, with you guys, I know I'm loved. I feel it. That's why I love you, too." While I never doubted our decision, Derrick's story reassured me.

An experience at our annual block party further confirmed the decision. Our former neighbor, Kathy, had recently moved away, selling her modest home for an impressive colonial. About 1 year later, she joined us for the party. Sitting in flimsy lawn chairs and laughing among friends

---

21 A recent study found that after accounting for age, gender, and one's personal financial worth, people in wealthier neighborhoods, compared to those in relatively poorer neighborhoods, were likelier to spend much, save little, and be materialistic. (This effect was stronger in younger people, presumably in their early 20s.) Therefore, when choosing your neighborhood, avoid gravel driveways with German imports. Instead, look for asphalt driveways with Subarus.

while watching a community gather, Kathy suddenly got quiet. She appeared distracted, lost in thought. "What's up, Kathy?" I asked. Staring ahead, eyes fixed on children scampering about, she said, "I can't believe I sacrificed all of this for bigger closets."

I'm sure 50 Cent is a nice guy. I'm sure he'd buy chocolate bars or Girl Scout cookies to support my children's fundraising. But, I'll pass sharing my fence with a neighbor who's willing to die making a fortune; I prefer sharing my fence with a neighbor who's willing to die making a life.

Connection matters. Closets don't.

Materialism's Price

The average American household income has doubled since the 1950s. Yet, happiness has stagnated, and depression has increased tenfold. This plateau in happiness and spike in depression corresponds with our accelerating materialism. For example, per a *USA Today* article from 2016, while leasing cars is rare in most countries, leasing cars had then increased nearly 30% in America. Meanwhile, between 2011 and 2014, 13% of Americans over 12 years old regularly took antidepressants, and between 1999 and 2014, people using antidepressants increased 64%.[22] When you start thinking, "Man, I really need..." turn to Jesus for reassurance. "Look at the birds in the sky; they do not sow or reap, they gather nothing into barns, yet your heavenly Father feeds them. Are not you more important than they?" (Matthew, 6:26). Consumerism demonstrates greed by satisfying our wants. God demonstrates love by satisfying our needs.

Consumer culture is convincing. But, we can leave its lies at the counter.

---

22 In his book, *The Body Keeps Score*, psychiatrist, Dr. Bessel Van Der Kolk, discusses the pharmacology industry. Because drugs are lucrative (in 2012, people spent over $1.5 billion on Abilify, an antipsychotic drug often used to treat mood disorders like depression), medical journals rarely publish studies on alternative treatments for mental illness (for a review of such studies, read Dr. Robert Motta's book, *Alternative Therapies for PTSD: The Science of Mind-Body Treatments*). Practitioners who promote these treatments—like volunteering, exercise, and prayer—are marginalized. I'm fine being an outsider. Actually, I love it.

Materialistic people have struggles beyond depression. Many also suffer from low self-esteem, anxiety, addiction, sickness, and nihilism. Worsening matters are their poor relationships created by narcissism, entitlement, and being manipulative. Because of these and other negative traits, materialistic people objectify others, using them for personal gain. This creates shorter, more conflictual relationships, ultimately increasing their loneliness and affecting their health like smoking 15 cigarettes daily. Life then becomes oppressive. Chaos ensues. That's when we learn that money can create tears—but friends wipe tears.

Like influenza, materialism is a virus. Once it infects part of us, it spreads throughout our bodies. In 1957, a vaccine for materialism was developed; however, it was originally only created for children. Thankfully, scientists are now conducting clinical trials with emerging adults. The doctor responsible for this vaccine has already treated numerous other maladies, including greed, egotism, and pessimism. Roll up your sleeve. Prepare for a slight pinch. Meet the world's most famous pediatrician, Dr. Seuss.

> And the Grinch, with his Grinch-feet ice-cold in the snow,
> Stood puzzling and puzzling: "How could it be so?
> It came without ribbons! It came without tags!
> It came without packages, boxes, or bags!"
> And he puzzled three hours, till his puzzler was sore.
> Then the Grinch thought of something he hadn't before!
> "Maybe Christmas," he thought, "doesn't come from a store.
> Maybe Christmas...perhaps...means a little bit more!"

Usually, Dr. Seuss's vaccine cures materialism. Sometimes, however, viruses are resistant. Especially when the genome is single-stranded RNA, as it unfortunately is with materialism. So, if you're still sick, there's hope. Another vaccine exists. It has been around for over two millennia, its success rate is 100%, and its creator—the first Doctor of the Church—is a perennial Nobel Prize in Medicine recipient. This vaccine, though, burns. Close your eyes. Breathe. Sometimes God's vaccinations hurt.

Come now, you rich, weep and wail over your impending miseries. Your wealth has rotted away, your clothes have become moth-eaten, your gold and silver have corroded, and that corrosion will be a testimony against you; it will devour your flesh like a fire. You have stored up treasure for the last days. Behold, the wages you withheld from the workers who harvested your fields are crying aloud, and the cries of the harvesters have reached the ears of the Lord of hosts. You have lived on earth in luxury and pleasure; you have fattened your hearts for the day of slaughter. You have condemned; you have murdered the righteous one; He offers you no resistance.

—James, 5:1-6

Start ignoring *Vogue*. Stop ignoring God.

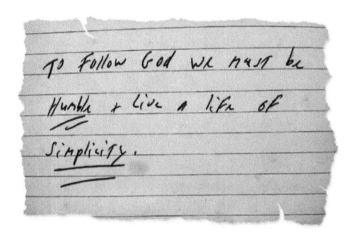

THE TREACHEROUS TREADMILL

"There are sufficient resources in the world for the needs of everybody, but not enough for the greed of even a significant minority." — Millard Fuller

Recall when you've craved something. A 3-Series. A beach body. A corner office. Unless you prolonged your newfound happiness, you likely returned to your emotional baseline. Welcome to the hedonic treadmill (i.e., emotional adaptation). A powerful, universal, and normal emotional response. The hedonic treadmill serves a significant evolutionary function: it helps us survive. Because of emotional adaptation, we're resilient. We "get over it." But, the hedonic treadmill also impedes thriving because we habituate to positive events. This time, we don't want to "get over it;" we want to remain happy. Therefore, we hit the treadmill. Again. And, again. And, again. Forget walking. Now, we sprint. Our destination, however, remains elusive.

Wanting more, we're left wanting.

In 1976, Steve Jobs co-founded Apple. Though he changed the world, his quest for world domination seemed insatiable. Investopedia estimates Jobs's ultimate net worth was approximately $10.2 billion. Putting this into perspective, if you spent $1,000 daily you'd finally be bankrupt after about 28,000 years! Many would give everything for this success. Sadly, some do; however, there's always a price. Steve Jobs died from pancreatic cancer. In a posthumous tribute featured in *Time* magazine, Jobs said of his children, "I wanted my kids to know me. I wasn't always there for them, and I wanted them to know why and to understand what I did… [Having children is] 10,000 times better than anything I've ever done." Steve Jobs only wore a black turtleneck and jeans. Since 1997, his salary was $1. So, I doubt financial greed fractured his relationship with his children. But, not even all the money in the world could fix it.

At Steve Jobs's funeral, his sister, Mona Simpson, gave an emotional eulogy describing his love for his family. Simpson said of Jobs during his final moments, "He looked into his children's eyes as if he couldn't unlock his gaze…Before embarking, he looked at his sister, Patty, then for a long time at his children, then at his life's partner, Laurene…Steve's final words, hours earlier, were monosyllables, repeated three times…'Oh, wow. Oh, wow. Oh, wow'." Thoreau reminds us, "A man is rich in proportion to the number of things he can let alone." Heed his wisdom before the last thing you let alone is your life. If not, your final words might be, "Oh, no. Oh, no. Oh, no."

Materialism is expensive. Then, there's buyer's remorse.

Pleasure, praise, and power might elicit happiness. But, beyond leaving our basic human needs of *competence, autonomy,* and *relatedness* unfulfilled, the high is fleeting.[23] Akin to the sugar rush from eating cookies, we eventually crash. So, we eat another. Then, another. Sometimes pounding a sleeve. That's the dirty little secret. That's why we remain perpetual hamsters on a wheel. The dopamine flooding our brain from achieving culturally-valued goals—like building a tech empire—maintains our addiction. Similar to gamblers at a casino, we pull the slot machine lever, praying for the big payoff. When it happens, after the flashing lights and bells cease, we remain empty. We then try our luck at blackjack—forever chasing the high.

Instead, we should cultivate gratitude. Appreciation is the strongest antidote for emotional adaptation. Especially because comparisons make us feel poor—even when we're rich. Thoreau wrote about this in *Walden.*

> However mean your life is, meet it and live it; do not shun it and call it hard names. It is not so bad as you are. It looks poorest when you are richest. The fault-finder will find faults even in paradise. Love your life, poor as it is. You may per-

23 Self-Determination Theory (SDT) maintains that people are motivated to realize their potential. According to SDT, when our basic human needs of *competence* (i.e., developing our skills), *autonomy* (i.e., managing our life), and *relatedness* (i.e., loving our mates) are fulfilled we thrive. Intrinsic values—like community, affiliation, and growth—satisfy these needs, whereas extrinsic values—like wealth, fame, and image—don't satisfy these needs. Living simply supports intrinsic values, thus aiding basic needs fulfillment and thriving. Materialism, however, supports extrinsic values, thus impeding basic needs fulfillment and thriving. Being materialistic will cost you money—and sometimes your life.

haps have some pleasant, thrilling, glorious hours, even in a poorhouse. The setting sun is reflected from the windows of the almshouse as brightly as from the rich man's abode; the snow melts before its door as early in the spring. I do not see but a quiet mind may live as contentedly there, and have as cheering thoughts, as in a palace.

Count blessings. Not sheep.

If you're exhausted from deferring debt, following fashion, or seeking sovereignty, get off the treadmill. Rest in Jesus. "Take my yoke upon you and learn from me, for I am meek and humble of heart; and you will find rest for yourselves. For my yoke is easy, and my burden light" (Matthew, 11:29-30). Heaven aside, eternal bliss is a mirage. No luxury, look, or leverage will make water appear in the desert. Living simply, however, could breach the levees.

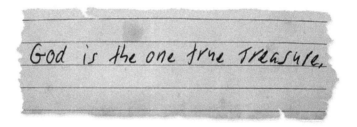

God is the one true treasure.

PARADOXICAL SIMPLICITY

"Voluntary simplicity means going fewer places in one day rather than more, seeing less so I can see more, doing less so I can do more, acquiring less so I can have more." — Jon Kabat-Zinn

Living simply gives us more time and widgets to thrive. Consider this. Minimum wage in New York State is now $11.80. If you worked full-time and squandered every penny on stuff after paying state and federal taxes, you'd have to work 1 month to buy the iPhone XS-Gold, 4 ½ months to buy Chanel's Classic Handbag, and 5 ½ months to buy Gucci's slim-fit safari jacket. Think what you could've done instead. You could've pursued challenges and experienced flow (fulfilling your need for *competence*). You could've clarified your values and lived accordingly (fulfilling your need for *autonomy*). You could've connected with loved ones (fulfilling your need for *relatedness*). Phones aid communication, handbags hold stuff, and jackets create warmth. Choose function over fashion. Choose simplicity over splendor. Choose life over lethargy.

Our time is worth more than overtime.

Living simply exchanges clutter for clarity. It might require accepting a lower salary and reduced spending. In exchange, you could more vigorously pursue rewarding life goals. Like leading an activist group, touring with your band, completing an Ironman Triathlon, starting a family, or entering the clergy. You'd also have more time and widgets for meaningful activities. Like reading, artistic and intellectual projects, time in nature, volunteering, or prayer. The bonus? These pursuits don't require a bonus. Again, heed Thoreau. "He is richest whose pleasures are cheapest."

In my positive psychology class, students complete five assignments to help them thrive. They can choose from about 50. Here's one for living simply:

> *Spend money on only the essentials (e.g., food and rent). When possible, walk, ride your bike, or use your skateboard instead of driving. Tear yourself away from your television, phone, and computer. Create windows of time to pursue meaningful activities like seeing friends, exercising, reading, hiking, visiting a museum, walking along the beach, painting, writing, or playing music. What was it like living simply? What was it like "taking back your time?" How did your view of materialism and living simply change? How likely are you to keep living simply?*

"Living simply" elicits images of thrift stores, organic gardens, and shabby shacks. This view, however, is superficial. Living simply is deeper. Paradoxically, it's also difficult. Therefore, when I created this assignment, I thought few students would complete it. Shockingly, most do. Even more shocking, they love it! Many often thank me for exposing them to living simply. Here are some reactions:

☺ *Thank you for teaching me how to use my time and energy better so I can do things that actually matter. I can't remember feeling so refreshed. I actually slept!*

☺ *This assignment changed my life. I finally read the book I've been dying to read. I also saw my old friend for lunch and went to the gym three times. No way will I ever return to my old ways!*

☺ *I never thought I could stay away from social media. But, I did. And it was amazing! I can't believe how much time I wasted on my phone. My boyfriend and I actually collected shells at Robert Moses. It was awesome!*

People often say emerging adults don't "get it." They should meet my students.

Learning how to live simply is tough in a materialistic world. Where cash is king and ATMs abound. Our role models are generally people who have million-dollar birthday parties, hangars for their cars, and signature sneakers. Models of living simply, however, exist. You must look for them. When you find one, spend time together. Listen. Observe. Learn how they live. It will be worth more than gold.

That's what I did with Professor Thieben. Beyond learning the fundamentals for living simply, I learned the details. The little things that make a big difference. For example, bookmarks get lost. They tear. They fall out. Therefore, Professor Thieben used a paperclip. Now, my children and I do, too. Professor Thieben also dressed simply, wearing his cloud-colored sweater vest more days than not. Until recently, I had the same Smurf-blue winter jacket for nearly 20 years. It worked. It kept me warm. It saved me from shopping. As a nod to Professor Thieben, I replaced the broken zipper with a paperclip. When he wished me happy birthday, Professor Thieben mailed me a handwritten or typed note on homemade 6"x9" stationary. The notes were generally identical. Here's a recent one:

```
                              April 25, 2017 A. D.

   Dear Jeff,

   I wanted you to know that I was thinking
   about you on the anniversary of your
   "natal day."

   Best to your bride and kids. Keep waving
   the flag of education.

                              God bless,

                              Mr. T

   CC: S. Loretta, JFK, Willie Nelson
```

Support your post office. Support your friends. Send notes—not texts.[24]

Materialism facilitates psychological bankruptcy. Living simply, however, facilitates psychological wealth. So, stop trying to keep up with

---

24 Professor Thieben's simple, low-tech practices gave him more time and widgets to thrive. For example, he didn't use email, and he didn't have an answering machine, call waiting, or a cell phone. Thus, he avoided the exhausting task of listening to voicemails, reading messages, and responding. His low-tech practices also helped him connect with people and keep the human touch alive. When he was with you, he was with you. Again, he taught me another important lesson: being unavailable makes us available. (See *Behind the Scenes* for how I've applied Professor Thieben's strategies.)

the Kardashians. Reject greed, selfishness, and vanity. Instead, embrace generosity, kindness, and humility. You'll get more return on your investment.

Be simple. Be alive. Thrive!

MATH MATTERS

"A lady once offered me a mat, but as I had no room to spare within the house, nor time to spare within or without to shake it, I declined it, preferring to wipe my feet on the sod before my door. It is best to avoid the beginnings of evil." — *Henry David Thoreau*

Math is essential for living. We use it to solve real-world problems (e.g., How fast can COVID-19 spread across continents?). We use it to solve everyday problems (e.g., Do I have enough eggs to cook French toast?). We even use it to solve psychological problems (e.g., How many designer jeans must I own to feel secure?). Understanding psychological math is the toughest. The formulas are complicated and change with life's seasons. The exams are also hard. Everybody, including me, occasionally fails. Embarrassed by our confusion, we skip extra help. We then seek the world's answers, becoming even more confused. Instead, we should seek God's answers.

Jesus lived simply. Unlike many people today, when He traveled, He packed light. His disciples did likewise. "He instructed them to take nothing for the journey but a walking stick—no food, no sack, no money in their belts. They were, however, to wear sandals but not a second tunic" (Mark, 6:8-9). Understanding values osmosis, Jesus also chose friends who shunned materialism. For example, aware that possessions possess, St. John the Baptist ate honey and locusts and wore clothes made from camel's hair. A true minimalist, Jesus even condensed the 613 Commandments of Mosaic Law (which includes the 10 Commandments) into two: *love God with your whole heart, your whole soul, and your whole mind*, and *love your neighbor as yourself*. Less is more.

Living simply also helped Jesus master His mission. Free of material distractions, and with like-minded friends, Jesus could honor His big rocks of rest, prayer, and service. Thus, He could then stay focused on connecting with God and completing His ministry. "No one can serve two masters. He will either hate one and love the other, or be devoted to one and despise the other. You cannot serve God and mammon" (Matthew, 6:24).[25] We, however, often spend more time and widgets on shopping, status climbing, and securing riches than fulfilling our destiny. Jesus knew better. "What profit is there for one to gain the whole world and forfeit his life?" (Mark, 8:36). Having disciples might feel fine. But, being God's disciple feels divine.

Jesus is a brilliant mathematician. He befriended the best students, attended the best school, and had the best teacher. Jesus knew how to live simply, and He knew how to thrive. Study His psychological math formulas. Memorize them. Apply them. You'll then pass the most important test: *LIFE.*

---

25 *Mammon* is an Aramaic word meaning "wealth" or "property."

Prospenity + pageantry ≠ paradise

Sandals + Service = Serenity

Clothes tatter. Cars rust. Compliments fade. Jesus remains.

God's love can surpass every human desire.

COMMANDMENT III TIPS

Thou Shalt
Live Simply

1. Clarify your values. Answer these questions:

What do I want said at my funeral?
What do I want written on my tombstone?
What would I do and who would I visit if I had 24 hours to live, and only I knew?
What domain(s) to thrive have I neglected (i.e., personal, social, spiritual)?
What gives me vitality and meaning?
What virtues do I want cultivated?
What kind of life did I imagine for myself as a child?

Sit with the discomfort if you realize you've gone astray from your values. Everybody does. Replace this distress with peace by following your values. Start small. Start slow. But, start. Now.

2. Guard against internalizing our culture's toxic materialistic messages. Treat your insecurity with psychotherapy—not retail therapy. Create a "Thrive" jar, contributing money otherwise spent shopping for your sessions. Also, toss fashion magazines and read your bible; spend less time "liking" friends and more time with friends; avoid cathedrals of consumerism and visit cathedrals of Christ. Furthermore, surround yourself with people

who live simply, not people who drank the "cultural Kool-Aid."
We become what we consume—and who we befriend.

3. Get off the hedonic treadmill. Before your next purchase, use
the "old," "broken," or "obsolete" product you're looking to replace in novel ways. Wait a week before clicking "place order."
Notice how your need is only a 2-day old want. Notice how you
feel and behave with less clutter and debt. Give thanks for what
you have. Count blessings. Not sheep.

4. For 1 week, calculate how many hours you spend 1) working
for material wants, 2) changing outfits, applying and removing
make-up, styling your hair, and exercising for appearance—not
health, 3) posting solely to get followers and, 4) shopping for,
buying, and returning items. Spend those hours the next week
on civic engagement, cultivating relationships, and personal
growth. Keep a journal. Reflect on your experiences. Then, make
a decision: Function? Or, fashion? Simplicity? Or, splendor?
Life? Or, lethargy?

5. Study Jesus' psychological math formulas. **Prosperity + Pageantry ≠ Paradise. Sandals + Service = Serenity.** Memorize
them. Then, apply them. Should you buy yourself another fashion accessory? Or, should you buy someone lunch? Should you
chill with people who think they're cool? Or, should you chill
with people you think are cool? Should you spend your life trying to impress others? Or, should you spend your life trying to
help others? With practice, you'll pass the most important test:
LIFE.

SOCIAL THRIVING

Having achieved personal thriving, you can now pursue social thriving. You must first *accept thyself*. Everyone seeks people's approval. But, thinking you <u>need</u> it for self-worth creates insecurity and, thus, superficial connections. The antidote? Unconditional self-acceptance. Accepting your being, essence, and soul—even without people's approval—provides the courage to be vulnerable and expose your true self. *Being real* will help you attract similar others and foster honest, enduring, heartfelt connections. With this caring community, you'll *love deeply* and have the support for spiritual thriving.

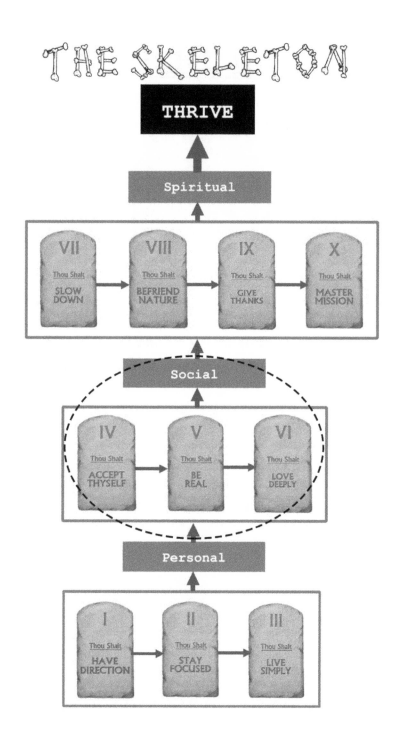

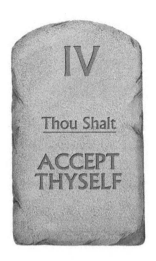

IV

Thou Shalt

ACCEPT THYSELF

Katrina, 26, always struggled with relationships. She was the misfit, the one rejected. The rumors, jeers, and teasing made her feel humiliated. They made her feel "defective." Consequently, she forever questioned her self-worth. Like everyone, Katrina wanted to belong and have deep connections. Yet, she often felt abandoned, filling the void with alcohol and fake friends. Tormented for years, her spirit ultimately broke. One night, Katrina had enough. She crammed 3,000 mgs of Zoloft into her mouth. Staring into the mirror, she fought the urge to swallow. Thankfully, she called her therapist. I'll always remember that Sunday night.

I vividly recall our first therapy session. After a limp handshake, Katrina slumped into the chair across from me. She sat quietly for several minutes, gazing downward. As time progressed, she began twirling her sweatshirt string and biting her bottom lip. Tears trickled down her cheeks. "If your tears could talk, what would they say?" I asked, handing her tissues. Katrina remained quiet. She eventually muttered, "I don't know…I guess…I'm just sick of being so depressed…feeling so alone. I just want to feel better…and…have friends." My eyes became glassy; however, I had hope. Despite Katrina's pain, and through the tears, I saw her potential.

Within a year, Katrina regained her life. She embraced sobriety. She left a safe job for her dream job. She also dropped her "friends" and discovered her tribe. What explains this dramatic transformation? With perseverance, commitment, and a willingness to temporarily experience more pain, Katrina convinced herself that she no longer *needed* people's approval for her self-worth. Even when rejected, she finally started accepting herself—as is. Katrina now refused "emotional scraps." Instead, she only welcomed the main course: *real* connection. Two years after terminating therapy, Katrina texted me, "I got engaged!!! Can you believe it???" Yes, Katrina, I can.

You don't need others' acceptance. You need self-acceptance.

COUNTERFEIT CONFIDENCE

"A truly strong person does not need the approval of others any more than a lion needs the approval of sheep." — Vernon Howard

Rejection stings. It can cause permanent scars. Sometimes, even death. Many factors contribute to how we cope with rejection. The obvious ones include genetics, personality, parental attachment, peer interactions, and traumatic experiences. There is, however, one surprising factor. It's something cherished. Something thought to foster greater educational attainment, higher employment, and stronger marriages. Instead, it fosters earlier sex and substance use, narcissism, and aggression. The fool's gold? *Self-esteem.* "Wait, I thought self-esteem was good," you may be thinking. I hate to give you the classic psychologist response. But, "it depends."

Society convinced your parents that high self-esteem was the Holy Grail. Therefore, they probably showered you with groundless praise saying you were "amazing," "smart," and "talented" for mediocre performances and work. Further, determined to maintain your (artificial) sense of self, your parents likely built your science experiments, carved your pinewood derby cars, and wrote (or at least really polished) your college essays. The irony is that their praise and your "success" was supposed to increase your self-esteem. Instead, it likely lowered it—making you anxious, insecure, and weak. So, after entering college or getting a job, you probably learned fast you weren't as wonderful as you thought. You were just...meh.

Striving to make you feel "good" about yourself, your parents also likely protected you from suffering and pain. Sometimes only hassles. Therefore, instead of helicopter parents, many of you had lawnmower parents. Clearing your life's path, they raised your floor—not your ceiling. Consider the 2019 college admissions scandal. Wealthy parents allegedly paid more than $25 million to fraudulently inflate their children's entrance exam test scores and bribe college officials. Beyond robbing honest students of college acceptance (an appalling offense), these parents also robbed their children of building the *3 Cs to Thrive*: **character, competence,** and **confidence.** Sadly, it seems these parents forgot a fundamental truth: adversity deepens our being.

We struggle when we don't struggle.

Self-esteem—counterfeit or authentic—creates needless pain. According to clinical psychologist, Dr. Albert Ellis, "Self-esteem is the greatest sickness known to man or woman." And, per social psychologist, Dr. Roy Baumeister, "The societal pursuit of high self-esteem for everyone may literally end up doing significant harm." Why? Because self-esteem is tenuous, outcome dependent, and promotes *conditional* self-acceptance. We, therefore, accept ourselves when we're accepted, and we reject ourselves when we're rejected. Because self-esteem makes self-worth conditional, it fosters *"if...then"* beliefs. The thinking goes like this: *"If* I have a date Friday night...*if* I have friends...*if* I get married...*then* I'm okay." Accept this proposition, and you must accept its inverse: *"If* I don't have a date Friday night...*if* I don't have friends...*if* I don't get married... *then* I'm not okay." When your self-worth is dependent on outcomes—

like getting people's approval—it becomes unstable and fragile. Winners then become "winners," and losers become "losers."[26]

Happiness shared is doubled. Friends matter. Companionship matters. Intimacy matters. But, will demanding someone's love help you get it? Or, will you keep making reservations for one? Let me explain. Imagine thinking you *must* have your partner's love. And, if you don't, it's *awful*, you *can't stand it*, and without it you're a *wretch*. If you strongly held these beliefs, and your partner rejected you, how would you feel? Optimistic? Calm? Annoyed? No. You'd feel hopeless, anxious, and angry. And, how would you behave? Independent? Forgiving? Confident? No. You'd behave needy, vengeful, and feeble. Hardly the way to regain your partner.

Now, let's again assume you strongly held these unhealthy beliefs. But, instead of your partner rejecting you, he or she accepted you. How would you feel? Really ponder it. Relaxed? Safe? Secure? No. You'd feel uptight, vulnerable, and worried. And, how would you behave? Trusting? Authentic? Bold? No. You'd behave suspicious, fake, and meek. Likely pushing your partner further away. Thus, aiming for closeness, you created distance. Aiming for connection, you created loneliness. Aiming for self-acceptance, you created self-hatred.

Getting what you want doesn't always get you what you need.

Life is better with love. You don't, however, *need* it to validate your worth. Your value is independent of your relationship status. Moreover, even if you don't awake with someone holding you, remember that you're always being held by the one who matters most: Jesus. "See what love the Father has bestowed on us that we may be called the children of God. Yet so we are" (1 John, 3:1). When the world beats you down—convincing you that you n*eed* others' approval for self-acceptance—look up.

---

26 Conditional self-acceptance applies to all pursuits. For example, we often only accept ourselves *when* we lose weight, *when* we leave home, or *when* we get hired. In Commandment IV, however, I focus on conditional self-acceptance relating to *needing* people's approval. First, it's the most common condition we set for self-worth. Second, it most directly influences our ability to love deeply. Highlighting it, therefore, made sense because Commandment IV (*Thou Shalt* **ACCEPT THYSELF**) is within the **Social Thriving** domain (see *The Skeleton*).

> G-od Created us out
> of Love. He wants us
> knowing We're more Worthy
> than the Pain and Rejection
> Would Have us Believe.

U.S.A.

"Because one believes in oneself, one doesn't try to convince others. Because one is content with oneself, one doesn't need others' approval. Because one accepts oneself, the whole world accepts him or her." — Lao Tzu

In my 20s, my self-acceptance was incredibly conditional on others' approval. Thankfully, I trained under Dr. Albert Ellis, creator of Rational Emotive-Behavior Therapy (REBT). I learned how thoughts, emotions, and behaviors are interrelated. I also learned about *unconditional self-acceptance* (U.S.A.). U.S.A. is the healthy alternative to *conditional* self-acceptance (i.e., self-esteem). Forever struggling with low self-esteem, I asked Dr. Ellis, "Considering the thousands of patients you've treated, how many people get U.S.A. in their gut, in their heart?" "Five percent," he quickly replied. "Really? Having U.S.A. seems impossible," I thought. Challenge accepted.

Here are the steps for cultivating U.S.A. that I've taken and have used with hundreds of emerging adults. The results have been life-changing.

Like me, however, you'll repeatedly fail at every step. When you do, shush your inner critic. Cultivate self-compassion. Then, try again. As Hamlet said, "There is nothing either good or bad, but thinking makes it so." This especially applies to what you think of yourself.[27]

Step 1: Accept Thyself

This refers to rating your behaviors, thoughts, and emotions—not yourself. Imagine you accidentally stood up your partner. It's healthy to think, *"Okay, I forgot to put the date in my calendar. That was stupid. Next time, I'll be more conscientious about keeping plans."* Here, you're rating your *behavior* (i.e., "<u>That</u> was stupid"). It's unhealthy, however, to think, *"I can't believe I stood up my partner. I should've been more careful. I'm so stupid."* Here, you're rating *yourself* (i.e., "<u>I'm</u> so stupid"). The former fosters hope and self-acceptance; the latter fosters despair and self-hatred. As Greek Stoic philosopher Epictetus said, "[People] are disturbed not by things, but by the view which they take of them."

Sometimes, your thoughts are lies.

In college, I tried dating Jennifer. Walking to our cars after a movie, I shared an observation. "Churches used to be the tallest buildings in villages. Then, it was castles. Now, it's big business. What do you think about that?" I asked. Crickets. We then said goodnight. Sitting in my car, I wilted. "Dude, are you kidding me?" I thought. "Did you honestly ask her about building evolution? Smooth. What a tool!" I felt alienated, embarrassed, and alone. Today, such rejection wouldn't phase me. Now, I'd think, "Jennifer finds sociological musings boring. Oh well. Thank God I realized this upfront. I'll put more time and widgets into other deep thinkers." Sticks and stones may break your bones, but rejection should only leave bruises.

---

27 Dr. Paul Hauck's work on U.S.A. inspired this approach. To learn more about it, read his book, *Overcoming the Rating Game: Beyond Self-Love—Beyond Self-Esteem.* You'll learn why U.S.A is the land of the free, home of the brave.

Step 2: Advance Thyself

Healthy obsessions create passion. Whether you're passionate about learning Brazilian jiu-jitsu, modifying cars, or writing a novel is irrelevant. Mastering something creates competence, and competence creates confidence. We then become courageous and more willing to take risks—including with rejection.

Robert, 28, was another patient of mine. Like many young men, he feared women. Making eye contact with them was painful, and talking with them induced panic. Robert loved fitness. Yet, gaming replaced training. Therefore, to help treat his social anxiety, aside from gradually exposing him to speaking with women, I encouraged Robert to restart weightlifting. Not to get the "right look." But, to gain confidence from setting and achieving goals. Within 6 months, Robert transformed himself. He strengthened his body—and his spirit. He now walked with his chest out, shoulders back. He held a stare. He said "Hello" first. He liked this new alpha attitude—so did women.

Find something to master. Find U.S.A. Find connection.

Step 3: Assert Thyself

Needing people's approval keeps us weak and pathetic. It makes us tolerate contempt, selfishness, and sometimes even abuse. Ensuring pain, not love. To regain our self-respect, to achieve U.S.A., we must become brave and assertive. People must learn that "Enough" means, "Do that again, and hell awaits." "Let your 'Yes' mean 'Yes,' and your 'No' mean 'No'" (Matthew 5:37). Make people heed you. Make people respect you. Be a savage.

One day, my mother left me a mean-spirited voicemail, littered with curses. After abusing me for over 30 years, I had enough. My mother was ill, almost terminally. So, I knew when I called back it would be our last conversation; however, I had to take a stand. Confidently, firmly, and with a slight edge I said, "Mom, it's Jeff. I got your message. I'm done letting you treat me like $&#@. You'll never bring your disrespect and craziness into my home. I love my kids too much. Don't call here anymore. It's over." After being a broken record (a standard assertiveness technique), I hung up. Three years later, my father left me a voicemail. "Jeff, it's Dad," he said, sniffling. "Your mother died in my arms last night." I drove to the beach and sobbed. I had to lose my mother to save my family—and my soul.

Relationships must often die before we resurrect.

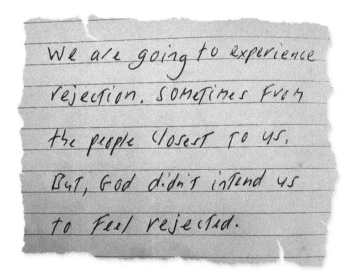

We are going to experience rejection. Sometimes from the people closest to us. But, God didn't intend us to feel rejected.

U.S.A. still evades me. It's a slippery little sucker. When I struggle *needing* people's approval, I try remembering what John the apostle said: "Do not be amazed…if the world hates you" (1 John, 3:13). I also look at my *"I AM ENOUGH"* tattoo on my left wrist. I'm then comforted knowing I'm okay—even *when* people reject me. You are, too.

THE PHOENIX

"To live is to suffer. To survive is to find some meaning in the suffering."
— *Friedrich Nietzsche*

We sometimes go to extremes for people's approval. To feel accepted and loved. This happened to Gianna, 25, a former student of mine and now friend. Gianna and I connected through our drive to thrive and love for God. Over several years, we took many walks around campus (see Commandment VIII). We discussed psychology, philosophy, and faith. Appreciating that life is suffering, we also discussed struggles. Being brave and vulnerable, Gianna told me her story. She inspired me before I heard it; she inspired me even more after.

Gianna forever battled anxiety and depression. At 12, she then began battling anorexia. This continued into her 20s. After hearing about Gianna's particular hardships, her family's history of mental illness, and her chaotic and invalidating home environment, I understood; it was textbook. Except for one thing. The more Gianna shared, the more I realized how, like me, she struggled *needing* people's approval—especially her father's—for her self-worth. I wondered if this contributed to her anorexia. So, I asked. Her response is below. Prepare to learn about courage. Prepare to learn about the dark side of self-esteem. Prepare to learn about U.S.A.[28]

Maybe If

How did *needing* people's approval, especially from your family and friends, contribute to your eating disorder?

A huge part of myself had always thought that I was sub-par (something I still struggle with sometimes today). I truly thought that I was never good enough at anything I did and that I was never going to excel in whatever I chose to do with my future. During some of my darkest times, I always wondered what my purpose was. Or, if I even had one. My life at one point was filled with extreme self-doubt and the inability to see my true worth, which led to so many years of severely destroying my body, overall health, and confidence. Most of these beliefs stemmed from my environment. Although there's a lot more that went into the development of my eating disorder, seeking approval and acceptance from others was a big one. Being the oldest of three, I was expected to be a good role model for my younger sisters. Having a sister with a disability made things even a bit more difficult.

Looking back at the time-periods where my eating disorder was severe, I remember one thing in particular that drove me to consistently use unhealthy behaviors: I needed control. There was so much that was out of control in my life, and looking to seek that control, I found it through food. Life at home was not great. A lot was going on, which in any family would be stressful. And, a lot of my needs came last.

---

28 Notice the *"if...then"* beliefs creating and sustaining Gianna's then toxic, fragile self-esteem.

> Let's face it, being a young adult in today's society trying to figure your life out is a very scary thing.

I was doing a large portion of getting my life together alone with no help. Being a commuter student during my undergraduate career, I had a very hard time connecting with other people and making friends. Especially because most of my days were spent either in class, in the library studying, or commuting to school via public transportation. I remember dreading going home, feeling completely unseen and unheard by everyone, mostly my family. I started thinking to myself very toxic thoughts. *"Maybe if* I was smarter…*maybe if* I was more successful…*maybe if* I was skinnier…*then* they would notice me more…*then* they would love me more…*then* they would appreciate what I do. *Maybe if* I pushed myself to become perfect… *then* people would like me more…*then* I could be a better daughter."* These thoughts became drilled into my head on a regular basis. And, because of this, I began seeking approval and validation from others because I was not receiving any at home.

Growing up, my father was my best friend. Once he became ill, all of that changed. My father and I at the time had a very rough and unhealthy relationship. And, a lot of my beliefs that I developed were shaped by what he would persistently tell me through his words and actions. Of all of the people in my life, he was the one that I sought the most approval from. And, it's one of the hardest relationships I've ever had to distance myself from, due to how toxic it was. I desperately wanted him to notice me and get that father/daughter relationship we use to have back. Up until the day I needed medical stabilization at the hospital, I made it my mission to become "the best Gianna I could be" day in and day out, which only ended up making me sicker. I remember sitting in my hospital bed thinking to myself, "It took getting this ill to finally be noticed. What in the world was I thinking? This is no way to live."

I now realize that I completely became someone I was not. Someone I was not proud to be. However, looking back at my journey, I wouldn't change a thing. The person I am now, the person who I'm becoming, is what I want to share with the world. Although it's still a work in progress, I'm learning a little every day. My biggest lesson?

> When I'm comfortable being in my own skin and I deeply love who I am—without needing others' approval—only then will I truly be happy.

Like a phoenix, Gianna rose from the ashes. No longer *needing* people's approval for her self-worth, she's now thriving. While I finished writing this book, she graduated from an accelerated nursing program at Thomas Jefferson University, pursuing her mission to help others struggling with eating disorders. Her goal is to "not only heal patients' bodies, but their minds as well." Gianna is now also more involved at her church.[29] Besides attending daily Mass, because she cultivated U.S.A., she also made new friends in the young adult ministry. Thankfully, with God's grace, Gianna also has a healthy relationship with food and exercise. Think a phoenix is only Greek folklore? Think again.

---

29 Gianna and her family recently moved around the corner from me in our one stoplight town. Our campus walks became neighborhood strolls. We also now attend the same church, St. Francis of Assisi. "Weird."

Brian Stieglitz/Herald

GIANNA CAPONERA BEGAN training with Anthony Bevilacqua eight months ago. Working out has been one of the steps toward her recovery.

'Strong is beautiful'
Woman reclaims her health with E.M. trainer

By BRIAN STIEGLITZ
bstieglitz@liherald.com

Exercise once left Gianna Caponera with injured knees, constant fatigue and, she said, "feeling miserable." But now it has given her back her strength, she added at the East Meadow gym where she works out with personal trainer Anthony Bevilacqua.

Caponera, 24, of Flushing, Queens, graduated from Hofstra University in December 2017 with a degree in psychol-ogy. She is gearing up to pursue an accelerated nursing program this fall. "A lot of personal experiences led me to want to be a nurse because of what I went through," she said, adding that her goal in the field would be to "not only heal patients' bodies, but their minds as well."

When she was 12, Caponera was diagnosed with anorexia. She described her years with an eating disorder as a cycle of seeking treatment, recovering, relapsing and seeking treatment again. "That's been my life . . . up until now," she said.

Caponera recalled hitting a low point while studying at Hofstra, when her anorexia was complicated by an accompanying diagnosis of an exercise addiction. She remembered taking spin and Zumba classes, and running four or five times a day. "I was so set on a goal that, looking back, was so unattainable," she said.

Fatigue, injured knees and

CONTINUED ON PAGE 14

May 2, 2019 – EAST MEADOW HERALD

...ED FRO... ...ONT PAGE

general unhappiness became the norm, she recounted. She began fainting frequently, and as a result was banned from attending certain cardio classes. "You don't know that you're not well until something bad happens," she said.

Finally, when her illness forced her to take a medical leave from Hofstra, Caponera was inspired to commit herself to becoming a nurse. Now, she calls recovery a constant "work in progress," and said, "Some days I wake up and feel fine. Other days I can't see what others see."

Bevilacqua, a personal trainer for 15 years, began working with clients in his East Meadow garage five years ago before opening a storefront gym on East Meadow Avenue. Caponera's mother, Florence Wilson started working out at the AB Fitness Center in January 2017 before recommending to Gianna that she try one-on-one personal training with Bevilacqua and his team, which she began eight months ago.

"It's just you," she said of her new workout regimen. "You're not comparing your work with the person next to you."

When working with his clients, Bevilacqua creates a meal plan for them to help them hit their goals, alongside working out. "You can't reach your goal without a good diet," he said.

Caponera said she once ate "as little as possible," and "whatever I did eat, I'd burn off. I was miserable."

Now she is trying food she was once afraid to eat — meats, for example — adding more protein to her diet, and eating with other people to ease her anxieties. She added that she has an incentive to eat more so she can have successful workouts.

Caponera added that she began seeing her body, once gaunt, change for the better, and her mentality changed with it. "It's not about being thin or losing weight," she said. "It's about being happy and healthy. Strong is beautiful . . . now I'm so happy when I see myself in the mirror."

"She's a very hard worker," Bevilacqua said. "I'm very proud of how far she's come."

Asked what advice she would give someone facing a similar struggle, Caponera said, "There have been so many times I've just wanted to say, 'Screw it.'" She paused and wiped a tear from her eye as Bevilacqua put a hand on her shoulder. Then she continued: "There are going to be good days and bad days. Be willing to put in the work. And accept help from people — don't push them away."

Gianna is a paragon of perseverance, bravery, and faith. While she once believed smaller dress sizes determined her worth, she now knows her worth comes from being God's child. "Even the hairs of your head have all been counted. Do not be afraid. You are worth more than many sparrows" (Luke, 12:7). Here's a poem Gianna recently wrote. It describes her transformation. It also encourages us to dig deep—especially when we're in hell.

> **"Reclaiming Freedom"** June 20 2019
>
> Reach for the impossible stars in the sky.
> Listen with open ears & loving compassion.
> For then you will find the answers you seek.
> Search for the light from inside of your Heart that was missing for so long.
> Burn as Bright as the sun,
> A rustling flame in a fire,
> Lighting up the night sky once again, or a dark room that's been locked up & hidden for ages— once that fire is lit,
> allow the Heat within your soul to flow through your veins & radiate outward—
> And finally then, will you rise above the Dust & the ashes that once kept you imprisoned. They will never be part of you again, & will finally, be set free.

One day, like Gianna, I hope to "burn as bright as the sun." I hope to be "lighting up the night sky once again." I hope to "finally, be set free." The next time you *need* people's approval for your self-worth, remember Gianna. A samurai. A knight. A Spartan.[30]

---

30 See ~~Deleted~~ Scenes for Gianna's full story. It demonstrates the strength of the human spirit and gives witness to God's grace.

"Strong is beautiful."

ONCE SHE BEGAN working out and changing her diet, Caponera said, she began seeing her body change for the better and her mentality changed with it.

Brian Stieglitz/Herald

Morning! Sorry to bother you this early but I had to share, ... freaking nuts- so I reread the accept thyself chapter this morning while I'm at work... I just realized that before you start talking about me, you put "the Phoenix." While I was away in CT last year for treatment, the first day I got there (and on my last day as well), they had these animal spirit cards- I pulled the Phoenix card on my first and last day. Out of 63 cards, that's the one I pulled. And it's in your book. And I never told you anything 🙈
Hope you have a great day!

ETERNAL ACCEPTANCE

"We love because he first loved us." — 1 John, 4:19

God loved us into existence. Unfortunately, our insecurities—particularly about getting others' approval—often distract us from this truth. We sometimes, then, doubt His love for us. We forget whether we're sinful or virtuous that God still protects us when we're afraid, consoles us when we're sad, and holds us when we're rejected. Reassuring us everything will be okay, and that *we're* okay—as is. God's love is the ultimate security blanket.

In antiquity, elders were revered. So, if you were younger, you had to approach them—except when the elder is God. After demanding an early inheritance from his father, the prodigal son squandered it on self-indulgence. Starving, he then returned home. Still off in the distance, his father ran to him, giving him hugs and kisses. Hearing about his father's compassion, the prodigal son's older brother became enraged. He said to his father, "Look, all these years I served you and not once did I disobey your orders; yet, you never gave me even a young goat to feast on with my friends. But when your son returns who swallowed up your property with prostitutes, for him you slaughtered the fattened calf" (Luke, 15:29-30). His father replied, "My son, you are here with me always…But now we must celebrate and rejoice, because your brother…was lost and has been found" (Luke, 15:31-32).

We're all lost, and we all must be found. Sometimes the home we struggle returning to is the home within our heart (i.e., our unconditionally accepted selves). We're often too scared, ashamed, or proud to seek God's help. He knows this. So, the next time you doubt your worth—thinking you *need* people's approval for love and self-acceptance—turn to God. And, remember to respect your elder. Run to Him. Break a sweat. He's waiting—with open arms.

Self-acceptance takes forever. God's acceptance lasts forever.

Trust God. And, Fall
into His Loving Hands.

COMMANDMENT IV TIPS

Thou Shalt
Accept Thyself

1. Listen for your *"if...then"* beliefs about *needing* others' approval for your self-worth. Then, vigorously dispute these unhealthy beliefs. For example, assume you think, *"If* I have a partner, *then* I'm okay."* Answer these questions:

Why must I be in a relationship?
Why am I a loser for being single?
Where's it written that I must be in a relationship?
How's believing that I'm a loser for being single helping me?
Why is being single awful?
Why is being single impossible to tolerate?

Your "new philosophy" will eventually be something like: "I really want to be in a relationship. I don't, however, *need* one. I'll keep trying to find true connection. But, even if I *never* find it, I'm still okay and can create a meaningful life." Eventually, you'll replace self-hatred with self-acceptance.

2. Do shame attacks. Deliberately act foolish in public. Walk a hot dog on a leash. Pay for an expensive item with coins (preferably on Black Friday). Walk around the track, throughout your neighborhood, or on a treadmill at the gym, dressed like your favorite Marvel superhero or Harry Potter character. While taking public transportation, stand up, scream every stop and the next

stop, and then sit down until you reach your destination. You'll eventually habituate to the "horror" of rejection.

3. Discover your passions. Ask yourself, "What have I always wanted to learn? What have I always wanted to achieve?" Then, do it. Be obsessive. Let your pursuit consume you. Make the time. Spend the widgets. Become a master. Recognize and savor your growth as you cultivate the *3 Cs to Thrive:* **character, competence,** and **confidence.**

4. Stop being weak. Start being strong. While giving "the look," structure your assertive communication by first stating the *fact* (e.g., You're late, again), then stating your *feeling* (e.g., I'm officially beyond annoyed), and then finally making a *fair request* (e.g., The next time you're running late, please call me). Make people heed you. Make people respect you. Be a savage.

5. Recall the prodigal son. Notice how his father runs to him. Notice how his father rejoices when he returns (even after he really screwed up). God does likewise with you. So, the next time your insecurity spikes and you think you *need* others' approval for self-acceptance, respect your elder and run to God. Break a sweat. He's waiting—with open arms.

V

Thou Shalt

BE REAL

Nathan grew up in Gladwin, Michigan. He liked riding bikes, shooting hoops, and recording music on his karaoke machine. Everything seemed fine—until it wasn't. Nathan's parents divorced. He first lived with his mother. Then, his father saved him from her abusive boyfriends. Soon after, Nathan graduated from Gladwin High School. It should've been a time for cheers. A cause for celebration. A bleacher seat, however, was empty. Months before, Nathan's mother was found on the floor—dead from an overdose. Life was already hard for him. But, it just got *real*.

Nathan's friends supported him during these dark times. One was particularly helpful. He accepted Nathan and encouraged his authenticity. He gave Nathan a safe space to explore his emotions, express his pain, and tell his story. They had sleepovers. They stayed up late talking. They passed notes in class. Then, life got in the way. Nathan got a job doing electrical work. His time was now limited, and they began losing touch. Nathan really missed his friend and longed for their deep conversations. Eventually, he lost focus at work and was fired. This meant more time with his friend. Reunited, they pursued their dream—together. Years later, they achieved it. Expressing gratitude to his friend for a lifetime of support, Nathan released a song bearing his friend's name, *Notepad*.

At 26, surprising many, Nathan exploded onto the world stage. Though discreet, his third album, *Perception*, debuted at No. 1 on the *Billboard 200*. Its first single, *Let You Down*, went triple platinum (having been purchased over 3 million times). Two years later, Nathan dropped his fourth album, *The Search*. It, too, debuted at No. 1 on the *Billboard 200*. Beating the bookie's favorite—and the immensely popular—Chance the Rapper. Unlike many rappers, Nathan doesn't curse. He prefers "droppin' clean records, but they nasty." He also doesn't glorify drugs, promiscuity, or wealth. Instead, he writes about *real* struggles, *real* pain, *real* life. Nathan became famous not in spite of being *real*—but because of being *real*. Hence, NF's slogan: *REAL MUSIC TILL THE DAY WE DIE.*[31]

COURAGEOUS CONNECTION

"The greatest gift you ever give is your honest self." — Fred Rogers

Sheep are social. They congregate when grazing. It's not, however, for connection—it's for protection. We, too, are sheep. And, we, too, congregate for protection. But, it's not from wolves devouring our body—

---

31 Nate, your music inspired me to explore my darkness and reside among ghouls, ghosts, and goblins. I can now protect myself with only a match. You've also helped me teach my children about virtue and God. Keep it *real*, dude. I'll try, too.

it's from loneliness devouring our spirit. "Be sober and vigilant. Your opponent the Devil is prowling around like a roaring lion looking for [someone] to devour" (1 Peter, 5:8). Like sheep, therefore, we move toward perceived friends. We feel comforted, we feel safe…briefly. Then, our insecurities circle. They snarl. They snap. They're starving. And, we're easy prey. Our shepherd calls, but we ignore Him. Forever scanning the pasture—waiting for our insecurities to attack.

Being *real* is manifested self-acceptance.[32] It's writing like nobody's reading, yodeling like nobody's listening, breakdancing like nobody's watching. Dr. Carl Rogers, psychologist and leader of the humanist movement, believed a "fully functioning" person must identify, accept, and follow their emotions and being. Consider Ava, 21, a volunteer park ranger with many "pets." Pancake, Toast, Sausage, Biscuit, and Gravy are the names of her Northern Water snakes. Bagel is her bat (who she calls her "sky puppy"), and Waffle is her 500 lb. black bear. Or, consider Heather, 23, a bait and tackle shop employee. She has bedazzled eyes with 1-inch faux eyelashes, "big hair," 2-inch rainbow fingernails, and she wears scarlet red lipstick. Heather enjoys giving workshops on lake fishing, field dressing deer, and hunting moose. "The most wonderful thing about Tiggers is that I'm the only one," said Winnie the Pooh's tiger friend. After creating Ava, Heather, and Tigger, God shattered the mold. He did likewise with you, too.

Everyone struggles being *real*. It can be painful. The consequences are potential shame, rejection, and loneliness. This can trigger issues like abandonment, defectiveness, and lovability; emotions like stress, anxiety, and depression; and behaviors like promiscuity, substance abuse, and self-harm. Our world praises "different." Diversity is encouraged. Black sheep are venerated—until they're vilified. Unlike sheep with fine wool used for designer clothes, black sheep have coarse wool used for rugs. People walk on outsiders. They use them to wipe their grimy feet. Want-

---

32 Keeping Commandment IV (*Thou Shalt* ACCEPT THYSELF), thus, facilitates keeping Commandment V (*Thou Shalt* BE REAL). Are you now understanding the sequential and systematic nature of keeping the 10 commandments to thrive (see *The Skeleton*)?

ing to be accepted by the flock, we post pictures desperate for "likes". We try saying the right thing, at the right time, for the right nod, by the right person. Sometimes, being fake prevents rejection. But, it always prevents connection.[33]

Playing it safe can be dangerous.

The benefits, however, of being *real* outweigh the costs. Authentic people are typically calm, satisfied with life, and happy. This is because synchronous traits, behaviors, and emotions create fulfillment and growth. We choose our path. We find our way. We run our race. But, only if we routinely choose authenticity over acceptance. Ralph Waldo Emerson thought being *real* was so difficult and critical for living your best-life-possible that it deserved a lifetime achievement award. He said, "To be yourself in a world that is constantly trying to make you something else is the greatest accomplishment." Being *real*, therefore, is more than a prerequisite for thriving—it's the essence of thriving.[34]

When we're *real*, so are our relationships. We attract similar others. People with comparable interests, pursuits, and values. People wearing the other pair of our mismatched socks. This facilitates memorable memories, travel companions, pillow talk, sounding boards, and intimacy. We learn about the human condition, our co-dependence, and our common humanity. We realize what makes life worth living. While hiking, my friend, Tom, asked me, "Jeff, are you happy?" A 2-hour conversation ensued. It was raw. We were vulnerable. We saw behind each other's curtains. The cobwebs. The props. The costumes. The masks. The mess. It got *real*. That was the first time we opened our sternums. I was nervous. I also feared judgment and losing a friend. Instead, I gained a comrade.

Friends know our secrets—and love us anyway.

---

33 NF's song, *Let Me Go*, perfectly captures the interplay among insecurity, perfection, acceptance, and rejection. Listen to it if you want to replace being fake with being *real*.

34 Longitudinal research (i.e., following the same group of people over time) with emerging adults found that being *real* facilitates life satisfaction. But, life satisfaction doesn't facilitate being *real*. Thus, while life satisfaction generally helps us live our best-life-possible, it seems other factors—like being *real*—are more important for thriving.

Connection requires courage. "Courage" comes from the Old French word, *corage,* meaning "heart" or "innermost feelings." Thus, courage is telling our story from our heart's abyss. It's the choice to be *real.* Easier said than done. Shame, the fear of loneliness created by vulnerability, engulfs us. But, while vulnerability facilitates shame and fear, it also facilitates true connection. Loving deeply requires facing our insecurities, limitedness, and existential anxieties of being. We must confront experiencing nothingness, feeling like a thing within a galaxy of things. We desire creating a sense of wholeness, a faith in living, and an opportunity for thriving. But, there's no guarantee. Deep connection requires taking risks. It's worth the palpitations. It's worth the panic. It's worth the pain.

Originals are priceless, while replicas have little value. Amedeo Modigliani's *Nu couché* sold for $170.4 million. Pablo Picasso's *Les Femmes d'Alger ("Version O")* sold for $179.4 million. And Leonardo da Vinci's *Salvator Mundi* sold for $450.3 million. Replicas for each, however, are generally several hundred dollars or less. Why? They look identical, right? Maybe. But, the originals get their value from their creator. We do, too.

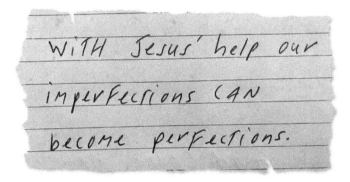

With Jesus' help our imperfections can become perfections.

"PURPLE HEART"

"Associate yourself with men of good quality if you esteem your own reputation; for it is better to be alone than in bad company." — President George Washington

Joe, 24, is the epitome of being *real*. Initially, you might think his authenticity is only superficial. He always wears his Sunday best, he's been rockin' a mountain man beard before it was trendy, and he carries a briefcase. After a short conversation, however, you'll realize that Joe's authenticity penetrates his skin. His hobbies are unique. His musical preferences are unique. His verbal expressions are unique. Have a cup of coffee with Joe (or, an aged lager, as he prefers), and you'll then realize that his authenticity even penetrates his heart. Like us, Joe's heart has four chambers and four valves. But, unlike us, it's also unique. It's filled with respect, integrity, and frosting. This explains why Joe is so polite, moral, and sweet.[35]

Intrigued by anatomy, I interviewed Joe about his heart. I learned that my biology teacher was wrong. The heart not only pumps life into our body—it also pumps life into our soul. Keep reading if you want to learn about the heart's true function. Forgive your teacher. He or she never met Joe.

G.I. Joe

Please tell me about "Joe" as a little boy. What was he like? How were his relationships? What were his interests and hobbies?

Joe, as a little boy, enjoyed a very close relationship with his mom and dad. I still do. Being an only child, I've always considered my parents to be my best friends. Although there were times when I would ask, "When am I going to get a baby brother or sister?" I al-

---

35 As evidence of Joe's sugar-filled heart, many of the quotes used in this book are from an inspirational daily calendar he got me for Christmas. Thanks, brother!

ways knew, in my heart, that I was my parents' sun, moon, and stars. They often told me, "God gave us one special boy, Joe, and that's you!" My parents and I moved together as one unit. We were always engaged in all sorts of activities and outings together. I remember our trips to Train Land in Pennsylvania, Sesame World, vacations to Lake George, family cruises to Bermuda and the Bahamas, taking Amtrak down to Washington D.C., doing the Pacific Coast Highway, Fort Sumter, Gettysburg, and Las Vegas, to name some of our adventures.

In addition to spending lots of quality time with my parents, I was very close with my grandparents on both sides of my family. I was particularly close with my mom's parents, Dolores and Joseph Ventre, and my dad's mother, Grandma Corrado. Unfortunately, my dad's father, Papa Corrado, passed before I was born. My Grandpa Ventre was a United States Marine Corps sergeant during the Korean War and was one of the most influential, significant role models in my life. He taught me so much in the short time that I knew him (he passed away when I was 12 years old). There's one lesson, though, that has always stuck with me:

> Be true to yourself and never compromise your integrity for anyone or anything.

Perhaps the greatest honor he bestowed upon me was telling me that he would select me to be in his platoon. That always meant more to me than I could ever convey in words. Grandpa was one of my heroes. He lived life with honor, dignity, and self-respect. He tried to instill those values in me. If you're listening, grandpa, I love you so much. Semper Fi!

I also had several close friends as a young boy, namely two of my neighbors, Christopher and Nicholas, who still live across the street from me today. We played all the time together, almost every day, in fact. We rode our bikes, walked down to Huntington Beach to play in the water and on the playground, and had Nerf wars in my basement. We also played video games and recorded "Crazy Kid" videos, whereby I would film them performing "Three Stooges-like" antics in my basement. It was hilarious!

I had numerous interests as a young boy. I was involved in the Cub Scouts and Boy Scouts, I loved playing with G.I. Joe and Lego, and I loved photography. I also fondly remember building many model airplanes with my dad. I was always interested in history, ever since I can remember. It's a passion that was kindled both by my dad and my grandpa. I have distinct memories of watching films such as, "Tora! Tora! Tora!" and "Thirty Seconds over Tokyo" with my dad and my grandpa after Sunday afternoon dinners. Those memories still warm my heart. In the third grade, I started playing the violin (albeit unsuccessfully). That was the beginning of my interest in music.

How does "Joe" as a boy compare to "Joe" as a man?

Today, I am much the same person as I was as a child. My overall worldview has endured. I believe that there is a fairness to the universe and that people are basically good. I continue to enjoy warm, close relationships with my family and friends. Our openness and authentic regard for each other remains a continued source of comfort for me.

My interests have also remained the same. But, they've grown and developed over the years to a whole new level. I continue to be very interested in scouting. I'm a member of The Order of the Arrow (the Boy Scouts of America's Honor Society), I became an Eagle Scout, and I trained to become uniformed leadership within Troop 113 as an Assistant Scoutmaster. I continue to participate in BSA events, as time allows, and may again attend Yawgoog Scout Reser-

vation with Troop 113 this summer. I enjoy "giving back" and helping our young scouts develop important values, skills, and character.
If you cultivate the right virtues, everything else falls into place.

My interest in history has propelled me into the world of what I
like to call, "Living History." Some people like to call this hobby,
"Historical Reenacting." Others refer to it as, "Grown men running
around with guns acting like fools!" I've been doing this for about
5 years. It's truly my passion to attempt to preserve our great nation's historic past. Over the years, I've amassed a highly specialized
knowledge of both sides of the American Civil War, the United
States Army in the 1850s, and various Volunteer Militia Companies
formed around Long Island in the late 1830s and 1840s. I also have
an interest in the Revolutionary War.

I teach about various facets of soldier life during these time-periods in American History at numerous venues, historical sites, and
societies. I try my best to be thorough in my lectures, and I'm extremely detail-oriented. I go to great lengths to make sure that my
uniforms, equipment, and information are as accurate as possible.
I even ensure the coffee I drink is authentic! Thankfully, there are
people out there who specialize in making associated accoutrements
to period specifications, utilizing period-correct materials. When
possible, I use original items that I've acquired over time. Perhaps
my most prized possession is my original 1839 manufactured M1816
Springfield musket. You should see it. It's awesome! This hobby has
great meaning for me, as I strongly believe in keeping history alive
through accurate reenacting and reporting. My parents tease me that
I must have been a general in the Civil War in a past life. That's why I
feel so much in my element during reenactments.

> We're passionate when we pursue
> things that reflect who we truly are—
> not who we "should" be.

I've also taken my music hobby far beyond any of my wildest expectations. I play upwards of 10 instruments and have a particular fondness for stringed instruments, such as the bass guitar, dulcimer, banjo, mandolin, strum stick, and the ukulele. I discovered that I'm partial to folk music and (what many call) "old-timey" tunes from the early 1900s. I've studied many great performers from that period, including Charley Patton, Lead Belly, Woody Guthrie, and Pete Seeger, to name a few. I've sought to emulate their music with regard to how they masterfully convey strong sentiment and emotion to their audiences. I'm greatly inspired by Pete Seeger's effortless ability to bring vast audiences together through the universal language of music. He's truly inspirational.

Another instrument that I love to play is the accordion. I own two accordions, a Hohner Panther button accordion and a Fradella piano accordion from the 1950s. I play both regularly and have developed an appreciation for Cajun, Tejano, and Polka music. Over the years, I've learned various two-steps and accordion standards that are immensely popular in Louisiana. I've also studied the late and great Amédé Ardoin. Music is in my veins!

My most important and meaningful musical endeavor, though, is my band, *BowTie Fridays*. Established in 2015, *BowTie Fridays* has performed all over Long Island, New York City, and Connecticut. We're taking over the world one state at a time! I play bass guitar and synthesizer. It's one of the most near-and-dear things to my heart. I truly love it. We have recorded records and are booking gigs all the time!

I have many hobbies. The common denominator that connects them all is the level of commitment, passion, effort and integrity that I feel for each.

You're a very *real* dude, Joe. What's the evolution of your authenticity?

Authenticity has always been something that has been greatly emphasized by my family, particularly by my parents. Authenticity, genuineness, and honesty are values that were instilled in me at a very young age. I can distinctly remember my parents (perhaps my mom, most especially) saying to me, "Don't ever lie to me, Joe. If you do, I won't ever trust you again. There is nothing in this world that you can't tell me and Dad, whether it be good, bad, or ugly. Whatever it is, we'll handle it together. Just don't lie. Know that Dad and I won't ever lie to you. We'll always tell you the truth, no matter how hard it may be to hear. For me, the worst thing you can be is a liar. Enough said. I love you so much. Now, come give me a hug!"

It hasn't always been easy for me to be true to myself. There's a lot of peer pressure and temptation to compromise one's own integrity and sense of right and wrong. But, I believe that my early life lessons and my warm upbringing with loving, supportive parents have helped me to remain *real.* I can say with conviction that I cannot remember a time when I compromised my core belief system. I'm very proud of that.

> As my grandpa always told me, "Never compromise yourself for the approval of other people. It doesn't work."

Describe the struggles of being *real.* How much were you rejected? How did you handle it?

Being *real* can present challenges. I can recall instances in the past where I was reluctant to disclose some of my hobbies and interests to people for fear of being judged as quirky or eccentric, or of being rejected altogether. For example, when I mentioned my historical reenacting hobby, sometimes people's facial expressions appeared to express, "This guy just likes to run around with guns and pretend that he's back in the 19th century. That's so weird!" Truthfully, it's not a hobby in which many 24-year-olds typically engage. But, I must say that, today, it honestly doesn't bother me to talk about my hobbies or interests with others. Even if they may perceive them as strange or unusual. Over time, I have come to realize that this is who I am, and I'm quite proud of who I am. I feel that I have a healthy self-acceptance and an attitude of, "I'm okay, you're okay." So, I don't need to compromise myself to be anything but *real* with others.

> Your real self is going to come out eventually anyway. So, you might as well be who you are from the beginning.

Well said! Does a particular story stand out about being rejected?

I've dealt with rejection, as have most people, during my lifetime. However, there's one period in my life, in particular, that stands out for me. It was during my undergraduate junior year at Hofstra. I was single and eagerly wanting to be in a committed relationship. I had experienced a monogamous, long-term relationship before, but not since high school. I was again yearning for that intimate connection with one special lady. I asked several girls out. But, typically, the relationships wouldn't go beyond the first date. Over time, I began to wonder what I was doing wrong. Was I being too intense, needy, or desperate? Was I defective in some way? I didn't want to hear the phrase, "Maybe we could just be friends?" again.

I spoke with my parents and friends about it. And, most often, their message to me was that rejection is an inevitable part of life that we all have to deal with. They similarly advised that I should continue to put myself out there and see what happens. And, that just because my relationships with these girls didn't develop as I had hoped, it didn't mean that I'd never find a special person one day. What it did mean was that these girls weren't the right match for me, and that I wasn't the right match for them. I learned that I wasn't to blame for my lack of a monogamous relationship. There was no blame, just the wrong matches, at that time. I thought about it and concurred that I needed to keep looking.

We can't cheat adversity…it happens. It's how we deal with it that matters. And, how we deal with it is truly a choice.

I truly believe that the loving counsel of my family and friends helped me reflect upon this challenging time in my life, and to ultimately learn valuable life lessons from it. I learned that rejection truly is part of the human experience. No one is invulnerable. So, I chose to keep going. I continued to put myself out there and took risks. I can happily report that, now, I'm in a happy, year-plus-long, committed relationship with my girlfriend!

Life often has a way of surprising us when we least expect it.

Thank you for sharing. I, too, struggled dating. How did you deal with the rejection?

The rejection that I felt while dating helped me to make *unconditional self-acceptance* (U.S.A.) my creed.[36] I came to realize that my happiness wasn't contingent upon the approval of others or the presence of one significant person in my life. I reflected and soul-searched about who I was as a person. I was an individual with personal strengths and weaknesses (like everyone else), who had a right to be who I am (like everyone else), and who had a right to be happy (like everyone else). I took this time to dispute my own unhealthy thinking, anxieties, fears, and self-doubts, and I came to realize that I was a pretty okay guy. I could be happy without a significant other. It wasn't my preference. But, it wasn't *necessary* for my happiness. I further came to understand that we cannot always make things happen just because we want them to happen.

---

36 You'll learn below why Joe knows about and understands U.S.A.

Things happen when they're supposed to happen, in their own time. Everything is in God's hands.

Wow. It seems like you did a phenomenal job convincing yourself that you don't *need* people's approval to be happy. What about now? Are you "cured?"

I think that we all want the approval of others, but I don't necessarily think that I struggle with *needing* it. I believe that I have a healthy sense of U.S.A. This helps me with being my own person and speaking my own truth. I think that if we, as people, are overly concerned with having others' approval, we may inadvertently compromise our own convictions, integrity, and real selves to get that approval.

I don't think that being someone you're not ever really works because it creates a distance between our real self and others.

When people create a false sense of self they're disconnected and distanced because their relationships are dishonest and misleading—not honest and *real*. I've come across people who I consider to be "chameleons," as they change who they are depending upon who they're with, just for approval. I can't imagine doing that because it's a type of lying. I was taught that it's more important to have your own self-approval, because that's the only way that you can ever truly attain self-respect.

> People who wear masks to gain approval may believe they've won the battle. But, they'll lose the war because they remain alone (emotionally), even with that approval.

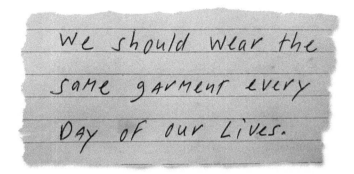

We should wear the
same garment every
Day of our Lives.

Okay. So, struggling with dating during your undergrad years stands out as a period of rejection. But, what about being accepted for who you are? Does a particular period or story about that stand out?

One story about being accepted for who I truly am occurred on the day of my Hofstra graduate school interview on March 6, 2018. I remember being incredibly nervous for my faculty interview. Nerves abounding, my name was called! My interview was with, wait for it, Dr. Robert Motta. Not only is he one of the most distinguished members of Hofstra's faculty, but he's also the *Director* of its Psy.D. School/Community Psychology Program! And, to make matters even more anxiety-provoking, he was my mother's professor and dissertation sponsor when she attended the Ph.D. School/Clinical Psychology Program at Hofstra back in the 1980s! I don't think that my anxiety level could be any higher than it was at that moment.

Dr. Motta began the interview with cordial introductions and niceties. He asked me only one or two questions about my undergraduate experience at Hofstra. Because I was so anxious, I elaborated much more than I needed to. He was kind and understanding, and nodded throughout my ramblings, likely thinking, "Wow, he talks a lot!"

After my verbal assault, Dr. Motta asked, "What are your interests, Joe? Tell me about your hobbies." Oh, no! Now, I was in a predicament. Civil and American Revolutionary War reenacting, a run-of-the-mill hobby for a young twenty-something, right? Not! I can remember a thousand thoughts instantly racing through my mind, all at the same time. How should I answer this? What should I say? Will he think that I'm quirky, strange, or bizarre in some way when I tell him about my reenacting? Will I jeopardize my chances of acceptance into the program when I tell him? I was afraid that I'd be judged and rejected for having such an atypical interest. But, because of my strong belief in myself, my integrity, and my level of self-acceptance, I knew I had to be honest.

Even if he thought I was strange, or that my hobby was eccentric, or that I wasn't right for the program, I'd still accept myself because myself is who I am.

After considering the many possible responses simultaneously swirling around in my head, I looked Dr. Motta squarely in the eye and finally said, "I'm a Civil War and Rev War reenactor, otherwise known as a Living Historian." I braced myself for the judgment. But, it never came. Rather, what I thought would be perceived as a quirky, idiosyncratic hobby was, instead, celebrated by Dr. Motta. Who I later learned is a Vietnam War veteran. Go figure!

> Once again, I was reminded that being authentic and honest about who you are—as scary as it is—helps you find and connect with like-minded people.

Dr. Motta seemed genuinely interested in my reenacting. He asked me many, many questions about it. A lively discussion ensued, my anxiety evaporated, and I was accepted into the program! This is one example of how my own self-acceptance gave me the courage to take the risk to reveal my true self. And, it paid off. To this day, Dr. Motta and I often talk about military history together!

Another story regarding me being *real* occurred when I was a fresh-man in high school. As with most high schoolers, fitting in with the "cool" or "popular" crowd was important to me. But, I have to say, that even at that age, I knew never to compromise myself or my be-liefs of right and wrong for the approval of others. No matter how powerful the desire to fit in had become.

I started spending time with a group of "friends" that year who seemingly enjoyed similar interests to mine. We all liked playing the same video games, enjoyed listening to the same type of music, and shared many similar thoughts and feelings. My friend group con-sisted of about seven people in all, two with whom (I thought) I felt particularly close. At the beginning, all was good. Then, as time went on, I began to see changes. Increasingly, when we all got to-gether, these two particular friends frequently thought of mischie-vous (sometimes illegal) things to do and pressured the rest of us to engage in their nefarious activities, including vandalism, destroying public property, and trespassing. I was uncomfortable with what they wanted to do and with their demands to participate. This was not my idea of fun, and I told them so. Time and time again, I rejected their pressure to comply and distanced myself from the group.

> *Being rejected hurts. But, being real sometimes requires you to (kindly, and with compassion) reject others.*

As time passed, their idea of fun became more and more danger-ous to me. They wanted to smoke marijuana, steal and drink alco-hol from our respective parents' houses, and view illicit sites on the Internet. I knew, without question, that these activities didn't align with my own personal value system. But, I distinctly remember being somewhat conflicted, as the desire to fit in was also very important to me. So, the question that I asked myself became, "Do I compromise my own values for the approval of these 'friends?' Or, do I stay true to myself and what I know is the right thing to do?" I decided to be true to myself.

Time after time, I found myself resisting their pressure, to which they would always respond, "C'mon, Joe. Everyone does this stuff!" My retort would typically be, "Not everyone…I don't, and my other friends don't either."

I couldn't compromise myself for their friendship, no matter how important their approval and acceptance seemed to be at the time. My own self-acceptance, self-respect, and ability to remain true to my own convictions was ultimately much more important. Needless to say, my decision didn't sit well with them. We severed ties, but they continued to frequently mock me for not doing what they were doing. The teasing and verbal attacks continued for months. But, I remained strong, even though it was difficult and, at times, enraging.

I often spoke with my parents and close friends about it. Although it was a tough time, I'm proud of myself for living by my values—and for not compromising my self-respect for others' acceptance. Eventually, the harassment subsided. But, my self-acceptance, self-love, and self-respect for staying *real* endured. Lesson well learned! By the way, by my senior year in high school, most of us were again friendly (just an aside).

Stressful grad school interviews and being teased…yep, been there, done that. How do you feel when people accept you for who you are? And, how did people fostering your authenticity influence your decision to pursue a career in psychology?

The joy of being accepted for who we really are is a feeling like no other. It's wonderful to be truly heard and fully understood by others. When I feel accepted for who I am, I can deeply trust and share my innermost thoughts, fears, and passions. When I feel accepted for who I am, I can take risks and grow.

Being accepted for who I am makes my heart feel light. It's a joyous, glorious, and jubilant experience.

This helps me in my hopes of becoming a psychologist, I think, because we, as professionals, need to fully accept our clients for who they truly are, just as we need to accept ourselves for who we truly are. Our clients can then, in turn, experience the joy of being fully accepted and understood as their true selves. As psychologists, I think that we need to create a no-judgment zone, an atmosphere of unconditional acceptance for our clients, so that they're comfortable with revealing their deepest, innermost thoughts and feelings to us. If this is accomplished, I believe that we have the greatest probability of helping them thrive.

My journey toward self-acceptance has instilled within me a great sense of confidence. With this self-confidence, I feel unstoppable. Having developed an honest, deep, and genuine faith in my own abilities and myself is truly an unparalleled feeling. It makes me feel as though I can accomplish whatever I set my mind to. And, guess what, I have!

> When we really accept ourselves and are real, we develop a psychological "safety net" that protects us from fear of failure and self-censure.

This net enables us to take risks because, in the event that we "fall" or fail, we'll be caught and remain safe and unharmed. We'll be ready to try again, without self-admonishment or self-loathing for "falling" because no real harm is done. We accept that, at times, we may not be successful. But, we also realize that there's success in the attempt itself.

My grandpa always said, "If you make a mistake, Joe, make sure it's one of commission, not omission." Carpe diem! Seize the day! Seize the opportunity!

Your grandpa is a sage. What about any other missions you may have besides being a psychologist? What role has authenticity played in you finding and pursuing them?

I long to touch people through my music, much in the way that one of my heroes, Pete Seeger, did. To me, it's truly a gift to move people emotionally, to help them heal in some way, whether through the language of psychotherapy, music, or other means. For me, deeply touching people's souls, being an agent of change, being someone who helps to promote inner peace, happiness, and joy in others is gratifying beyond words. I truly believe that my musical endeavors will be lifelong. Music is a part of my personal fabric!

Another mission that I've identified is my interest in educating others about our nation's great history. I'm passionate about sharing historical information that can be easily "lost" or inaccurately transmitted to others, particularly to our youth. A relatively short period of time has passed since I was in elementary school, middle school, and high school. But, I've observed a significant, disturbing difference between today's youth and those of my era, with regard to the level of apathy, disinterest, and lack of passion about our magnificent country and her past.

> It makes me wonder: If we don't value and respect others' history—what makes them who they are—will we not value and respect our own?

I feel that one of my missions is to teach about how the freedoms and the personal and civil rights that we enjoy (and often take for granted) today, as United States citizens, didn't come without incredible sacrifice and a willingness to fight for deeply held convictions. If history (and the lessons that are recorded from associated events) aren't passed on, they'll be forgotten or, even more horrific, never learned in the first place. This is incomprehensible to me.

One of my grandma's dear friends, Joe Ambrosino (Joe A.), a Korean War veteran, will be 88 years old in April 2020. He holds an executive position in Merrick's Veterans of Foreign Wars (VFW) post. And, to this day, he lectures to numerous Boy Scout troops across Long Island about what it was like to fight in a war and to defend our country. He's impassioned in his talks and tries hard to teach that the freedoms that we enjoy were hard earned and came at a steep price, often stating, "If you have free will today, thank a veteran." It's one of his bumper stickers, in fact (yes, Joe A. still drives at 87 years young!).

I admire Joe A. He, like my grandpa, has taught me that, "You can't know where you're going unless you know where you've been." I'm thankful for our nation's past. I honor it. I'm grateful for and humbled by it. I feel blessed to be a free citizen. I'll continue to teach about it to all who will listen (sometimes difficult, as I can drone on for hours…oh, well…that's me). After all, it's one of my passions and life missions.

Finally, I would like to be a loving husband and father one day. This life mission, I believe, comes from a long line of exemplary husbands and fathers in my family, starting with the shining example of my father, Louis Corrado. Truly, there are no words that can adequately describe my dad in either role. But, the following immediately come to mind: loving; good; tolerant; kind; dependable; patient; compassionate; accepting; passionate; brilliant; strong; role model; hero. My dad is a beacon of goodness. My mom says he's a "special soul," and that I'm very much like him.

We tend to be like the people we're most around. Thankfully, God blessed me with a phenomenal inner circle—my family.

In my life, I honestly cannot remember one time when my dad didn't accept me for my real self, with all my thoughts, beliefs, and behaviors (unless he believed that they'd somehow put me in harm's way, and then there was a discussion about it). My dad is the very definition of "accepting." That's one of the reasons why he's such a great psychologist. I'm blessed to have had him as my first and most important role model and as an example of how to relate to others, how to resolve conflicts, how to appropriately express feelings, and how to love. His example has consistently helped me to cultivate my own sense of self-acceptance over the years because he accepted me for who I am. It was all okay, I was all okay. There was nothing that was bad or wrong about me. Yes, I sometimes acted foolishly. But, that didn't make *me* a fool! My dad made sure I knew that.

> Being raised with this basic belief—that I'm okay even with my flaws and quirks—was invaluable to me and my feelings of self.

My grandpa also provided me with a beautiful example of how to be a good husband and father. He adored my grandma, and they enjoyed 49 years of marriage together before his passing. My mom frequently speaks about how he, as her father, often imparted wisdom from his own experiences to explain things to her and my aunt when they were growing up. Even today, my mom looks to the heavens and says, "Dad, you were so right," when one of his life lessons once again rings true. I can only aspire to live up to these wonderful examples when I do eventually marry and have children.

It's one of my missions to make my role models proud of me, as they've made me proud of them.

You clearly have very supportive and loving relationships. How has being *real* helped you love so deeply?

I've been immensely fortunate to have been raised in a loving home with two truly incredible parents. They completely accept me for who I am. They're my first teachers so, if they accept me, I can accept myself, just as I am. I can be *real* because I'm not afraid to be myself. I've been given permission to always be the authentic, real me. Because I know that I'm deeply loved and accepted, I can, in turn, deeply love and accept myself—and others. I can, without fear, project my true, authentic, real self to the world without consequence. While also respecting, appreciating, and encouraging others' authenticity, too.

The support, love, and acceptance that I've been shown throughout my life has given me a very special gift: the ability to see the good and the light within myself—and others—and the ability to be true to myself.

The ability to know and express my real self has enabled me to deeply connect with others and to establish and maintain honest, true, lasting relationships. My family, friends, and girlfriend know who I truly am and, because of that, relate to me on an honest, meaningful level. We're genuinely connected because there are no barriers, masks, or false selves getting in the way. Like I said before, you might as well be your real self because your real self will eventually emerge anyway.

Being *real* has enabled me to determine which relationships are the most meaningful in my life. Through an examination of my own value system, I was able to "trim the fat" and associate myself with a circle of true friends who honestly and openly think and behave similarly to myself. Being *real* enabled me to find more like-minded people with whom I could establish real relationships (similar to me being *real* with Dr. Motta and us connecting). I don't need to work to fit in with a crowd.

And, like you and I have discussed, this saves a ton of time and energy for more important matters—like living the best life we can.

Being *real* has also taught me about vulnerability. I have several amazing friends, from my *BowTie Fridays* bandmates, to my Hofstra "brothers," to my girlfriend…we all share the same personal values. We all truly know each other and truly like each other as people. We're comfortable around each other. We have the courage to be *real* around each other without pretense or fear of rejection. We can be who we are in our purest, most unadulterated forms. This, to me, is true intimacy, true connection.

> When we put ourselves out there to others in a raw way, we risk a great deal. But, this vulnerability is ultimately the key to creating real relationships.

The mask, the false self doesn't work. It only creates distance, and distance creates loneliness. I'm a firm believer that, when you accept yourself and when you're *real* with others, you can then be vulnerable. This paves the way for beautiful human connections. I'm blessed with the ability to enjoy extremely close relationships with my family, with my close friends, and with my girlfriend.

I can honestly say that all my relationships have been greatly enhanced by my ability to be *real* with others.

You again mentioned how courage is important for being *real*. Can you please expand on this?

The fear of rejection or judgment can set up roadblocks to being *real*. It takes courage to side-step these roadblocks. I think that we need to be courageous, particularly in this day and age where peer pressure to be/act/think/look a certain way is so much a part of our culture. Especially with social media. While using it to touch base with people is fine, too much of it can really interfere with you being *real*. Again, my parents were crucial figures in fostering the belief that I'm okay just the way I am. I distinctly remember both of them telling me time and time again, "Who cares what other people think? What do *you* think? Use your own head. Always stay true to yourself. If you can't tell yourself the truth, you're in trouble." It took some time for that message to really solidify. But, now in my 20s, I wholeheartedly agree with it.

My own faith has also greatly contributed to my courage to move past the roadblocks of judgment and rejection. Over time, I have come to realize that God created me this way *for a reason* and that He has bestowed particular interests and talents upon me *for a reason*.

> God created me this way. I take great pride in the work He did to make me the person I am today!

If you could savor a beer with anyone, who would it be? Why?

It would probably be Pete Seeger. I've always admired his ability to bring vast groups of people together. If you look at the live videos of his shows, the emotion in the venues is palpable, and the connectedness created by his music is nothing short of miraculous. The power of his music bonds people together in ways that are unexplainable. I'm so inspired by, not only his talent, but by him as a person. Interviews with Pete Seeger have revealed him to be a loving, sensitive, kind-hearted, and good-natured individual who conveys messages of peace, compassion, and non-violence to the world. What greater gift can someone give to others?

Okay, final question. What advice can you give other 20-somethings who want to be *real*, but who are paralyzed from the fear of rejection and loneliness?

For me, the presence of supportive and warm figures in my life aided tremendously in fostering the courage to be *real.* My parents taught me that there's no option, no debate. Tell the truth to yourself and others—the rest will follow. Their acceptance of me, in turn, has fostered my own sense of acceptance, awareness, and efficacy. Their love, warmth, and support instilled in me a profound sense of competence and confidence that enables me to be myself. I can tell them anything, and I know it will be okay. I learned from the best and by example. So, my first piece of advice is to surround yourself by loving, supportive people who encourage you to be you, and who love you for who you are. If someone tries making you into someone you're not, walk away. It's not worth it.

My second piece of advice is simple, yet it takes immense courage: Just be you! You're awesome—as is. You know who you are. You know what you think and what you believe. You know how you feel. Don't be afraid to communicate you to others. People will admire and respect you for it. But, more importantly, you'll admire and respect yourself. It's not impossible. It's something we're all capable of, if we commit to it. So, be strong. Be brave. Go for it!

> And, when you struggle being real—
> and we all do—ask God for help.
> He's as real as it gets!

Joe was wounded in battle. He took shots on the playground, in his neighborhood, and at mixers. Minié balls hit him. Bayonets sliced him. Yet, he fought hard. He was strong. He was brave. God graced him with a loving, supportive platoon. Eventually, Joe won the war. A paragon of authenticity, I award him the "Purple Heart." Joe, you're a true soldier. I salute you, sir.

Life is a battle. Fight for something noble—like being *real*.

"I AM"

"The Lord is my light and my salvation; whom do I fear? The Lord is my life's refuge; of whom am I afraid?" — Psalm 27:1

People often say they'd do "anything" for a date, dinner plans, or diamond ring. For some, it's worth giggling at gossip, self-deprecation, or another drink. For others, it's worth bruises, belittlement, or walks of shame. And, for people truly desperate for connection, it's worth death. But, when have you heard someone say being *real* is worth death? I never have—until considering Jesus.

Upon arrest, Jesus stood before Caiaphas and the entire Sanhedrin.[37] The Sanhedrin wanted Him dead to retain their power and wealth. So, they sought false testimony against Him. They got none. Until two witnesses came forward saying, "This man said, 'I can destroy the temple of God and within three days rebuild it'" (Matthew 26:61). Caiaphas asked Jesus to respond to this accusation. He kept silent. Enraged, Caiaphas then asked Jesus if He was the Messiah, the Son of God. Even knowing the consequences, Jesus replied, "I am" (Mark, 14:62). He was then scourged and crucified. Had Jesus denied his essence, He might have avoided torture. He might have saved His life. But, He would've then lost his soul—and abandoned His mission. Being *real* might cost us mates. It might cost us dates. It cost Jesus His life.[38]

Staying true to ourselves is one of the toughest commandments to keep for thriving. We must be honest, courageous, and vulnerable. We must tolerate doubt, fear, and rejection. We must also accept possibly sleeping alone, sitting alone, and eating alone. But, we needn't feel alone. Jesus, the most rejected person in history, saved you a seat at the lunch table. Sit beside Him. Share your snack. Make a friend.

---

37 The Sanhedrin was the supreme council and tribunal of the Jews led by the high priest (who was then Caiaphas).

38 The Roman governor, Pilate, was afraid of crucifying Jesus. His wife told him, "Have nothing to do with that righteous man. I suffered much in a dream today because of him" (Matthew, 27:19). Pilate, therefore, ordered Jesus' scourging—what the Romans called "the halfway death"—hoping it would appease the bloodthirsty townspeople. During the scourging, Jesus was tied to an upright post, His hands above His head. Each strike from the flagellum (i.e., whip) ripped His skin because of the sheep bones, rocks, pottery shards, and steel attached to it. Pieces of muscle, sinew, and bone went airborne. A red mist appeared. After dozens of strikes, His back, arms, chest, buttocks, and legs were shredded. His bones were exposed. The soldiers then revived Jesus, dosing Him with water. The scourging continued. Then, the "fun" began. Soldiers dressed Him in a scarlet military cloak. They placed a crown of thorns on his head and drove the thorns (several inches long) into His skull by striking Him with a reed. They knelt before Him, saying, "Hail, King of the Jews!" He was then crucified. The next time you deny your essence fearing ridicule, loneliness, or rejection, consider what Jesus did to be *real*.

Stop playing the game. Start a new one.

If we follow Jesus
we will be rejected
by many people.

Thou Shalt
Be Real

1. Show your true self. Start slow. Be cautious—yet courageous. Begin telling someone about your quirks. Maybe you eat peas individually. Maybe you only wear pajamas emblazoned with bears, donuts, or Yetis. Maybe you obsessively read about serial killers. If the person seems trustworthy, share your views on more serious matters, like chastity, cohabitation, or childcare. If you don't connect, try again with someone else. You must strengthen your courage to strengthen your connections.

2. Stop trying to numb your fear, loneliness, and shame. Put down your phone. Put down your drink. Put down your work. Instead, confront your suffering. Learn about yourself. Go deep. Walk in the darkness. Tolerate bumping into things before your eyes adjust. What monsters lurk? How do they hurt you? Why are they there? Who unleashed them? Stay in the dark until you have answers. When you do, cultivate self-compassion. Write a letter to your 5-year-old self. What would you tell him or her? Follow your advice.

3. Tolerate ambiguity, and stop demanding certainty. Ask someone out...though he or she might "have plans." Take the job interview...though there are 200 other applicants. Run the marathon...though you might collapse. Audition for the lead role... though you've only been an extra. Trust yourself. Cultivate courage. Have faith.

4. Recall Joe, the paragon of authenticity and "Purple Heart" recipient. Review his insights: *"Your real self is going to come out eventually anyway. So, you might as well be who you are from the beginning,"* *"When we really accept ourselves and are <u>real</u>, we develop a psychological 'safety net' that protects us from fear of failure and self-censure,"* and *"God created me this way. I take great pride in the work He did to make me the person I am today!"* Meditate on his wisdom. Then, embody it.

5. Remember what Jesus experienced to be *real*. Carefully read Matthew 27 and Mark 15. Sit with it. Pray on it. Imagine His anguish and despair. Had Jesus denied His essence, He might have avoided being tortured, humiliated, and crucified. But, He also would've lost His soul—and abandoned His mission. Jesus *had* to be Himself. You do, too.

Mom and Dad were fighting, again. This time, Mom didn't threaten Dad with the rifle. She didn't run toward traffic threatening suicide. Dad didn't punch through sheetrock. He didn't rip the phone off the wall and demolish it. Nonetheless, this fight felt different. It was more volcanic. The fireworks were louder and brighter. Curses spewed, and the screaming escalated. Dad smashed the vacuum cleaner to the floor—shattering its glass panel. Shards rained on JJ. Working around the glass, he kept eating his tuna casserole. It was another day at Disney.

Growing up, JJ experienced more than emotional abuse. Sometimes, it was a wooden spoon to his thigh. Other times, it was a belt to his bottom. Occasionally, it was a hand to his face. Things changed when JJ was around 8. His Oscar the Grouch doll could no longer protect him, having lost too much blood fighting ogres. Therefore, soon after, his purity was poisoned—and his childhood died. During his first photo shoot, JJ wore his favorite sky blue E.T. pajamas. Unlike E.T., however, he didn't want to phone home—he wanted to leave home. Bruises fade. Welts subside. Handprints disappear. But, the scars from losing his innocence remain. Even now as an adult, JJ feels them stretch when sensing rejection, abandonment, or danger. He feels them tear when seeing an adult hug a child too long. He feels them bleed when realizing that a room suddenly got dark. JJ likes to think he's a confident man. But, he's still a scared little boy.

Thankfully, God showered JJ with grace. He gave him the right friends, at the right time. They taught him about compassion, support, and love. They reoriented him. They showed him the way, giving him a new roadmap for love. JJ was then able to find other loving relationships. At 23, a beautiful, intelligent woman winked at him and said, "Hello." Six years after our first date, my wife and I started a family together.[39]

DUI

"Parents are like shuttles on a loom. They join the threads of the past with threads of the future and leave their own bright patterns as they go." — Fred Rogers

---

39 After writing this sentence, I heard my son say to my daughter, "I walloo, Julianne." So much for trans-generational domestic hell. God isn't just great—He's awesome!

We're born to be loved and to love deeply. We feel it when Mom kisses our boo-boo, or when Dad pats our back. Embraces, an arm around our shoulder, and intertwined fingers warm our hearts. Likewise with animals. Elephants hug each other, play together, and "run to the door" after being reunited (contrasting many people). Birds, like the Brewer's sparrows and chinstrap penguins, share food to forge bonds and demonstrate cooperation and altruism. Mother-baby blue whale pairs caress one another. Loving deeply, it seems, is in our DNA. God resides in us all.[40]

In the 1960s, psychologist, Dr. Harry Harlow, demonstrated the significance of love on development. He isolated infant rhesus monkeys from their friends and mothers. Secluded, the monkeys suffered. They stared blankly. They circled their cages. They self-mutilated. Some starved themselves—even to death. When re-introduced to the group, many monkeys stayed alone, still suffering. Yet, they found solace holding their cloth diapers. "Aha!", thought Dr. Harlow. "Infants might innately desire clinging to something soft, comforting." Dr. Harlow then gave the isolated monkeys two surrogate mothers. One "mother" was made of wire and wood, yet she held a milk bottle. The other "mother" was covered in foam rubber and soft terry cloth, yet she had no milk bottle. When given the option, monkeys chose feeling loved over feeling satiated. Fasting from food is one thing, fasting from love is another.

We need food to survive. We need love to thrive.

Monkeys raised by their biological mothers always fared best. Compared to surrogate mothers, biological mothers raised more confident, loving children. Their offspring better navigated the "playground." They knew how to share the ball. They knew about taking turns on the swings. If a bully flexed, they stood firm. Because their mother loved them, they

---

40 Spindle neurons are brain cells that help generate social emotions like empathy, trust, guilt, embarrassment, and love. Scientists previously thought only human brains had spindle neurons. But, we now know that they're also in the brains of great apes, elephants, and marine animals including humpback whales, sperm whales, fin whales, orcas, and bottle-nosed dolphins. Research determining how these animals express love and related emotions remains underway. Nonetheless, we know that they're wired to love deeply. We are, too.

thought others would, too. Thus, they were successful with dating and mating. Thanks to their matriarchal model, female monkeys also became better mothers. Monkey see, monkey do. Mothers, therefore, are more than milk dispensaries—they're also love dispensaries.

Similar to monkeys we, too, learn how to love from our parents. They're our first driving instructors; we drive under their influence. They also provide our roadmap for love. Sometimes, the map helps us find love. Other times, it gets us confused or lost. Having worked with thousands of emerging adults, it seems many had incompetent instructors and are using the wrong map. Some find themselves in sketchy neighborhoods or refueling at creepy gas stations. Others keep reaching dead ends or crashing. Exaggerating? Consider these stories of multi-car collisions and a peaceful road trip.

Domestic Driver's Ed

Betrayal

Rebecca, at 14, learned about her father's pornography addiction and affair. Now 24, she's incredibly promiscuous. But, Rebecca "only" sleeps with four new guys per semester. She also tolerates her boyfriend's drug problem, flirting, and cheating—until scratching his car with a screwdriver. "Whose car were you really destroying?" I asked. "I don't know," she replied with malevolent eyes. Destroying "Dad's" car was cathartic.

Contempt

Paul's father hated women and was sexually charged. In elementary school, Paul recalls his father wearing a shirt saying, "Tattoos aren't Just for Sailors and Whores." He also recalls a sign in his father's workshop that read, "Fishermen Have Longer Rods." Paul's father routinely told him, "Women are here to make our lives hell." Predictably, Paul's father treated his mother cruelly. "My dad was really mean to my mom," Paul said. "But, she never got her act together." Paul, now 25, emotionally and physically abuses his girlfriend, a pattern since his teens. He's also sexually aggressive. Like father, like son.

Love

Rose always felt supported. Growing up, her parents attended every sporting event, recital, and religious ceremony. If they couldn't, a grandparent substituted. Rose's father listened to her practice piano and taught her how to play football. He also took her bike riding and to dog festivals. Rose's mother taught her how to crochet, quilt, and make her mema's famous chocolate chip cookies. She even turned Rose's hair into a frosted donut for Crazy Hair Day. Rose, now 28, is an artist and volunteer puppy raiser for the Guide Dog Foundation—childhood dreams. She's also engaged to Dan, a gentleman.

Some parents are skilled drivers. They always use their blinkers, follow the speed limit, and drive like they're transporting precious cargo. Other parents, however, are inept drivers. They jump curbs, swerve into other lanes, and drive into oncoming traffic—with their children unbuckled.[41] If your parents failed Driver's Ed, look for other instructors. It can be aunts, uncles, friends (like with JJ), or even neighbors. Our first choice, however, should always be God. He passed Driver's Ed. He's a certified instructor. He even started His own driving school.

God delights in us, as we should delight in each other.

---

[41] This is often because our grandparents struggled driving, too. If your parents passed along to you the wrong roadmap to love, try replacing your anger toward them with compassion. Assume they did their best. At 44, I finally do. Hopefully, you can, too.

GREAT PARTNER SYSTEM

"All you need is the plan, the roadmap, and the courage to press on to your destination." — Earl Nightingale

A Luddite like Professor Thieben, I avoided GPS. My first experience was disastrous (though hilarious). Traveling to Boston, I entered a residential cul-de-sac. The GPS kept prompting, "Go straight. Go straight." I wanted to listen. Doing so, however, meant driving through a house. I froze. "What should I do?" I thought. "The GPS said go straight." I called my wife. She told me to turn around. If your roadmap for love is getting you lost, you, too, should turn around. Replace your **Good-Enough Parent System** for a **Great Partner System**. You'll arrive where you belong— surrounded by love.[42]

Back Roads

Like any journey, the beginning is essential. Initially take the wrong road, and you'll be frustrated and overwhelmed. Maybe even angry. You

---

42 By "good-enough" I really mean "subpar." But, there isn't a synonym for "subpar" starting with "g." Therefore, "good-enough" had to be good enough.

think you know the back roads. Then, you get distracted. Sometimes, your memory fails. Other times, you drive in circles or daydream—missing turns, traffic lights, and stop signs. Your trip is then derailed. So, pay attention while navigating the back roads to love deeply, and you'll eventually reach the main roads. If not, you may be lost—and lonely—forever.

Thriving relationships require people to have similar values. This fosters a deep connection. Our culture, however, often promotes a shallow connection. Yes, physical attraction matters. Somewhat. Values matter more (see Commandment III). After briefly assessing the person's appearance, thoroughly assess their values. My wife and I did this on our second date. Thankfully, we both valued personal growth. Buildings remain standing because the pillars are apart. If they were adjoining, the building would eventually collapse. Likewise with relationships. Therefore, if my wife and I decided to stay together, we agreed to support a "Jeff," a "Cara," and a "Jeff and Cara." Yes, it would've been our last date if either of us disregarded relationship architecture. But, we preferred learning this after our second date—not our second child.

Waistlines expand. Hair thins. Butts droop. Values remain.

FRIENDSHIP CT

Friendships are the foundation of love and life. But, what's friendship? My friends, Keith and Stephanie, are raising a kindergarten class of cherubs. Over coffee, Keith said to me, "You're like a brother. Stephanie and I love you and Cara very much. We respect you both immensely. God forbid something happens to us, would you be our children's legal guardians and raise them?" That's friendship. After telling my friend, Matt, that I finally confronted my sexual abuser, *he* cried and hugged me. That's friendship. I confessed to my friend, Sal, that my sin is killing me (see Commandment X). He then squeezed my hand saying, "Me too, dude. Let's pray for each other." That's friendship. If friends are life's treasure, I'm rich like King Solomon. Follow this roadmap to love, and you could be, too.

It's almost cheesy and old-fashioned to suggest being friends before lovers. Yet, science supports this. Romantic BFFs report more teamwork, laughter, authenticity, honesty, and security; they also report steamier sex. Reading a speech from Plato's *Symposium*, Aristophanes discussed soulmates. He said humans originally had four arms, four legs, and a single head with two faces. When the humans threatened to conquer the gods, Zeus halved them. Miserable, the two halves roamed Earth searching for their soul's other half. Once united, they could again love deeply. With God's grace, I hope you find your soulmate—and best friend—like I did.

Some have a "friend with benefits." But, everyone benefits from having a friend.

Loving relationships take considerable time. Giving someone the last 10 minutes of our day conveys they're a pebble—not a big rock. It happens. Everyone gets overwhelmed. Everyone gets distracted. Everyone forgets promises. It becomes corrosive, however, when it's habitual. At best, chronic nighttime chitchat maintains the status quo. Noah's ark wasn't built in a day. Neither is deep connection.

One day, my then 12-year-old son, James, and I shared 15 hours together. Afterward, we discussed our day. I asked him, "Buddy, if someone wanted to know what this day meant to you and why spending time together is important, what would you say?" Here's his response:

> When my dad and I spent the whole day together, it felt amazing. I loved being unplugged and out in nature with him. I loved doing things together that we both love because, although it is good to share other passions with people, doing

something we both love makes me feel more connected with him. I love that. We spent lots of time giving each other our full attention. I think that made the day really great. Giving someone your full attention is important if you want to have a good relationship with them. It helps you connect with the person and learn new things about them.

Another critical part of having a good relationship with someone is time. You need to give time and attention to the person you are trying to build a relationship with. That is why we had a great day hiking, driving (while listening to NF), cooking, and talking. We did so many things together, and I think that this experience, as well as future ones, will keep our relationship strong. Forever. Even when I have my own family and kids.

Another way to spell "love" is T-I-M-E.

Nods. Smiles. Chuckles. Glib responses. We act like we're listening. But, we're usually not. People are only listening to each other—their brains in a neurological waltz—9% of the time. Here's a classic example.

Me: *May I have a medium coffee, please?*
Barista: *Small or large?*
Me: *Medium.*
Barista: *Small or large?*
Me: **Medium.**
Barista: **Small or large?** (a <u>small</u> and <u>large</u> cup shoved in my face)
Me: *Oh, sorry. Large, please.*

We talk to watches. We talk to doorbells. We talk to refrigerators. Yet, we ignore each other—missing opportunities to connect. Social psychologist, Dr. Shelly Gable, suggests that our response to *good* news better predicts relationship satisfaction than our response to *bad* news. A typical response to, "Hey, hun. I got promoted to assistant marketing director!" is "Cool." That conveys mild interest and care. The best response, called *active-constructive responding*, is something like, "Wow! I'm so proud of you. You must be thrilled. What are your new responsibilities?" Indifference and monosyllabic mumbles weaken relationships. Attentiveness, questions, and fist bumps strengthen relationships.

Listen more. Talk less. Celebrate more. Criticize less.

Trust is the biggest stress buster in relationships. Hypervigilance wastes our widgets and impedes creating thriving relationships. It also distracts us from connecting and encourages annoying reassurance seeking. Blasting someone with rapid fire "♥ me?" texts repels even the most devoted. We want connection. We want intimacy. Yet, trusting others can be terrifying. Start small. Trust me when I say I understand.

Aware of their nakedness, Adam and Eve hid. Responding to God's call, Adam said, "I was afraid, because I was naked" (Genesis, 3:10). We, too, hide and are afraid when we're "naked." Some of our thoughts, behaviors, and feelings might be considered bizarre, disgusting, or evil. Fearing rejection, we stay clothed—emboldening shame. Sometimes, we wear fashionable fig leaves. Other times, we wear snowsuits during heatwaves. But, when we shed some layers, when we trust our partners, we weaken shame and start connecting. We start loving deeply. Be courageous. Be vulnerable. Be the first to get "naked."

Trust is the road to intimacy.

Main Roads

Congratulations! You've successfully navigated the back roads to loving deeply, and you're now traveling the main roads. The windows are down, the music is blasting, and the sun is radiant. Cruise control is tempting. Resist. You might rear-end the next car. You might get drowsy. You might miss the exit (like I frequently do…seriously). Avoiding accidents requires concentration, awareness, and sustained effort. Slow down. Get off your phone. Hush backseat drivers. And, please, stop pounding gummy bears. You're almost there.

We like spending money. The average American has $38,000 in personal debt, excluding home mortgages. Only 23% report carrying "no debt." This is suffocating, stressful—and often avoidable. It's explained by a basic banking principle: too many withdrawals, too few deposits. This principle also explains why so many relationships go bankrupt. Rather than making deposits into our relationship, like leaving a card on her pillow, writing *XOXO* on the mirror when he showers, or skipping Guys' Night because she's sick, we keep making withdrawals from our relationship, like texting while he's talking, being late for her work party, or ignoring the dishes. Unlike Ebenezer Scrooge, don't wait for the spirits

of Christmas Past, Present, and Yet to Come to visit you to start gener-
ously giving your partner empathy, patience, and love. Instead, start now.
You'll then realize that small deposits are big—and the return on your
investment is huge.

Invest less in financial bonds. Invest more in emotional bonds.

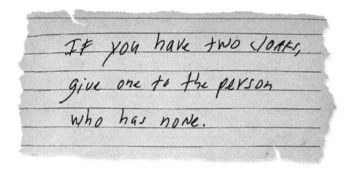

APPRECIATION FWY

Like a werewolf, ingratitude can emerge when relationships get dark.
When this happens, we hear the corny joke—not the apology. We taste
the dry chicken—not the warm meal. We see the scribbled note—not the
love note. You can protect your relationship with the silver bullet: appreciation. But, if you keep taking your partner for granted, the werewolf
will howl in the distance, and ingratitude will eventually attack. Clamp-
ing your relationship in its jaws, then eating the carcass and lapping the
blood. Languishing relationships have a 1:1 ratio of positive to negative
interactions. Thriving relationships, however, have a 5:1 ratio of positive to negative interactions. Appreciation helps create a healthy proportion—and keeps the moon covered.

My daughter's principal, Dr. Toscano, sent weekly videos during the
COVID-19 pandemic. On Mondays, students got a weekly challenge.
The first one was to make their beds and send her a picture. Here's the
email my daughter, Julianne, sent Dr. Toscano:

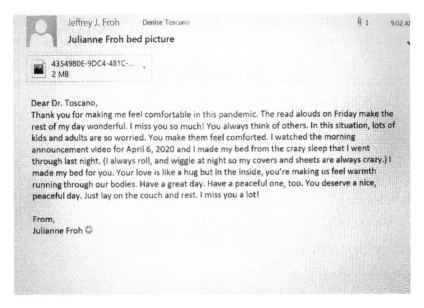

Jeffrey J. Froh   Denise Toscano   📎 1   9:02 AI
Julianne Froh bed picture

4354980E-9DC4-481C-...
2 MB

Dear Dr. Toscano,
Thank you for making me feel comfortable in this pandemic. The read alouds on Friday make the rest of my day wonderful. I miss you so much! You always think of others. In this situation, lots of kids and adults are so worried. You make them feel comforted. I watched the morning announcement video for April 6, 2020 and I made my bed from the crazy sleep that I went through last night. (I always roll, and wiggle at night so my covers and sheets are always crazy.) I made my bed for you. Your love is like a hug but in the inside, you're making us feel warmth running through our bodies. Have a great day. Have a peaceful one, too. You deserve a nice, peaceful day. Just lay on the couch and rest. I miss you a lot!

From,
Julianne Froh ☺

Dr. Toscano called Julianne. She said, "Hi Julianne. How are you? I just wanted to tell you that your email made my day. I miss you, and I love you." Responding to every student via email would be arduous. Calling every student would be impossible. But, when we feel appreciated, we make the impossible possible. Knowing the roadmap to love that my parents gave me, you'll understand why this interaction made me well with tears. If JJ's children can learn how to express appreciation and love deeply, so can you.[43]

Gratitude warms our heart and ignites our love.

TOUCH TPKE

Touch is powerful. It promotes growth in premature babies, reduces pain, decreases autoimmune disease symptoms, lowers glucose levels in children with diabetes, and improves the immune system in oncology patients. Social psychologist, Dr. Dacher Keltner, has discovered that

---

43 Soon after sending this email to Dr. Toscano, Julianne became overwhelmed completing schoolwork and cried. I wrapped a blanket around us and held her while playing with her hair. She calmed down and took a nap. Sometimes, we all need our terry cloth monkey.

even 1-second touches to the forearm can convey negative and positive emotions. Therefore, when my student, Casey, became emotional during her presentation, showing support and empathy, I briefly touched her shoulder. She later emailed me saying, "The tap on the shoulder I got from you after I sat down was so reassuring. It really meant something to me." We smother our partners during the honeymoon phase. Before long, however, we sleep on opposite sides of the bed. We forget how our partner's hair tickles our face. We forget how our partner's heartbeat lulls us to sleep. We forget how our partner twitches and smacks our face. Hold hands. Hug. Snuggle. (Maybe wear a hockey mask.)

Being close emotionally requires being close physically.

Numerous phobias exist. Most recently identified is *désmefsiphobia*, the fear of commitment.[44] Unfortunately, *désmefsiphobia* is rampant among emerging adults. Therefore, most swipe left. Few swipe right. Some commit…just enough. A FOMO subtype applying to relationships intensifies the phobia. People fear they'll miss out on someone "better." If, however, they committed to one person, they'd overlook attractive alternatives. Thus, though the flowers may be brighter in your neighbor's yard, committed gardeners won't notice. Commitment, therefore, makes you feel like you're not "missing out." Ironic, huh? Commit to someone, and you may miss the high from first kisses. But, *désmefsiphobia* will make you miss the high from loving deeply. If you want to experience a love that has created wars, commit to someone. You'll then learn why falling in love was worth falling on a sword.

Say "Yes" to someone. Say "Yes" to love.

---

44 *Désmefsi* is "commitment" in Greek.

DREAMS EXPY

Most relationships have a faint pulse. Like defibrillation, supporting each other's dreams prevents relationship arrhythmia by shocking its heart. Every December, my family and I have a dream session.[45] They're invigorating. We learn what makes our eyes sparkle. We learn what stars we wish upon. My wife dreamed of running a 10K. For Mother's Day, we registered her for one and surprised her at the finish line with flowers and balloons. My son dreamed of climbing a mountain. We summited Cadillac Mountain. My daughter dreamed of becoming the Class President. Next June, she'll be on stage addressing the 2021 graduating class of James H. Boyd Intermediate School. I dreamed of publishing this book. You're reading it. Helping facilitate dream creation, I hung rainbow Christmas lights in my children's bedrooms. Dream catchers ain't got nuttin' on *Dreamland*. Create your own dreamlands. Christmas lights are optional (though they're damn cool!).

Chasing dreams together creates memories. Catching dreams together creates union.

---

45 Matthew Kelly's book, *The Dream Manager*, inspired this family tradition.

My wife and I have written, what we think is, one of the greatest love stories. Together for 21 years, we still surprise each other with a sugar-laden latte. We still hold hands during our daily walks. We still cuddle. Each year has surpassed the previous one. Following God helped— big time! "I give you a new commandment: love one another. As I have loved you, so you also should love one another" (John, 13:34). But, largely because of my childhood trauma and **Good-Enough Parent System**, we've blown tires. We've thrown off our alignment. We've worn out gears. Thankfully, aside from being a world-class driving instructor, God is also a world-class mechanic. "If you live to be a hundred," said Winne the Pooh, "I want to be a hundred minus one day, so I never have to live without you." When you feel like Pooh, you've nailed it. You've reached Heaven on Earth. It's possible. Use the right roadmap to love deeply.

LOVE ANYWAY

"How wonderful would it be, while we discover faraway planets, to rediscover the needs of the brothers and sisters orbiting around us." — Pope Francis

Our relationships should be a witness to God's love. Per Jesus, the second greatest Commandment is, "You shall love your neighbor as yourself" (Matthew, 22:39). St. Francis of Assisi also urged us to, "Preach the gospel at all times, and if necessary use words." We should heed their wisdom. Even more, we should emulate Jesus. He loves everyone—including His enemies. Jesus' love transcends hate, pain, and time. Jesus was different. He was a rebel. He changed the world. So can we.

While another ice age is doubtful, a cold front looms. Dress warm. Drink water. Stock your fridge. People will mock you, judge you, and reject you. They may spit on you, punch you, and kick you. Jesus experienced this—and worse (see Commandment V). He loved anyway. Nailed to the cross, Jesus said of His sadistic torturers, "Father, forgive them, they know not what they do" (Luke, 23:34). Alongside Jesus were two criminals also being crucified. One criminal reviled Him and challenged Jesus to prove His divinity by saving their lives. The other criminal, however, acknowledged Jesus as God. Dying and suffering—6-inch spikes driven into His extremities and splintered wood piercing His torn flesh—Jesus said to the penitent criminal, "Amen, I say to you, today you will be with me in Paradise" (Luke, 23:43). I beg God for the strength to forgive like Him, sacrifice like Him, and love like Him. I never will. But, I'll die trying. You should, too.

Jesus uses the best roadmap to love deeply. He'll show you the way. "I am the way and the truth and the life" (John, 14:6). When traveling with Jesus, you'll always land on the ✗. Unlike following a pirate map, however, you won't find diamonds, rubies, and pearls. Instead, you'll find the ultimate treasure: love.

No Jesus. No love. Know Jesus. Know love.

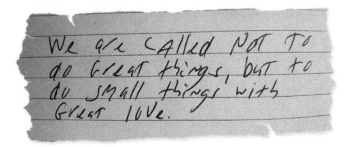

We are called not to do great things, but to do small things with great love.

COMMANDMENT VI TIPS

Thou Shalt
Love Deeply

1. Assess your loneliness. Be honest. Then, do some math. Calculate your ratio of 1) selfies to group pics, 2) hours on FaceTime to hours with face time, and 3) minutes spent holding a phone to minutes spent holding a hand. If any of these ratios exceed 1:1, favoring self-absorption or cellular-love over time spent with others, consider your level of egotism and technology addiction. Then, recommit to loving deeply.

2. Study your roadmap to love. Are the exits marked? Are the street names blurry? Is it missing some pages? Test it. If you find love, keep using it. If you're driving in circles and reaching dead ends, toss it. Replace your **G**ood-**E**nough **P**arent **S**ystem for a **G**reat **P**artner **S**ystem. Getting lost gets old. Road trips rock!

3. Pay attention when traveling the back roads to loving deeply. You can get distracted. You can become forgetful. You can daydream. Look for potholes, debris, and construction. Keep your eyes on the road.

VALUES ST: Share similar healthy values. Looks change. Values remain.

FRIENDSHIP CT: Take walks. Take adventures. Ask for two spoons. Be BFFs.

TIME AVE: Give each other extended windows of time—unplugged.

LISTEN LN: Listen more. Talk less. Celebrate more. Criticize less.

TRUST CIR: Be vulnerable, and fight shame. Expose your true self. Get "naked."

4. Having successfully traveled the back roads to loving deeply, you can now take the main roads. Resist cruise control, silence your phone, and hush backseat drivers. Accidents happen.

GENEROSITY HWY: Graciously give your partner patience, empathy, and compassion.

APPRECIATION FWY: Recognize your partner's kindness. Express gratitude.

TOUCH TPKE: Hold hands. Snuggle with and caress your partner. Be affectionate.

COMMITMENT CSWY: Fight your *désmefsiphobia.* Take the risk. Commit.

DREAMS EXPY: Chase dreams, and catch them—together.

5. Jesus created the best roadmap to love deeply. Use it. When you're hurt and betrayed, give forgiveness. When your relationships weaken, make sacrifices. When the world nails you to your cross, love anyway. Trust God, heed Him, and follow Him. No Jesus. No love. Know Jesus. Know love.

Spiritual Thriving

With personal and social thriving attained, you now have the foundation for spiritual thriving. Start by listening for God's whispers about your mission. The world's incessant white noise, however, muffles His voice. To hear Him, you must *slow down*. You must rest, recharge, and let your mind wander. You must also *befriend nature*. Frequent God's playground to learn life lessons and feel Him stir your heart. You'll then realize God created you deliberately and that your life has a purpose—because you have a purpose. *Give thanks* to God for including you in the cosmic puzzle. This appreciation for life will fuel your drive to *master* your *mission* and thrive.

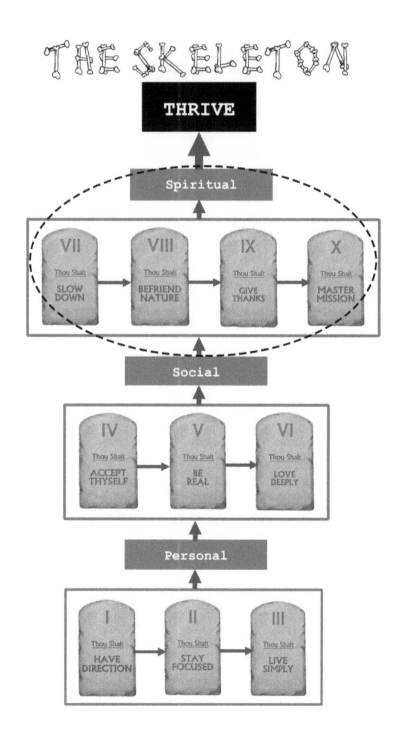

VII

Thou Shalt

SLOW
DOWN

Henry grew up just outside Boston in Concord, Massachusetts. Concord was mainly agrarian and, for some time, safe from the Industrial Revolution's tentacles. People traveled via foot or horse. Noisy factories and piercing train whistles were absent. Until, when Henry was 25, the Fitchburg Railroad was built, replacing a peaceful existence with the rat race. Henry appreciated quadrupedal vermin in forests—not bipedal ones scampering about his town. He also appreciated the slow, old ways and questioned if these changes would hurt people's souls. After graduating from Harvard, he held several odd jobs. People encouraged him to pursue law, business, ministry, or teaching. Writing, however, stole Henry's heart. So did communing with God in nature.[46]

At Harvard, Henry was exposed to *transcendentalism*. The movement began because of a religious controversy with the Unitarian church. Some ministers thought the church had become too rational and the pathway to God being taught was too dogmatic. There was too much emphasis on bible study and listening to sermons, and too little emphasis on using one's intellect to create a consciousness of God. Transcendentalists segmented life into three stages: 1) learn the wisdom of the past, 2) develop a relationship with nature (to discover ethical truths and commu-

---

46 Unlike Henry, few understand the effects of technology on civilization. To increase your awareness, read Jacques Ellul's book, *The Technological Society*, and Nicholas Carr's book, *The Shallows: What the Internet is Doing to our Brains*. Technology isn't our servant—it's our master. And unless we're careful, it will diminish and prevent humanity. I think it already has.

nicate with God), and 3) share one's insights with others. This philosophy, Henry believed, explained why people sought adventure and their
mission. He wrote, "If a man does not keep pace with his companions,
perhaps it is because he hears a different drummer. Let him step to the
music which he hears, however measured or far away." At 28, Henry listened to his own distinctive beat.

From 1845-1847, Henry retreated to the woods. Living even more
simply than as a boy, he built a humble abode far from civilization. Slowing down almost to a halt, every week Henry tried working for one day
and reading, contemplating, connecting with nature, and developing his
consciousness for six days. He wrote, "I do not wish to be any more busy
with my hands than is necessary…My instinct tells me that my head is
an organ for burrowing, as some creatures use their snout and forepaws."
Henry knew how to use his time and widgets. That happens when you
follow your mission.

Most importantly, Henry desperately wanted communion with God.
He wanted to feel Him. He wanted to see Him. He wanted to hear Him.
Henry recognized and experienced God in the smallest moments.

> As I stand over the insect crawling amid the pine needles
> on the forest floor, and endeavoring to conceal itself from
> my sight, and ask myself why it will cherish those humble
> thoughts, and bide its head from me who might, perhaps, be
> its benefactor, and impart to its race some cheering informa
> tion, I am reminded of the greater Benefactor and Intelligence
> that stands over me the human insect.

Some people learn from reading. Some people learn from listening.
Henry learned from watching insects.

Henry knew he needed to slow down to listen to God and thrive.
He needed to retreat. To be in silence and solitude. To build an invisible

moat between him and the world. This let Henry David Thoreau write one of the most influential books ever, *Walden*.[47]

NEAR DEATH

"Most of the things we need in order to be most fully alive never come from pushing. They grow in rest." — Mark Buchanan

Everyone seems stressed. Per a recent stress survey by the American Psychological Association, 75% of Americans experienced at least one stress symptom in the last month, while another 45% lie awake at night. Further, 36% are anxious, 35% are irritable or angry, and 34% have stress-induced fatigue. The most stressed? Emerging adults. Unless they slow down, 20-somethings will limp across the finish line—if they even complete the race.

Stress is a quiet killer. And, like a burglar, it's stealing our lives. Chronic stress accelerates aging by shortening our telomeres (i.e., the "end caps" of our DNA). It's also linked to suppressed thyroid function, hyperglycemia, and decreased bone density and muscle tissue, as well

---

47 Mr. Thoreau, if you're reading this, thank you for teaching me about living fully. I allowed about 500 words to tell your story. I hope I demonstrated reverence for your life—as you did for God and His creation.

as lowered immunity, higher blood pressure, and increased visceral fat (which is related to heart attacks, heart disease, and strokes). Chronic stress also increases our risk for liver cirrhosis, lung ailments, and cancer. Further, inflammation created by undue stress hormones (e.g., cortisol) facilitates autoimmune disorders and possibly even Parkinson's disease. Mild stress causes apathy. Moderate stress causes thriving. Excessive stress causes death.

A healthy sleep schedule can delay us meeting the Grim Reaper. Yet, zombies abound. Sleep deprivation is an insidious form of torture. It impairs basic biological functions that help us cope with stress and grow. For example, people kept awake for 24 hours had decreased brain activity in the prefrontal cortex (which controls attention, anticipation, and planning) and the thalamus (which controls emotion, memory, and motor activity). So much for all-nighters being productive![48] Sleep deprivation has also contributed to soldiers dying from friendly fire. Sleep, therefore, even helps us distinguish friend from foe—and decide when to pull the "trigger." Male lions sleep 18-20 hours daily. They're the King of the Jungle. If you slept 7-9 hours nightly, maybe you could be the king or queen of your jungle.

We carry enough luggage. Lose the eye bags.

Exacerbating our stress is our internet and cell phone addiction. It's depleting our widgets, intensifying our anxiety, and harming our health. Nearly 90% of Americans check their emails, texts, and social media accounts "often" or "constantly." People generally engage with their phone 2,617 times daily (the top 10% do this 5,427 times). And, in a sample of emerging adults, 67% of men and 25% of women preferred an electric shock to sitting quietly with no phone. Seems unbelievable, right? Observe a crowd. Recently, near hundreds of people, I said to my family, "Look around. This generation will develop the worst hunchback." Days later, I read about "text neck." Beyond causing spinal damage, cell phone

---

48 Per the Centers for Disease Control, the effects of being awake for 24 hours is comparable to having a blood alcohol content of .10%. That's nearly 13x the legal limit for driving. Drunk driving is dangerous. So is sleep deprivation.

addiction is also shrinking our brains, decreasing our empathy, and increasing our stress. Disconnect from your phone. Avoid joining "Generation Hunchback." Instead, look up. God prefers eye contact when He's talking to you.[49]

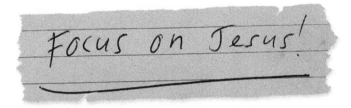

Focus on Jesus!

An old soul, I've been forever touting limited cell phone use. Some of my classic lines include, "Spare me the message if you wouldn't lick an envelope," "I'll know you're running 2 minutes late when you're 2 minutes late," and "Don't text me *Loved seeing you* minutes after we hugged good-bye." When I use my bullhorn, some politely nod, some scan Facebook, others leave. I can be annoying. But, my diatribes are driven by love and a passion to help people live their best-life-possible. Unknowingly, I've been channeling Thoreau.

> *For my part, I could easily do without the post-office. I think that there are very few important communications made through it. To speak critically, I never received more than one or two letters in my life—I wrote this some years ago—that were worth the postage...And I am sure that I never read any memorable news in the newspaper. If we read of one man robbed, or murdered, or killed by accident, or one house burned, or one vessel wrecked, or one steamboat blown up, or one cow run over on the Western Railroad, or one mad dog killed, or one lot of grasshoppers in the winter—we never need read another. One is enough.*

---

49 People with internet addiction have shown brain atrophy. Areas affected include the frontal lobe (which helps us "get stuff done"), the striatum (which governs and regulates social behaviors), and the insula (which fosters empathy development). Further, every buzz jolts our nervous system, spiking our stress hormones, and igniting our fight, flight, or freeze response. Instagram? Or, peace? TikTok? Or, love? YouTube? Or, thriving? Your call (or text).

Disable news alerts. Unsubscribe from listservs. Ignore texts. No response is a response.[50]

> Hey Dave, thanks for thinking of me. As we get to know each other, which I'm enjoying, you should know I'm very anti tech and obsessed with staying focused (never been on social media, etc.) Therefore, I'm not big into texting and I don't watch videos, etc people send me. I am, however, big into talking with loved ones and going for walks together, especially in nature. FYI so you know I'm not ghosting you; I'm trying to live a value congruent life.

Delivered

Our body, mind, and soul need rest. We must unplug for extended periods to hear God and discover our mission. Ralph Waldo Emerson realized this, saying, "Let us be silent that we may hear the whisper of God." When we slow down, we feel God stirring our hearts and guiding us toward our destiny. "Call to me, and I will answer you; I will tell you things great beyond reach of your knowledge" (Jeremiah, 33:3). Slowing down, however, seems impossible—and counterintuitive. Mustn't we keep grinding to be successful and create a life worth living? Hold my hand. Let's skip down memory lane.

LONELY SWINGS

"People say nothing is impossible, but I do nothing every day." — Winnie the Pooh

---

50 After several failed attempts of escaping from prison, I'm finally free. I recently swapped my smart phone for a flip phone. I never realized how much I missed a home-cooked meal.

We rarely play. We think having a catch, climbing rocks, and riding bikes is only for children. Talk about naïve. Play helps us thrive. It boosts our health, keeps us sharp, and fosters our connection with people—and God. "All work and no play makes Jack a dull boy," said Jack Torrance, the axe-wielding writer in Stephen King's, *The Shining*. True. But, it also facilitates emptiness and abandoning our mission. Play is anything but child's play.

Like a strong work ethic, we also need a strong play ethic. Play teaches us teamwork, negotiating, respect, trust, and compassion. Negative emotions—like those facilitated by stress—narrow the scope of our thoughts and actions, whereas positive emotions—like those facilitated by play—broaden the scope of our thoughts and actions. Thus, play helps us see and experience life as a child, not an overwhelmed adult. Play also increases our happiness by triggering the release of natural feel-good chemicals (i.e., endorphins), thereby promoting well-being and reducing pain. Further enhancing health, play also improves our memory and overall brain function, helping us remember good times, increase our competence, and deepen our wisdom. "We don't stop playing because we grow old; we grow old because we stop playing," said George Bernard Shaw. Remaining a child at heart, thus, is good for our heart.

Be playful. Live as if you're dying. Because you are.

My friend Sal and I have been meeting monthly for 13 years. Jesus tells us to, "Come away by yourselves to a deserted place and rest a while" (Mark, 6:31). So, we usually walk the beach or hike. One evening at Caumsett State Park, nearing a majestic several hundred-year-old oak tree, the sunset resembled a Bob Ross painting. Mixtures of cadmium yellow, phthalo blue, titanium white, and alizarin crimson filled the sky. We paused. We observed. We stood quietly. A gentle voice whispered to me, "Look up." We then watched a Cooper's hawk fly directly overhead, gliding with the breeze. Its white belly and wings reflected the colors of God's gift. Sal and I shared the moment without sharing the moment. I then realized something: if we don't play and slow down to discover our mission from God, our "beauty"—like that of the tree and hawk—will remain hidden. And, beauty can only inspire if it's revealed.

Like flora and fauna, children's stories also teach life lessons.[51] Two years ago, my family and I saw *Christopher Robin*, a film about my favorite anthropomorphic bear. Christopher, Winnie the Pooh's old friend, was a playful boy turned lifeless man. Done believing in Heffalumps and Woozles, Christopher now only believed in productivity and profits. He ignored his wife. He neglected his daughter. Pooh reminded Christopher that, "Doing nothing often leads to the very best of something." Eventually, Christopher regained his passion for adventure, family life, and play. A reformed workaholic, I related with Christopher. Sadly, too much (see Commandment I).[52] I had flashbacks of choosing overtime instead of playtime. Of answering conference calls instead of God's calls. I

---

51 Recall Dr. Seuss's vaccine for materialism.

52 If you're a budding or entrenched workaholic, read Dr. Juliet Schor's book, *The Overworked American: The Unexpected Decline of Leisure*. Hopefully, you'll gain perspective.

cried throughout, holding my daughter's hand. Reassuring my wife that she remains a priority, and desperate to teach my children the power of play, I later surprised each of them with a Winnie the Pooh doll and note stuffed inside his shirt. Here's what I gave my wife:

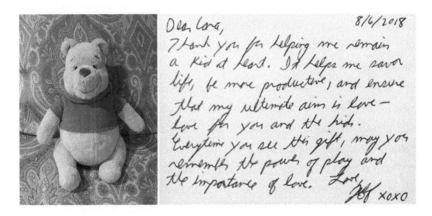

We hear God while praying. We hear God while playing. Pooh knew this. Now, I do too.

God wants us thriving. He encourages rest. He encourages balance. He encourages play. "The city shall be filled with boys and girls playing in her streets" (Zechariah, 8:5). Bruise your knee, get a splinter, and stain your clothes. You'll awake your inner child, experience peace—and commune with God.

Find your "off" switch. Find your mission.

SLOW 'n STEADY

"I think 99 times, and I find nothing. I stop thinking, swim in silence, and the truth comes to me." — Albert Einstein

Since a boy, I've been perfectionistic. In kindergarten, only the top gymnast got a trophy. I loved counting my missing teeth in its reflection.

In religious ed, I cried hearing only one student got an "A+" on the *10 Commandments* test. Whew. Close call.[53] I masked insecurity with success until my teens when I discharged childhood rage upon the world. Eventually, God's light overpowered my darkness. He sent angels. He sent messengers. He sent Professor Thieben (see Commandment III). Devils, however, are always devils. Therefore, though I stopped terrorizing others, I started terrorizing myself. Personal damage soon replaced property damage.

Insecurity creates needless suffering. Especially when, like me, you overcompensate with unrelenting standards. In grad school, I danced with Death. Trying to impress my advisor, I distributed research surveys at campus events—and Christmas parties. Getting published was rare; my term papers even got published. Graduating in 5 years was improbable; I stood on stage alone. My pathological obsession with excellence yielded much reward: coveted fellowships, national presentations, and gainful employment. It also, however, yielded much pain. I routinely had bronchitis or walking pneumonia, I nearly collapsed in the shower from exhaustion, and I frequently experienced panic attacks. Eventually, I burnt out. At 27, the stress awakened a sleeping dragon: bipolar II disorder. If only I slowed down.

Ashleigh, 25, is the yin to my yang. I make your heart race; Ashleigh makes your heart rest. I hustle; Ashleigh strolls. I look like I'm always chasing prey; Ashleigh looks like she's always chasing rainbows. Don't mistake her innocent aura for passivity or weakness. Ashleigh is gritty. She's an academic Navy SEAL. And, she's crushing grad school—without crushing her spirit. We spent several hours together discussing her life philosophy. Ashleigh shared her struggles, her weaknesses, and her wisdom. I learned much from Ashleigh. Hopefully, you will, too.

---

53 I'm now writing a book on the 10 Commandments. Am I still proving myself because of that transient feeling of "failure?"

Wonder Woman

Please describe your work ethic with school, athletics, and jobs growing up and now in your 20s. What influenced it?

Coming from a family with very high-achieving parents, a strong work ethic was instilled in me from the beginning. I remember my parents speaking to me about what I wanted to become when I was a little girl. Having those future-oriented conversations helped me develop a very driven mindset.

Sports were really a culmination of unfortunate events. I accidently kicked someone in the face at 5 years old during soccer. My first swim meet ended with me choking on water after diving off the blocks for my butterfly stroke. In 10th grade, I was on the school basketball team. I didn't score a single point during my career. My parents now describe those seasons as "painful to watch."

Throughout these highs and lows, my parents attended every single game, every single meet, and every single ceremony where I received an academic award. My work ethic and passion for success, therefore, was shaped and reinforced by a very loving and encouraging family that boosted me up when I was down. I was always encouraged to keep going and to never quit something I started.

> Effort is always more important than outcome.

Describe the benefits of being super-driven for so many years.

As you know, I'm now in a doctoral program for psychology. I worked really, really hard to get where I am today. I spent countless hours studying for the GRE when my friends were getting adult jobs where they have since grown and traveled up the ranks. This was a choice I made, which is both awesome and frustrating at the same time. Between internships and working in schools, psychology students don't get paid. You really need the intrinsic motivation to keep pushing you through. This "Beast Mode" mentality makes you develop into a naturally hard worker. However, it's hard to compartmentalize it into just one area of your life. The beast spills over into every other area. My mom jokes and often calls me "Captain Marvel," the most powerful woman in the superhero universe. When I'm doing homework, studying, interviewing, working at our family business, or preparing for an upcoming family event, I'm usually giving 150%.

While it's tough to give it your all, it pays off and it feels really good when other people praise your hard work.

Another cool thing is that if you're a "Beast Mode" person, you probably learned it from someone else. So, it means you have inspiring people in your life. My mom is the epitome of "Beast Mode." She was a Radio City Rockette, turned lawyer, and now helps my dad in his business. She's very talented and works very hard in everything. My dad is a veterinarian and is just naturally brilliant in everything related to math and science. Growing up, I knew I had two very cool parents. I wanted to work hard to be just like them.

My sisters must have noticed this, too. My middle sister, Lauryn, is in nursing school. And, my youngest sister, Caroline, is in a physician's assistant program. There's a common joke in my house thanks to my mom. After my mom was dealing with me crying over a 30-page paper, my sister Lauryn freaking out about dispensing medication for diabetic ketoacidosis, and Caroline crying about finding time to study biochemistry in between volleyball workouts, she jokingly coined the family phrase, "Why do we all do such hard $&#@?" My whole family goes "Beast Mode", and it has become a joke! Are we stressed out of our minds? Yes. Do we all overwork sometimes? Yes. However, we all love what we're doing. And, it shows! "Beast Mode" feels awesome—until it doesn't. Even Captain Marvel isn't an impervious superhero. She, too, experiences fatigue and energy depletion.

> The only superhero is Jesus. And, good luck being like Him!

What about the consequences of "Beast Mode?" Does a particular story stand out?

The consequences I experienced were complete exhaustion, anger, and moodiness. I also shut a lot of people out to focus and study more. I was very preoccupied with impressing other people and being the best at literally everything. At school, I *had* to get the "A." At work, I *had* to be the most pleasant, kind, perfect, bending over backwards to make someone else happy person. I put immense pressure on myself.

I would come home from work or school and completely crash from "putting on the show."

I'm very "Type A." I would really panic when certain days wouldn't go perfectly. Perfection becomes such an essential part of who you are that you feel the need to cut out everything else that could possibly get in the way. The cycle is dangerous. You become lonely, angry, obsessed with recognition, and you're destroyed when you fall short. It really stinks.

Did you have an "aha" moment when you realized always going and never slowing down was toxic? If so, can you please describe it?

After my second semester in grad school, I had a big "aha" moment that showed me the consequences of going non-stop.

After a tough semester, I was completely exhausted. I could barely keep my eyes open during the day. I would come home from school and actually be too tired to eat. I stopped going to the gym because I needed that hour to do more work. I gained weight. I felt sick with worry when I went to bed, and I was in a panic when I woke up the next morning. My relationships suffered. I couldn't function because I was obsessed with perfection and people pleasing. I constantly worried about getting the best grades, being the best daughter, and being the best girlfriend.

I actually went to the doctor because I thought something was seriously wrong with me. Maybe my inexplicable fatigue was Lyme disease? Maybe an underlying thyroid issue? After a bunch of tests, I learned I was completely "fine." I definitely didn't feel fine.

My doctor pushed anti-depressants and anti-anxiety medication to deal with the "stress of being in a doctoral program." I refused all of these medications because I wasn't depressed. I wasn't anxious. I was burnt out beyond belief. My knowledge in psychology helped me to realize I was just completely drained. Shot. Done. Exhausted. I was a victim of my own go-go-go lifestyle.

> When we refuse to slow down, our bodies take over and slow us down.

Knowing that I needed a big-time change, I completely revamped how I lived. I took off Friday afternoons. I went cycling twice a week. I strategically planned date nights to look forward to. I bought more tickets to shows and concerts. I printed out recipes to cook with my family. I shut off my phone and emails for extended amounts of time. I started to stop worrying about what other people thought about me and started to think about how I felt about myself.

Now, I don't feel guilty about going on long drives with my mom to visit my sisters at school. I don't feel like a slacker when I go on breakfast dates with my boyfriend, Matt. I take vacations. I go for hikes. I'm finally focused on being my best—not perfect. I regained my life. I'm now performing better at school, in my relationships, and in my family. Who knew?

I came to terms with the fact that slowing down isn't slacking off. Slowing down helps you become exceptional. And, becoming exceptional takes time. Becoming someone you're proud of takes time. You can't rush through this. I was beating myself up to become the perfect version of what everyone wanted me to be. I learned to love myself through self-care and self-compassion.

> *Slowing down helped me finally love who I am and who I am becoming.*

Slowing down is extremely difficult. I applaud you for doing it. What helps you maintain balance?

Slowing down *is* incredibly difficult! A wise professor once told me that when you think you can't slow down, that's exactly when you *need* to slow down. I live by this motto.

Self-care used to make me feel selfish. Now, it's something I look forward to. Slowing down is absolutely self-care. My favorite way to do this is to be with the people I love. I used to have family dinners and date nights where I was obsessed with time. I would have a calendar in my head that was planned out by the half hour. I would allot myself an hour and a half to eat dinner with friends. When the waiter would be slow to bring the check, my leg would start to twitch. (The nerve of not being on my schedule!) Now, I plan my days around what I want to prioritize. I can finally relax at dinners because I know I need this time to recharge. My new, healthy mindset helped me regain control of my emotions.

Also, though I'm still time-conscious, I'm no longer my calendar's slave. I'm its master!

I'm also very aware of how my body feels. It's okay to acknowledge that your body hurts from the stress of the week. It's okay to realize that your emotions are all over the place. Everything you're feeling is okay. It's all about how you respond to it. Do you push through to the point where you can't function the next day? Do you lash out at the people trying to help you? Do you shut out the world and obsess about how you're not doing enough? Yeah...I did those things, too. But, I'm changing. I'm getting there.

> **Slowing down is the new "Beast Mode."**

Are there any tips you can give us for slowing down personally and professionally? For example, I know you limit cell phone use and that you're pretty much off of social media. Can you please tell me about these and other practices?

I'm a very big believer in not being too involved in social media. I've intentionally shut myself off from the world of Facebook, Instagram, Twitter, Snapchat, TikTok, and anything else that you can think of. Yes, I'm 25 years old. Yes, I know how weird this is. But, whatever. I don't care. I never liked the social media world. I never understood how people feel "connected" in that way. Isn't it stressful to monitor how many people like your photos? Isn't it excruciating to put yourself out there for people to judge your life and your looks? You know they do!

I choose to live my own life with a very select group of people. I'm not embarrassed to admit that I have very few "true friends." If I had a Facebook account, we're talking maybe seven people. I don't have time to keep up with social media. I don't want to be on my phone looking at other people. Have you noticed how often you do this?

You're sacrificing your own precious time—and true connection!

Once you cut yourself off from the drug of social media, you begin to live in this alternate universe. You notice the "zombie dates" where couples (of all ages) go out to eat and stare at their phones. The disconnection in the world is palpable. We should all try to slow down and disconnect from the constant busyness of the world. Try a day, then a week, then a month. See how it goes. Believe me, you'll feel the relief. You'll feel the peace. If you're like me, you'll never want to go back to your old ways.

You could also sit by the ocean, go to a concert, go for a hike, and do it for the sake of doing it instead of posting it on some site for people to think you're living your best life. Reconnect to the world. Really feel it. Have you experienced a sunset without obsessing over taking the perfect picture? Have you ever been to a concert where you left your phone in the car? Are you living in the moment? Or, are you living on your phone?

> **Slow it down. Just be.**

What do you enjoy doing when you're not working and you're trying to slow down?

I love to go to the beach in the summer and in the winter. I love to go on vacations to new places and be immersed in new cities and cultures. Being in places that remind you how small you are is somewhat calming to me. The things I'm worrying about are probably pretty small in the grand scheme of life.

I also love to get a maple latte at Southdown Coffee in Huntington Village and drive to Caumsett State Park with my windows down. I love walking to the overlook by the mansion and going all the way down the big hill until I get to the water. I like to sit on the grass and listen to the ducks, listen to the birds, and feel the wind blow around me. This is extremely calming to me. I love to go to art museums and just sit in a random room for an extended amount of time. I like to sit and be aware of the world around me.

Awareness slows you down!

I love to sit and talk with my boyfriend, my mom, my dad, and my sisters. We usually talk while cooking or baking. My sisters and I go watch the sunset whenever they come home. I like to experience the beauty of the world while being with people I love.

I also love to sit with a cup of coffee and people watch. I remind myself that everyone is stressed out about something. Each person is struggling. Everyone loves and hates. They have pieces of themselves that they wish they could change.

> *Being connected to a common pulse of humanity helps me slow down.*

What specifically did you struggle with trying to slow down?

The problem with doing everything is that it's very rewarding. I'm someone who can do many things at once and do them all fairly well. This is a quality I both love and hate about myself. Take for example my last semester in grad school. I took a full course load (17 credits); I had an internship three days a week (7:15 am - 2:30 pm); I became an adjunct professor and taught an undergraduate class; I was a clinic-coordinator; I was a therapist and saw six clients a week (1 hour each); I attended weekly supervision sessions (4 hours); I worked 11 hours a week at my job at an animal hospital; and I was involved in my family and my relationship. My days began at 5:30 am and ended around 11 pm every night. It was hard. Really hard.

I managed it all very well, though. And, I got straight As. Talk about reinforcement! I did, however, flirt with burn out. It was rough. But, sometimes you have to do what you have to do. You just can't push this hard with everything every time.

You have to slow down, become aware of what you're doing, and be smart.

I love being the "girl who can do it all." It's cool. It's sexy. I'm "Wonder Woman," as my boyfriend calls me. It feels good. However, there's always a downside. When my internship ended at 2:30, and I had to rush home to work from 3-8:30, that was stressful. When I fell asleep during the movie my boyfriend bought tickets for a month in advance I felt like a horrible girlfriend. When I had to buy under eye cream to hide the bags under my eyes—and, let's remember, I'm only 25—I felt like I wasn't living my best life. We slip up. We take on more than we can handle. It happens.

Over time, I've learned to cut out the stuff I don't need.

Now that I'm applying to very competitive internships, this craziness has paid off. But, at a big cost. Grad school is supposed to be an unbalanced time. If I slowed down too much, I would have a very bare resume. There's a fine line between too little and too much.

God helped me immensely this past semester. I vividly remember praying on my way to my internship and prior to teaching the undergraduate class every day. I needed a significant amount of strength and blessings. He helped me tremendously. He reminded me of one of my favorite prayers: "God, grant me the serenity to accept the things I cannot change, the courage to change the things I can, and the wisdom to know the difference." Slowing down has helped me to do this.

Okay. So you definitely struggled personally. What about socially? Did being "Wonder Woman" affect how you dealt with people? Did it strain your relationships?

As I mentioned, I'm a relentless people pleaser in remission. So, the struggle to slow down definitely affects me interpersonally. It's tough. I worry about letting someone down. I worry about being judged for not being the best every time. However, I truly believe I worry less these days. My "Type A" personality will always be present. Thankfully, with God's help, I've learned to dial down the intensity a bit.

I have to intentionally say the golden word: No. Being a psychologist, I know I needed some hard-core exposure therapy saying this word to get over my fears. When I feel the need to please, I have to identify it, feel it in my body, and force myself to say, "No!" If I didn't force myself to do this, if I gave in to my fears, I'd still be running around like crazy and burning out. Now that I'm more familiar with slowing down and have more confidence from setting limits on people, I feel ok politely saying, "No."

> Prioritizing your time isn't selfish.

You've told me before that slowing down has helped you perform better in school and at work, and that it has also helped you manage your anxiety and strengthen your relationships. What about spiritually? Have you seen benefits in this area, too?

Definitely! I took a year off after graduating from my undergraduate studies. I didn't know if I wanted to become a physician's assistant, a nurse, or a psychologist. This was stressful. I had to work full-time during this year off. It wasn't all fun. Believe me, there was a panic to get my life together. If I continued to rush into things, I would go full speed ahead in the wrong direction. So, I slowed down. I thought about my values and my mission.

> I kept asking myself, "What is God calling me to do?"

Through countless bike rides at Caumsett Park, deep conversations with my parents, and lots of prayer, I realized God is calling me to make lives better. I love people. I love human stories. The good, the bad, and the ugly. I love the privilege of having someone confide in me. I feel honored when people are vulnerable and bring me into their world.

During my year off, I was flooded with a great deal of gratitude. In particular, I really became aware of how blessed I am to have the family I grew up with. My parents are freaking incredible. They're textbook amazing parents. My two sisters, Lauryn and Caroline, are my best friends. We love each other. And, we "do the hard $&#@" together! Also, my grandparents have been married for 56 years. They're the cutest couple I've ever met. Their love inspires me every day. Friends come into my house and leave saying, "I've never seen such a loving family. You're so lucky." I am. I'm very blessed.

Having heard this so many times, and after slowing down during my gap year and finally listening to God, I realized with immense clarity that I had to work with individuals and families who didn't have the same home life that I did. I have been shown love, compassion, and kindness tenfold throughout my life. This is why I can show this to my clients. Being a psychologist is the perfect professional mission for me.

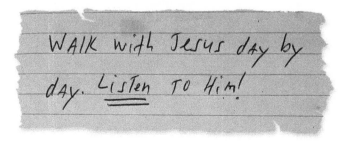

WALK with Jesus day by day. Listen TO Him!

In my personal life, my spiritual calling is to be the type of parent that my parents have been for me. I want to be a wife and a mom. This possibility makes me giddy with excitement. This is perhaps where I feel God calling me the most. To build a family in love is the biggest mission of my life. During my gap year, when I had the forced opportunity of truly slowing down, I met my boyfriend, Matt. Coincidence? I don't think so. He is the Superman to my Wonder Woman (and he slows me down when I'm moving too fast). My family and Matt have shown me that I'm worthy and capable of love and belonging. It's because I received love that I'm able to cultivate and give love. I'm *very* aware this is a rare gift. It's the biggest blessing in my life. And, I *have* to share this with others. I just *have* to.

I love 1 Corinthians 13:4, *"Love is patient, love is kind."* I have this verse in three different places throughout my house as a daily reminder. Slowing down and giving people kindness and respect is impossible when you go solely after self-serving interests, as we commonly do in our very busy lives. God, however, helps to guide me back on track. I try to bring love and kindness into everything I do. Like the rest of us, I fall short many, many times.

> God is calling us to connect with each other. Unfortunately, we're often too busy to hear Him.

I often wonder how I can pay God back for the life my parents gave me. He has granted me the opportunity to become a psychologist and work with those needing patience, kindness, compassion, and love. How lucky am I? What a beautiful job. What a gift. As Mairead said in the **Give Thanks** Commandment in this book, *"Sitting with someone and really listening to them is one of the most loving things we can do."* I couldn't agree more.

Wow! So, slowing down helped you hear God and discover your mission. That must have been incredible. Do you recall when you first heard Him speak to you about this? What was that like? Were you scared? Excited? Overwhelmed? Grateful?

Working with my first client in the Positive Psychology Institute for Emerging Adults was when I first really heard God speak to me about my mission. After months of dealing with the same presenting problem, my client broke down and had a psychological "breakthrough" as to why her relationships were so dysfunctional. She cried in session and gave me a hug at the end. This moment of connection and the ability to really help someone was when I first heard God loud and clear. It was scary because I realized the power of being someone that could make a difference. I was humbly overwhelmed, and I thanked God for what He has given me. This is my calling.

This is how I will make a little piece of the world a little bit better.

Your mission sounds amazing. Can you please tell me more about it?

My mission is to become a psychologist and use positive psychology techniques in therapy to make lives better. My goal is to have a private practice to help people recognize their potential and to find their own missions. I especially enjoy working with young females to enhance their self-compassion and regain control of their self-worth. I also plan on getting married and having children to share and experience my life with. My future husband and I will raise strong and kind children who know they are loved deeply, just as my parents demonstrated for me. I hope to travel more and teach my children about the beauty and excellence in the world around them. I can't wait for that!

Before we end, what final words of wisdom do you have for other 20-somethings who are struggling to slow down?

My advice is to do it. Slow down! You must carve out the time to intentionally put the phone down, put the schedule down, and re-enter your life. If you're struggling, dig deep and understand why you have an issue slowing down. Is it the disease of pleasing others? Is it your own unrelenting standards? What is getting in the way of hitting pause? Reject the message that we must constantly do everything all the time. Learn how to become selective with what gets your time and energy. Stop being a people pleaser. Start saying, "NO!" If you do, you'll hear God.

> We must slow down to listen to what God is calling us to do.

Also, the next time you start feeling burnt out, turn toward the people who love you and want to help you. Including God. Stop shutting them out. Take comfort in slowing down with a hug or an impromptu study break when your boyfriend brings you flowers and your favorite chai latte. Take a break after a few hours of studying to go to the gym and sweat the stress out. Stop obsessing, and take pride in the work you've accomplished. You know what will happen if you do these things? You'll end up accomplishing more.

Ashleigh occasionally sped. Sometimes to avoid being late, sometimes to avoid being unemployed, and other times to avoid being average. But, she generally remained under redline. Between 1993-2017, maximum speed limit increases on American roadways facilitated over 36,000 deaths. Slowing down and obeying the law could've saved these lives. Slowing down and obeying God's law—like resting for a day to commune with Him—could save your life, too.

Slow 'n steady wins the race. It also helps us find our mission.

TOUGH LOVE

"The only thing worse than being blind is having sight but no vision." —
Helen Keller

We desire thriving. Yet, we hesitate. Angst engulfs us. Doubt para-
lyzes us. Some seek distraction; others seek God. Potential failure, however, elicits half-hearted petitions. We pray for polishing, slight edits to
our story, tweaks to our being. God, though, aims high. He solicits conversion. "Unless a grain of wheat falls to the ground and dies, it remains
just a grain of wheat; but if it dies, it produces much fruit" (John, 12:24).
Petrified of accepting our mission and the concomitant responsibility, we
ignore God. We become selectively deaf and blind. A loving father, God
keeps calling us. He keeps nudging us—even if it means watching us fall.

Saul was an epic sinner. For years, he persecuted Christians. While
traveling to Damascus to further destroy God's church, a light from the
sky suddenly flashed around him, and he fell to the ground. A voice said
to him, "Saul, Saul, why are you persecuting me?...I am Jesus...get up and
go into the city and you will be told what you must do" (Acts, 9:4-6).
Upon standing, Saul realized he was now blind. Three days later, Ana-
nias, Jesus' disciple, restored Saul's sight, saying to him, "Saul, my brother, the Lord has sent me...that you may regain your sight and be filled
with the Holy Spirit" (Acts, 9:17).

Falling often precedes rising.

Saul then proclaimed God's word. He became "an instrument of salvation to the ends of the earth" (Acts, 13:47). Embracing his mission, Saul
(now called "Paul") said, "The Holy Spirit has been warning me that imprisonment and hardships await me. Yet I consider life of no importance
to me, if only I may finish my course and the ministry that I received
from the Lord Jesus, to bear witness to the gospel of God's grace" (Acts,
20:23-24). People often begged Paul to stay in their town. But, committed
to his mission, he left them, saying, "What are you doing, weeping and

breaking my heart? I am prepared not only to be bound but even to die in Jerusalem for the name of the Lord Jesus...The Lord's will be done" (Acts, 21:13-14). Some people die for money. Other people die for their mission.

Unless we slow down, our mission will remain unknown. Rather than emulating St. Paul and doing what we <u>must</u> do, we'll instead do what we <u>want</u> to do. Never adding our piece to the cosmic puzzle. Never leaving an eternal fingerprint. Don't wait to be knocked down. Don't wait to become blind. Listen for God's whispers, look for His signs, and surrender to His calling. Then, fulfill your destiny.

Pray for a conversion. Pray for a life worth death.

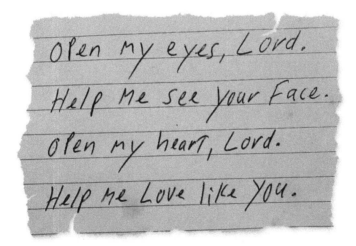

Open my eyes, Lord.
Help me see your face.
Open my heart, Lord.
Help me love like you.

COMMANDMENT VII TIPS

Thou Shalt
Slow Down

1. Consistently sleep 7-9 hours nightly. The Vedas say, "All intelligences awake with the morning." Therefore, rise at least 1 hour before dawn. Decline invitations for late dinners. Instead, suggest breakfast or lunch. Stop using your cell phone for an alarm clock. Spend $10 and buy one. Even better, open your windows. Birds know when you should rise.

2. Regularly unplug for extended windows of time. For the first hour of your day, keep your phone off. Build an invisible moat between you and the world. Use your brain's prime time to grow in mind, body, and spirit. Read. Exercise. Pray. Save your widgets, and don't waste them on pointless texts, emails, and notifications. Also, stop using a mobile office. Instead, drive in silence, listen to music, or enjoy an audiobook or podcast. Work hard, but set limits. Create balance—not stress.

3. Be childlike, and foster a strong play ethic. Host game nights, ride your bike, join a running club, or snowshoe. Go backpacking, cliff camping, or spelunking. Paint, have a catch, sleigh ride, or snorkel. Climb a tree, kite surf, or learn hip-hop dance. While playing, feel God's presence. Enjoy Him. He's better company than your phone.

4. Channel Ashleigh, the rainbow-chasing paragon of perspective. Recall her inspiring words: *"Slowing down helped me finally love who I am and who I am becoming," "Being connected to a*

common pulse of humanity helps me slow down," and *"We must slow down to listen to what God is calling us to do."* Ponder Ashleigh's wisdom when you're trying to slow down. Then, follow it.

5. Slow down to hear God. Begin your day with 15 minutes of meditation or prayer. Light a candle in a dark room, and rest in silence (see #2 above). Get comfortable. Sit straight, place your hands on your lap, and put your feet on the floor. If your eyes are open, watch the candle flickering. If your eyes are closed, look into the darkness. Take 10 deep, slow breaths from your belly, not your chest. While still breathing deeply and slowly, draw your attention to your heart. Notice the warmth around and within it. Focus on it. Feel it permeating your body. After bringing awareness to God's presence, ask Him *the* question: *What must I do with my life?* Stay still, keep breathing deeply and slowly, and remain mindful of the warmth throughout your body. Carefully listen for God speaking to you. Feel Him stirring your soul. Feel Him guiding you. Over time, this habit will help you find your mission. When you do, pursue it. Be brave. Pray for a conversion. Pray for a life worth death.

VIII

Thou Shalt

BEFRIEND NATURE

John and his family emigrated from Scotland to the U.S. settling in Wisconsin. Growing up, he often clashed with his strict, religious father. But, he found solace in nature. In his 20s, John spent several years at the University of Wisconsin studying botany, chemistry, and geology. There, he drew attention for his creative genius and poor decorum. Thankfully, rather than wasting widgets polishing his manners, John spent them pursuing his mission: preserving America's natural treasures.

At 29, John injured his eye working. Bedridden, secluded in a dark room for 1 month, John emerged ever more excited to wander across America. After walking 1,000 miles to Florida and then visiting Cuba, John moved to his promised land: California. "The mountains are calling, and I must go," he said. The rugged mountains and the vastness of Yosemite stole his heart. John's response to Yosemite was euphoric, heavenly, and religious.[54] While discovering Yosemite, John survived on little food. Yet, he thrived spiritually, studying Ralph Waldo Emerson's works and befriending nature. John's spiritual relationship with nature taught him that everything is interconnected. "When one tugs at a single thing in nature, he finds it attached to the rest of the world," he observed. As with St. Paul, blindness made John see.

---

54 In his documentary, *The National Parks: America's Best Idea*, Ken Burns wrote, "If Yosemite was a temple, [John] would become its high priest."

After traveling for about another decade, John revamped his strategy for preserving America's national resources. He had to change collective minds and federal laws. "Through all the wonderful, eventful centuries... God has cared for these trees, saved them from drought, disease, avalanches, and a thousand straining, leveling tempests and floods; but he cannot save them from fools—only Uncle Sam can do that," wrote John. In 1890, because of his determination, Congress approved the protection of Yosemite. And, in 1892, with government support, John co-founded and became the first president of the Sierra Club, thus starting the environmental movement.

Nature gave John a new family and a path. She forged his connection to God. She helped him discover his mission. "Protect what you love, and what you love will protect you," said my daughter, Julianne. Spoken like a true follower of John Muir, *"Father of the National Parks."*[55]

55 Ralph Waldo Emerson, Henry David Thoreau, and John Muir fostered each other's love for nature. Emerson, however, was the leader. In the mid-19th century, Emerson led the *transcendentalist movement*, which Thoreau and Muir followed and helped progress. Emerson was Thoreau's mentor and friend. He inspired and encouraged Thoreau to write nature poetry, which he began doing in the 1840s. While Muir admired Emerson, he admired nature more. When Emerson offered Muir a job at Harvard, he declined, saying he was still busy doing fieldwork. Muir later confided to a friend, "I never for a moment thought of giving up God's big show for a mere profship!" Thanks to these three men, we better understand, recognize, and appreciate our spiritual connection to nature. Thank you, God, for Emerson, Thoreau, and Muir. May we feel their spirits swirling about the sky, forests, and mountains.

NATURAL MEDICINE

"Nature itself is the best physician." — Hippocrates

Pill commercials are deceptive and terrifying. While people frolic in fields or savor a sunrise, a soft, warm, trustworthy voice whispers innocuously to us. *"Common side effects include constipation, headaches, drowsiness, nausea, and insomnia. More serious side effects are increased blood pressure, internal bleeding, cancer, suicidal thoughts, and death."* This might explain why Americans spend exorbitantly on natural remedies. According to a national survey from 2016, Americans spent $30.2 billion on "complementary health approaches" like meditation, chiropractic care, and yoga. And, because we love the quick and easy, 42% of this paid for herbal supplements. Pills, though, only sometimes cure life's ills.

Imagine if I told you a wonder drug existed that could help you feel better, live longer—and even find your mission. Amazingly, this product exists. The FDA doesn't regulate it. There are no negative side effects. You can access it whenever. And, it's free. The miracle pill? Nature. Philosophers and religious leaders have extolled for millennia nature's role in thriving. Yet, people typically only experience nature while walking from their homes to their cars and then to noisy, stressful, and artificial environments. Like ecosystems, our bodies have four interrelated components: *physical, intellectual, emotional,* and *spiritual.* When one component is off, every component is off. We then flounder trying to discover and pursue our mission. Befriending nature, however, helps us maintain ecological balance.

Get lost in nature. You'll find your way in life.

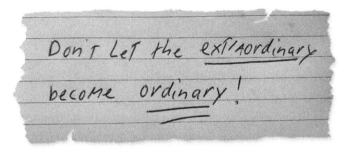

Don't Let the extraordinary become ordinary!

Physical

Strong, healthy bodies help us braille the world. They support adventure, exploration, and discovery. Yet, we take better care of our pets. While 83% of dog owners visit their vet annually, only 30% of people visit their doctor annually. Healthy living is an act of faith. "Do you not know that your body is a temple of the Holy Spirit within you…?" (1 Corinthians, 6:19). So, make an appointment with nature. Tend to your body. Tend to your spirit. Tend to God.

Noise creates stress. How? By triggering our adrenal glands to secrete adrenalin and cortisol (i.e., a stress hormone). For example, people who listened to aircraft noise while sleeping woke with increased vascular damage, inflammation, and cortisol levels. Compare this to nature's "quiet room." Spending two nights in the forest, relative to two nights in the city, lowered people's cortisol level. As did 20 minutes sitting or walking in nature at least three times weekly for 2 months. (Adding another 10 minutes made cortisol plummet.) Rustling leaves is 20 decibels, and a babbling brook is 40 decibels, whereas an alarm clock is 80 decibels, and a subway car's interior is 95 decibels. Push pause, hit mute, and power down. You can then ponder life, hear God—and discover your mission.

Take a hike. Not an Uber. Take your pals. Not your pods.

Chronic stress is deadly. Partly because it impedes heart health (see Commandment VII). Nature can help. Data across 20 studies involving 732 participants found that people who walked or sat in a forest, compared to those doing likewise in a city, had significantly lower blood pressure. A recent experiment extended these findings showing that walking in a forest, compared to walking in a city, caused significantly higher heart rate variability (indicating more relaxation and less stress) and lower heart rates. Anecdotal data support this. Here's my resting heart rate (RHR) during 1 week at Yawgoog, an 1,800-acre reservation. My RHR was 63 amid packing. It decreased to 58 while adjusting to my mosquito net covered "bed" and wolf spider roommate. It then remained at 51 or 52 throughout my trip. Professional athletes have RHRs in the 40s. Bring it, Xanax!

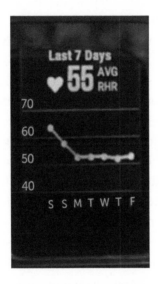

Still skeptical nature is curative? In a classic study, patients who recently had their gallbladders removed were randomly assigned to 1 of 2 conditions: a window facing a brick wall or a window facing nature. Patients with a nature-view had shorter hospital stays, fewer painkillers post-surgery, weaker pain medications, and more positive nurse notes. So, if you're hospital bound, request a nature view. Bribe the nurse with flowers. Then, ask him or her to leave them by your window.

Stress is stressful. Nature nurtures.

Intellectual

Thoughts must float about like clouds. Gradually, they reshape, eventually crystallizing into wisdom. Our thoughts first resemble flat, expansive, low-lying stratus clouds. They then resemble cumulus clouds with multiple layers. Finally, our thoughts resemble wispy cirrus clouds reaching for Heaven. Like clouds, our thoughts will only tickle the stratosphere under expansive skies. Opening your door to the exterior opens the door to your interior.

Creative people make life better. They make us learned, lively, and loving. How? They observe. They daydream. They walk…in nature. For example, Aristotle walked around the Lyceum's tree-filled groves while teaching students about science and philosophy.[56] Dr. Edward Jenner, per his eulogy given by Dr. William Dewees, contributed to the smallpox vaccine and other scientific advancements by finding "the height of his ambition and the zenith of his power to benefit mankind while walking with nature." And St. Thomas Aquinas created the "Five Ways" (i.e., five logical arguments for God's existence) during brisk walks around the cloister neighboring the Basilica of Saint Sabina in Rome. Befriending nature, therefore, facilitates creativity; creativity facilitates openness; and openness facilitates finding our mission. Elevating our heartrate in nature, thus, elevates our mind.

Hofstra University, where I work, is a registered arboretum. Trees wear nametags in Latin. Thousands of tulips beautify campus during our annual tulip festival. Appreciating our urban garden, I always hold walking meetings. The creative juices flow. During our "*Walk 'n Talks*", students and I have sculpted dissertations, dissected thorny data, and pondered theories. I've even invited colleagues for strolls. They're surprised when I say, "How about we talk while walking? It will be even better if your phone stays behind." Though initially hesitant, they always leave saying, "Wow, that was so…relaxing…energizing…and productive.

---

56 Aristotle founded the Peripatetic school at the Lyceum. "Peripatetic" comes from the Greek, *peri*, meaning "around," and *patein*, meaning "to walk."

I have to do that more. Thank you!" Don't thank me. Thank God, the master artist. "All things came to be through him, and without him nothing came to be" (John, 1:3). German polymath Friedrich Nietzsche said, "One must give value to their existence by behaving as if ones very existence were a work of art." Within you, thus, resides a statue to be chiseled, a musical to be produced, a screenplay to be written.

Your mind is bursting with colors. Grab a paintbrush. The world is your canvas.

Emotional

Stiff necks. Shallow breaths. Scattered brains. Many of us, including me, resemble exposed nerve endings. We twitch. We jump. We react. The slightest thing triggers a cascade of negativity. Find your mission? You can't even find your phone! (Good.) We think only a head transplant will relieve our brain fog. It won't. Ask Frankenstein. Instead, befriend nature, relax, and recharge. Otherwise, you'll lose more than the forest for the trees.

Recall how noise impedes physical health? It also impedes emotional health. In people living near a major airport, a 10-decibel increase in aircraft noise was related with a 28% increase in anxiety medication use. Further, people living near noisy streets, compared to quieter ones, are 25% more likely to have depressive symptoms. "When life feels too big to handle, go outside. Everything looks smaller when you're standing under the sky," said author and social activist, L.R. Knost. Science supports this. Walking in the woods for 50 minutes, compared to walking along a four-lane road, reduced anxiety and negative self-talk while also increasing positive emotions. I grew up on a main road, and I was anxious, depressed, and angry. I now live on a back road, and my children are calm, zestful, and loving. Sure, other variables also help explain this difference. One thing, however, is certain: a noisy outside facilitates a noisy inside.

Our world is flooded with unnecessary distractions (see Commandment II). Filtering this requires many widgets. But, these distractions already depleted our widgets, limiting our ability to connect with people. Nature, however, protects us from modernity's madness. She creates a peaceful, inviting, loving home. A space for intimacy and connection. Like any loving mother, nature gives us her best so that we, too, can give others our best. When we do, we create the supportive, secure relationships needed to explore and find our mission.

My children and I are obsessed with building snowmen. We pray for blizzards to play in God's snow globe. Each year, we strive to build a bigger snowman. This one was 8 feet tall. We shared laughs. We shared love. We shared celebratory hot chocolate. These tender moments become bittersweet when you realize it might be the last one. That's why they must be savored. That's why they must be created—deliberately, consistently, and lovingly. During these playful times, I learned about my children's mission. James dreams of going to the Air Force Academy and entering the Space Force. Julianne dreams of becoming an architect, interior designer, and published author. Befriending nature with my children, thus, helped me support them with finding their mission. It was worth the numb extremities and icy beard.[57]

---

57 While awaiting edits for this book, Julianne and I, along with our friend, Tom Vacchio, wrote a children's book about family time. Julianne's dream might soon come true. Stay tuned!

Build a snowman. Build a relationship. Build a life.

Spiritual

With plants, fragmentation fosters vegetative reproduction. With people, fragmentation fosters vegetative symptoms (e.g., distraction, fatigue, and insomnia). We thrive when we feel whole; we feel whole when we're connected to something larger than ourselves. Time in nature facilitates this sense of oneness by fostering transcendent emotions like gratitude, joy, awe, and love. "Heaven is under our feet as well as over our heads," observed Thoreau. Agreed. Death isn't a prerequisite for experiencing Heaven. Go outside.

A transcendentalist, Thoreau desired a deep connection with God. He believed less time with people and more time with wildlife increased his divine consciousness (see Commandment VII). John Muir agreed, saying, "Keep close to Nature's heart...and break clear away, once in a while, and climb a mountain or spend a week in the woods. Wash your spirit clean." Thoreau, therefore, retreated to Walden Pond. Unfortunately, even there he experienced human peacocks spreading their large, colorful, patterned plumage to impress and attract others. Their flashy display might have made an insecure person feel small, trivial, and isolated. Thoreau, however, was confident with his chosen life. Of his human neighbors, Thoreau wrote in *Walden*:

> *Often, in the repose of my mid-day, there reaches my ears a confused tintinnabulum [tinkling bell] from without. It is the noise of my contemporaries. My neighbors tell me of their adventures with famous gentlemen and ladies, what notabilities they met at the dinner table; but I am no more interested in such things than in the contents of the Daily Times. The interest and the conversation are about costume and manners chiefly; but a goose is a goose still, dress it as you will.... I delight to come to my bearings—not walk in procession with pomp and parade, in a conspicuous place, but to walk even with the Builder of the universe....*

This pompous yakking distracted Thoreau from higher pursuits. Noise is noise. Whether it's from a plane, car, or braggart.

Compare this to wildlife. Thoreau found his furry, feathery, and scaly neighbors welcoming, humble, and kind, making him feel expansive, significant, and connected. Again, writing in *Walden*, Thoreau said:

> *Every morning was a cheerful invitation to make my life of equal simplicity, and I may say innocence, with Nature herself.... The Harivansa [A French work] says, "An abode without birds is like a meat without seasoning." Such was not my abode, for I found myself suddenly neighbor to the birds; not by having imprisoned one, but having caged myself near them....*

The birds welcomed Thoreau with open wings. They took him into their nest, gathered twigs for him to sit, and kept him company. After a few conversations, Thoreau learned that he and the birds were members of the same cosmic family with the same heavenly father. The birds befriended Thoreau. We, however, often ignore our neighbors. And we wonder why we're so sad and lonely. Who's the birdbrain?

Discovering God's plan for us requires much time in silence and solitude. People talk excessively. We communicate excessively. Marketers market excessively. It's exhausting and distracting. Nature, however, provides the perfect respite to recharge and ponder. That's when we question ourselves. That's when we discover ourselves. That's when we hear God's voice gently guiding us toward our mission.

Nature gives recreation so we can have re-creation.

HIDDEN TEACHERS

"I went to the woods because I wished to live deliberately, to front only the essential facts of life, and see if I could not learn what it had to teach, and not, when I came to die, discover that I had not lived. I did not wish to live what was not life, living is so dear...I wanted to live deep and suck out all the marrow of life...." — Henry David Thoreau

"Teach" comes from the Old English word, *tǣċan*, meaning "direct," "warn," and "persuade." Learning, therefore, isn't the ultimate goal of teaching—it's helping students thrive. This is news to our education system. Need proof? You received a life of tests rather than tests of life. Fret not. The master teacher who inspired geniuses like Galileo Galilei, Vincent van Gogh, and William Shakespeare is still teaching. Her class is just beyond your door and still in session. Step outside. Open your eyes, open your mind, and open your heart. Prepare for *Life 101*.

Nature is our perennial master teacher. We learn how all life cycles have three common stages: birth, growth, and death. We learn how everyone—and everything—is connected. "For as in one body we have many parts, and all the parts do not have the same function, so we, though many, are one body in Christ and individually parts of one another" (Romans, 12:4-5). Sergeant Sun teaches us to start and end our day with beauty, keep our inner fire burning, and shine light on others—not ourselves. Mother Mountain teaches us to reach new heights, rise to the top, and enjoy the view. Sister Sky teaches us to stay awed, expand our horizons, and befriend the dark. St. Waterfall teaches us to roar with passion, create peace, and go with the flow. Nature University has world-class teachers. The lessons are endless—and life-changing. Everyone can attend. Many, however, don't.[58]

You won't get detention, suspended, or expelled if you skip nature's class. The consequence is worse: you'll tire, stagnate, and meander. "Of all the paths you take in life, make sure a few of them are dirt," suggests John Muir. Follow his advice.

Get outside. Get dirty. Get living.

---

58 Bears, bats, and bumblebees hibernate to conserve widgets. Are you weary? Maybe you need sleep. Birds migrate for food and improved nesting locations. Are you avoiding change? Maybe you should spread your wings and fly away from home, a relationship, or your job. Lobsters teach us about dominance hierarchies and how confidence, competence, and courage help us survive—and win. Swans, sea horses, and gray wolves teach us about monogamy and the stability it gives life and society. Dogs teach us about loyalty, making friends, and learning new tricks. Cats teach us about purring, pouncing, and occasionally lying low. Animals, insects, crustaceans, and fish teach us more about life than we realize—and definitely more than YouTube University. If only we befriended nature.

Life Lessons

I recently attended class in Shenandoah National Park and Montauk Point State Park. My teachers were distinguished lecturers. Past students include President Herbert Hoover, Charles Lindbergh, Edsel Ford, and Andy Warhol. I learned about virtue, suffering, authenticity, purpose, and courage. Great teachers make us uncomfortable. They challenge us to see life anew. Prepare to squirm. Prepare to learn. Prepare to thrive.

Brother Bird

Class started at 5:30 am—sharp. I found a front row seat on the porch overlooking the Blue Ridge Mountains. I sat, quietly. A nerd, I arrived first. So I thought. Brother Bird was waiting, prepared. Do you think running late is rude? Or, do you think it's exercise? Do you plan? Or, do you improvise? Do you lead by example? Or, are you a hypocrite? **Lesson #1:** *Cultivate virtue.*

Brother Bird loved teaching. His passion was infectious, likewise his gratitude. You could tell by his mastery, clear instruction, and care for his students. "This is the day the Lord has made; let us rejoice in it and be glad" (Psalm 118:24). Brother Bird knew this might be his last lecture, and he was savoring it. Did you find your mission? Or, a job? Do you thank God for blessings? Or, does busyness distract you? **Lesson #2:** *Be passionate and grateful.*

Throughout class, Brother Bird always gave his best. He graciously shared his brilliance, wanting nothing back. He also kept it *real*. Remaining authentic, Brother Bird only sang his songs. He wouldn't sing covers. Do you sing your heart out? Or, do you lip-sync? Do you give your divine gifts freely? Or, are there strings attached? Do you stand on life's stage? Or, do you hide behind the curtains, decaying from regrets? **Lesson #3:** *Boldly share your talents.*

Like Professor Thieben, Brother Bird kept the human touch alive. He was gentle and warm. Respectful, he also approached me quietly; I sometimes only detected his presence from a moving branch or bush. When I spoke, he listened and expressed agreement by nodding or flapping. Are you confident and meek? Or, arrogant and weak? Do you allow silence in conversations? Or, do you chirp too much and fill pauses with platitudes? **Lesson #4:** *Respect others.*

Be inspiring and uplifting. Help people fly like a bird.

Father Fog

Brother Bird and Father Fog co-taught class. Father Fog's gloominess was annoying, and it dampened our dialogue. Brother Bird asked the sun for help. The sun then removed Father Fog from the classroom. Do you consider God an ally? Or, do you consider Him an adversary? Do you ask the Son to help lift your fog? Or, like me, are you sometimes too stubborn, ignorant, or ashamed? **Lesson #1:** *You need the Son.*

The next day, Father Fog returned to class. This time, he stayed longer and tried dominating the lesson. Father Fog was cocky; he thought he knew everything. His thinking was also myopic and dark. Brother Bird had enough, and he again asked the sun for help. Father Fog fought hard. The sun, however, fought harder. Several hours later, Father Fog finally left. This time, for days. Are you forbearing with the Son when

He tries lifting your fog? Or, do you expect results yesterday? Do you let people explain their views? Or, do you control conversations? **Lesson #2:** *Be patient.*

During Father Fog's absence, I realized something: he lied. A lot. He said everything existed within his clouds. But, when he left, I saw towns, farms, and mountains beyond the horizon. Opportunity, love, and hope transcended his boundaries. The world wasn't bleak like Father Fog said. "The people who walked in darkness have seen a great light; upon those who dwelt in the land of gloom a light has shown" (Isaiah, 9:1). Do you think God can help people change? Or, do you think sin will always win? Do you think your fog clouds your vision? Or, do you think it reflects reality? **Lesson #3:** *Light follows darkness.*

Fog makes us blind. The Son makes us see.[59]

Professor Wildflower

Skyline Drive is a 105-mile road running through Shenandoah. Professor Wildflower and colleagues border much of it. Trilliums, bluets, wild geraniums, and jacks-in-the-pulpits display their natural beauty. Bubblegum-pink wild azaleas and golden ragworts make you pull over.

---

59 My family and I took every picture of nature in this book. But, while attending class in Shenandoah, I couldn't get a picture of Brother Bird or Father Fog that captured their beauty. Therefore, I got their pictures from the National Park Service's gallery of Shenandoah. I hope these pictures, along with the others, encourage you to befriend nature, listen for God while attending her class, and support John Muir's mission by visiting our national parks. It will inspire you to find and follow your own mission.

It's like driving in a rainbow. "Earth laughs in flowers," wrote Emerson. With its 862 wildflower species, Shenandoah must then always be crying from laughter. Do you recognize and appreciate your unique petals? Or, do you feel like every other daisy? Do you boldly bloom? Or, do you wither? **Lesson #1:** *Show your true colors.*

Skyline drive gives access to numerous trails and, thus, courses taught by Professor Wildflower. Walking along the road looking for one, I noticed something I didn't while driving. Majestic butterflies—including eastern tiger swallowtails, great spangled fritillaries, and monarchs—surrounded Professor Wildflower as she taught. They danced, fluttering about, enjoying her company while listening to her lessons. Sometimes, they sat with her. Other times, when Professor Wildflower needed rest, they gave her space. Professor Wildflower and the butterflies respected, accepted, and loved each other. It was *real*. Do you think being authentic creates thriving relationships? Or, do you think it creates heartache? Do you think a tulip should always act like a tulip? Or, do you think it should act like a rose when in a rose garden? **Lesson #2:** *Authenticity attracts beauty.*

Let your colors shine brightly. You'll draw similar hues.

Dr. Woods

Minutes into class, I understood why Dr. Woods was a Distinguished Teacher of the Year recipient. Hiking along the Appalachian Trail in Shenandoah, I was taken aback by the order in her classroom. I first noticed that plants, trees, and animals lived and worked harmoniously. For example, photosynthesis forms plants, animals eat them, animals die, and then plants feast. During a rain shower, I then realized how precipitation falls, rises, and then falls again, creating a classroom environment that facilitates learning, living, and thriving. I asked Dr. Woods about how she created the perfect system. "I didn't create it," she said. "God did. I just try living as He planned while using the gifts He gave me to pursue my mission." Do you believe in creation and evolution? Or, only evolution (find the *Easter eggs* in this book ☺)?[60] Do you think life has a purpose? Or, are you nihilistic? **Lesson #1:** *God created everything—including you—deliberately.*

Walking about class during a break, I met Dr. Woods's family. I mainly spoke with Uncle Chestnut and Cousin Red Oak. I also met Aunt Maple, Poppa Birch, and Grandma Ash. Her niece, Yellow Poplar, was relaxing by the stream. Unlike typical families, most members were healthy. Intrigued, I asked Dr. Woods about this. "We all value deep roots," she said. "So, we periodically drop our leafy friends for more energy to build a stronger base." Fascinated, I probed further. "You also seem to occasionally smother each other, stifling growth," I replied. "How do you separate?" "We lose our lower branches to have more resources for growing our upper branches," she said. "If we don't get taller, we'll never reach the sun, limiting our potential and never fulfilling our mission." Do you have deep roots? Or, are they shallow? Are you willing to cut draining relationships? Or, are you too scared or weak? Are you reaching for Heaven? Or, slipping toward Hell? **Lesson #2:** *Keep growing.*

Stay grounded. Remove deadwood. Reach for the Son.

---

60 I need you saving room for dinner. So, here's one more jelly bean: *The beginning of our universe is so incalculable that it's as precise as throwing a dart from space and hitting a bullseye just a trillionth of a trillionth of an inch in diameter on Earth.*

Sensei Ocean

Montauk is one of my favorite towns. Unlike the neighboring Hamp-
tons, Montauk is chill, simple, and brimming with natural beauty (not
silicon and Botox). Montauk's spirit resides in my heart. So much so,
that my first tattoo is sunrise at Montauk lighthouse within a larger sun.
In Sensei Ocean's class, I've watched false dawn sitting upon rocks sur-
rounding the lighthouse; I've roasted s'mores over moonlit campfires;
I've also surfed many waves, caught many fish, and built many sand castles. During a recent family vacation, I returned to Sensei Ocean's class.
I centered myself, emptied my mind, and inhaled the salty air. Watching
his ever-rolling waves I wondered, "What are you telling me? What are
the lessons?" During an hour of silence and solitude, I took these notes.
The message is manifest. The dissonance is debilitating. Nature is the ultimate mirror of truth.

Montauk:
Lessons from The Atlantic Ocean

- A Humpback whale surprised me. A seal surprised me. People love surprises.
- Be persistent. Sand castles + obstacles will crumble. Cliffs will erode. You'll remain.
- Be inviting. Be welcoming. Be a good host(ess).
- Be yourself. Even if some dislike you.
- Life ebbs + flows. There are highs + lows. Roll with it. Be fluid.
- Life is messy. There's turmoil. To be alive is to suffer. Figure it out. It's worth it.
- Add peace to the world. Even when life is crazy.
- Be aware of your natural rhythms. Embrace them. Never apologize. Use them to thrive.
- The ocean is generous. We should be, too.
- Be silent when possible. Roar when needed.
- The ocean gives life. It only takes when needed. Do likewise.
- The ocean provides a respite. Create a warm, loving home. Life is hard.
- Provide for loved ones.
- Let people struggle in the surf. Hold their hand. Lovingly. But, let them grow.

I learned more from Sensei Ocean in 1 hour than I did from a year's worth of reading. These are my overall takeaways. Do you swell and crash upon shores during nor'easters? Or, do you always try resembling a lake? **Lesson #1:** *When life is chaotic, be strong and respond accordingly.* Do you adjust to storms? Or, do you fight the tide? **Lesson #2:** *Be fluid.* Do you teach people how to swim? Or, do you always throw them a life preserver? **Lesson #3:** *Know when to keep people afloat, know when to let them* *gasp.* Do you accept that sometimes you can't provide perfect swimming conditions? Or, do you show resentment with a powerful undertow? **Lesson #4:** *Give what you can, when you can—never apologizing.*

Sensei Ocean is gentle, yet strong. Humble, yet bold. Loving, yet dangerous. My biggest takeaway? He's everything I dream to be. And, everything I'm not.

Make a splash. Regardless who seas.

Befriending nature helps us live our best-life-possible and thrive. In nature, we learn honest, inspiring, and timeless lessons. Learning from this master teacher, however, requires attending her class and being engaged. Nature has forever been, and still is, teaching us about life. Have you stopped listening? Have you become truant? Our noisy world muffles God's voice, but nature's quiet classroom helps us hear Him. Rest in nature's arms. Be reverent. Be still. Discover your mission.

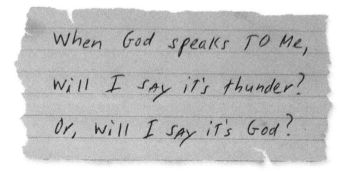

When God speaks TO Me, Will I say it's thunder? Or, will I say it's God?

THE RIGHT RESPONSE

"God has not called me to be successful. He called me to be faithful." — St. Mother Teresa

Artists often depict angels as friendly winged humans with halos. Scripture, however, describes something different. Angels are more ferocious than tame, more frightening than peaceful. Some held flaming swords. Others had four faces, four wings, and many eyes. The cherubim weren't cherubs. Hollywood also got it wrong (typical). Unlike Castiel from *Supernatural* and Clarence from *It's a Wonderful Life*, angels don't always protect us from sin and stupidity. They aren't always nice. Some angels are even evil (think Satan, the fallen angel). Thus, according to Scripture, the first words spoken by angels when visiting someone often were, "Fear not" or "Do not be afraid." This introduction helps when you're regarded as more savage than saint.

Now, consider Mary. She must have been terrified when the angel, Gabriel, visited her. Imagine her shock, confusion, and panic upon his arrival. Yet, Mary's curiosity about God's message made her stay. Gabriel told her she'd give birth to Jesus. A virgin, Mary asked Gabriel how this was possible. The angel said, "The Holy Spirit will come upon you, and the power of the Most High will overshadow you. Therefore the child to be born will be called holy, the Son of God…for nothing will be impossible for God" (Luke, 1:35, 37). Mary replied, "Behold, I am the handmaid of the Lord. May it be done to me according to your word" (Luke, 1:38). In this brief, history-changing interaction, we learn two profound lessons. **Lesson #1:** *Anything is possible with God.* **Lesson #2:** *Saying "Yes" to God is always the right response.* Mary had the right response. We should, too.

Mountains, oceans, and wildflowers do what they <u>must</u> do. Thankfully, so did Mary. Nature and Mary understood and accepted God's plan for their lives. Their belief is reflected in a recent church bulletin: "When we look at our lives and try to distill the important lessons, we some-times discover a spiritual insight: We needn't be anything other than who God has made us be." Sitting atop a throne of lies, the world stifles our growth. We become easier to manage because clones create conformity. God warns us about this: "Do not conform yourselves to this age but be transformed by the renewal of your mind, that you may discern what is the will of God, what is good and pleasing and perfect" (Romans, 12:2). Run away from the Pied Piper. Run toward God.

Mary didn't negotiate with God. She didn't give Him stipulations. She didn't ask to read the fine print.[61] Instead, she surrendered. Emulate Mary. Trust God's messengers, feel His nudges, and follow His bread-crumbs. Like Mary, be obedient. Then, prepare to suffer and be rejected. Prepare also to be fulfilled—and to find your mission.

Our mission isn't about us. It's beyond us.

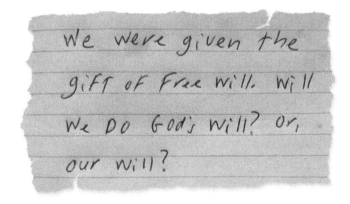

We were given the gift of Free will. Will We Do God's will? Or, our will?

---

61 I applaud Jesus for reading the fine print (see Commandment I). Now, I applaud Mary for *not* reading the fine print. Why? Jesus was asked to sign *Satan's Contract*. Mary, however, was asked to sign *God's Contract*. Doubt Satan. Trust God.

COMMANDMENT VIII TIPS

Thou Shalt
Befriend Nature

1. Go for long silent walks in nature. Unplug. Walk mindfully, sensing the earth beneath your feet. Feel the stillness, inhale deeply, and savor the smells. Note the dampness and temperature. Is rain impending? Is a snowstorm brewing? Appreciate your restored mind, body, and soul. Use this clarity and the widgets to find your mission.

2. Lie in the grass and watch the clouds or wish upon a star. Jump in a lake hooting and hollering or summit a mountain. Build a snowman, go canoeing, or bird watch. During these activities, feel your connection to nature. Recognize your dependence on her. Thank her for bringing you joy and peace. Thank her for sustaining your life. How do you best express your gratitude? Protect her—as she protects you.

3. Study God's handiwork. Notice the balance, order, and harmony. Watch birds dance in the sky. Sometimes, it's a solo. Other times, it's a duet. Occasionally, it's a mosh pit. Get intoxicated from a flower's fragrance. Pick one tree annually, and observe the colors change daily. Appreciate how each individual canvas changes subtly and has unique color patterns. God loves details; love is in the details.

4. Nature is our perennial teacher. While befriending nature, ask her, "What are you telling me? What are the lessons?" Be still. Be

quiet. Listen and observe. Take notes. Create a study group, and use these lessons from distinguished lecturers.

Brother Bird: 1) *Cultivate virtue.* 2) *Be passionate and grateful.* 3) *Boldly share your talents.* 4) *Respect others.*
Father Fog: 1) *You need the Son.* 2) *Be patient.* 3) *Light follows darkness.*
Professor Wildflower: 1) *Show your true colors.* 2) *Authenticity attracts beauty.*
Dr. Woods: 1) *God created everything—including you—deliberately.* 2) *Keep growing.*
Sensei Ocean: 1) *When life is chaotic, be strong and respond accordingly.* 2) *Be fluid.* 3) *Know when to keep people afloat, know when to let them gasp.* 4) *Give what you can, when you can—never apologizing.*

5. Get comfortable and close your eyes. Be still. Once you're settled, imagine an angel appearing to you and giving you your mission. Let the shock, confusion, and panic engulf you. Feel your heart race. Feel your chest tighten. Feel your palms sweat. After feeling this anxiety for several minutes, picture the angel, Gabriel, visiting Mary and telling her that she'd give birth to Jesus. Be inspired by Mary's bravery and trust in God. Let the awe undo and replace your anxiety. Then, mentally or aloud repeat the lessons from Mary's response to God: 1) *Anything is possible with God*, and 2) *Saying "Yes" to God is always the right response.* With much effort and God's grace, like Mary, you'll eventually find your mission and do God's will—not your will.

IX

Thou Shalt

GIVE THANKS

Growing up, Dorothy's parents rarely discussed God. Yet, she always felt Him in her heart. Quietly, she believed "every soul has a tendency toward God." Reading spiritual books strengthened her desire to know Him. Like me, however, while attending college, she also strayed. She became exceedingly attracted to communist ideology, making her reject Christianity because of its "hypocrisy." But, unlike Hansel and Gretel, God's breadcrumbs helped Dorothy return home.

A series of events rekindled Dorothy's faith. After several arrests, some love affairs, and an abortion (which she thought sterilized her), one particular event at 27 sparked her religious conversion: another pregnancy. Life got *real*. So did her love for God. Dorothy abandoned her old ways and made God her North Star. Like when she was a little girl, she again felt Him in her heart. Gratitude for creation provided fertile soil for Dorothy's faith to grow, igniting her passion to personify the gospels and give witness to God's love. A paragon of gratitude, Dorothy knew that appreciation creates abundance—but only if you notice and give thanks to God.

Dorothy's gratitude for her daughter, Tamar, was radiant. "Give thanks to the Lord, who is good, whose love endures forever" (Psalm 118:29). Dorothy wrote, "No human creature could receive or contain so vast a flood of love and joy as I often felt after the birth of my child. With this came the need to worship, to adore." Like any loving mother, Dorothy wanted the best for her daughter, which often meant living differently than she had. Therefore, Dorothy wanted Tamar befriending theists—not vagabonds. She wanted Tamar embracing faith, fellowship, and church teachings—not a bohemian lifestyle. She wanted Tamar knowing and loving God—not rejecting Him. Consequently, Tamar was baptized and received into the Catholic Church. Shortly after, so was Dorothy.

Gratitude for life born within prompted Dorothy's religious conversion. It also motivated her to spread the Good News (i.e., *euangelion* in Greek). Thus, giving thanks to God for life energized Dorothy to identify and master her mission. With French Catholic social activist, Peter Maurin, Dorothy started reforming society and the church. Together, they founded the *Catholic Worker Movement* and its accompanying newspaper. Practicing works of mercy, they also started soup kitchens and self-sustaining farm communities. "Loving thy neighbor is not just good for the neighbor, it is essential to our souls," she said. Dorothy's legacy continues today in well over 200 *Catholic Worker* communities worldwide. In 2000, the Vatican began her canonization process. Becoming a saint takes many years. Actually, a lifetime. Consider Dorothy Day.

BASICALLY ZERO

"There are only two ways to live your life. One is as though nothing is a miracle. The other is as though everything is a miracle." — Albert Einstein

Physician, Dr. Ali Binazir, calculated the probability of our existence. He first determined the odds of our parents meeting. He then determined the odds of them talking, reuniting, committing to a relationship, and having children. Finally, he determined the odds of the exact sperm and egg combining to make us—and every ancestor! After his exhaustive, meticulous calculations, he concluded, "The odds that you exist at all are basically zero." To illustrate, he explained, "It is the probability of 2 million people getting together each to play a game of dice with trillion-sided dice. They each roll the dice and they all come up with the exact same number. For example, 550,343,279,001." And you thought winning the Powerball lottery was hard!

A miracle is an almost impossible event. Thus, existence is a miracle. If God as the potter and you the pottery makes you uncomfortable, I understand. Remember, I've spent more years as an agnostic or atheist than as a theist. But, be open-minded. How you explain your existence directly affects the mission you pursue and your likelihood of mastering it. Consider Scripture as evidence that your life is a divine gift. "God created man in his image; in the divine image he created him; male and female he created them" (Genesis, 1:27). "Before I formed you in the womb I knew you" (Jeremiah, 1:5). "For you created all things; because of your will they came to be and were created" (Revelation, 4:11). Still doubtful? Okay. Maybe science will help you realize that God is the supreme benefactor—and giver of life.

Getting pregnant is inconceivable. Like an amateur hitting a homer off Max Scherzer. Exaggerating? Let's delve. First, you must have sex five consecutive days before and on the day of ovulation to increase your odds of pregnancy. "Daily sex for nearly a week...hhmmm...we can do that!" you say. Really? Only 26% of married couples have sex weekly (daily…ha!). Further, most couples only have sex bi-weekly, monthly—or even less. Good luck procreating being platonic. *Strike one.*

Assume you and your spouse agree to a rabbit-like sex frequency during that fertile window. Home run! Nope. About 30% of women have irregular ovulation. For these couples, keeping a sex calendar can be stressful, frustrating, draining—and an extinguisher for bedroom fire. Eventually, many of them lose hope. So, even if something goes down, you'll soon realize that it takes more than getting "lucky" to get lucky. *Strike two.*

Now, assume the stars align. You two sealed the deal. In 9 months, your stork will arrive. Right? Maybe. You're still at bat. Keep your eye on the ball. About 200 million sperm are released when a man ejaculates. Yet, only one sperm fertilizes the woman's egg. What makes the journey to the fallopian tubes so treacherous? If the sperm is strong and healthy (less than 10% are), it must then navigate adverse acid, defeat murderous mucus, outmaneuver wicked white blood cells, and avoid disastrous dead ends. Of the approximately 10,000 sperm reaching the uterus, about 1,000 hit the fallopian tubes and around 200 get to the egg. Yet, only one enters it. If not…. *Strike three.* Back to the dugout.

"Wow, creating life seems impossible," you say. Indeed. And, there's more to consider. Almost 15% of couples are infertile. Even if you win the fertility lottery, beware: more than two cups of coffee daily can decrease fertility, as can certain medications (even common ones like Motrin and Advil). Further, women either overweight or underweight are more likely to have an ovulation disorder, so are women exercising beyond 5 hours weekly. Men have their own problems. Sperm require testosterone. Excessive testosterone, however, can impede sperm production. No sperm, no zygote. Men should also avoid tobacco, marijuana, and other drugs. It's also wise for men to curb exposure to radiation, heat, and cell phone use (because radio waves can damage sperm). If not, they'll have testy testes. Making love is necessary for making life. But, it's insufficient. You need help. You need prayer. You need God.[62]

So, does a coin flip explain your existence? Or, does God's love? The answer determines your gratitude for life and, thus, your drive to thrive. Sit with this. Chew on it. Wrestle with it. Dorothy Day did. She then changed the world. So can you.

You received your life as a gift of love. Now, give your life as a gift of love.

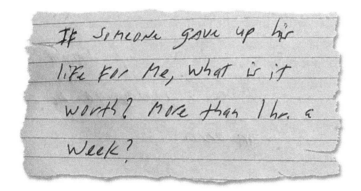

BANDANAS & BLESSINGS

"Children are grateful when Santa Claus puts in their stockings gifts of toys or sweets. Could I not be grateful to Santa Claus when he puts in my stockings the gift of two miraculous legs? We thank people for birthday presents of cigars and slippers. Can I thank no one for the birthday present of birth?" — G.K. Chesterton

---

62 After two traumatic miscarriages (see Commandment I), my wife and I tried preventing more heartache by taking rare surgical steps to make another pregnancy *impossible*. Several years ago, we began lightly discussing adoption. But, we hesitated. Two months ago, I again raised the issue. One month later, I raised it again. Cara then revealed that she recently researched adoption online; God was stirring her heart even more to expand our family. Eight days later, we learned that she was pregnant. There's miracles, then there's miracles. God found a way—because He *is* the way. Guess who's getting another tattoo?

Mairead, 21, still walks with a shadow—even at night. It's the spirit of her archenemy: the Hydra. With nine heads, the Hydra is one of the deadliest monsters. Sever one head, and two appear. One head is even immortal. Like Hercules, when Mairead fought the Hydra, she enlisted comrades: family, friends, and God. The battle was hard. It took years. She was cut, she bled, and she broke bones. But, she eventually emerged victorious. With a loud battle cry, Mairead raised the Hydra's immortal head for all to see. She then buried it. Kneeling before God, she prayed that it remains in the netherworld—forever.

I was blessed to interview this warrior. No research study could better capture how gratitude for life energizes people to master their mission. Throughout this book, I've woven the thread that we struggle when we don't struggle. Few will struggle like Mairead. And, few will thrive like Mairead. Her story is raw, heartfelt, and moving. May it inspire you to see life as a gift. May it inspire you to thank God for your health and suffering. May it inspire you to love the life you live—and live the life you love.

No One Tells You

Please tell me about your story. How did it unfold?

It was February 2006. I was playing in a CYO basketball game. I was running, dribbling the ball, and a girl tripped me, sending me flying to the floor and landing on my left arm. All I remember is lying on the ground at half court near the bench crying, holding my left arm. The dramatic second-grader inside me thought it was broken. That was the only thing I kept telling my parents on the drive home.

My dad thought I was being dramatic. That I was just the third child of four acting out for attention. How could he not? That would be the response of any typical Irish father with four kids. However, 24 hours went by and the pain didn't subside. In fact, it escalated.

My game was on a Sunday. On Monday, I stayed home from school. I remember sitting at the kitchen table, my mother sitting to the left of me, and all I kept saying was, "Mom, it really, really hurts," while bowing my head in my folded arms in excruciating pain. I had an appointment with the orthopedist on Wednesday. I remember thinking, "How in the world am I going to make it until Wednesday?"

Wednesday came. There I was in the orthopedist's office, being escorted back to X-rays. "How cool? I get to wear a lead apron," I thought. Little did I know that what I was about to find out and experience for the rest of my life was anything but "cool."

And then, Thursday came. Oh, how this day is forever seared in my brain. My mother and father were both here this time. Naïve 7-year-old me thought, "HA! My arm really is broken!" I was given a chapter book with an orange cat on the cover that I borrowed from my teacher's classroom, and I was told to stay in my chair in the waiting room while my parents went to speak with the doctor. There I sat, reading my cat book. Proud of myself for being a "big" kid by sitting there all alone. Then, an X-ray technician motioned me to the back of the office to get more films. As I walked by, I remember looking to my left and seeing both my parents in chairs across from the doctor, tears in their eyes, looking back at me. At the time, as a second-grader, I thought nothing of this. But, in hindsight, it remains one of the most memorable and gut-wrenching memories of my journey.

The second wave of X-rays were complete. I then went back in the waiting room to read that cat book. Shortly after, my dad came to sit next to me. He said, "Mairead, tomorrow we're going to the doctor in New York City. Isn't that really cool?" Again, not really "cool."

Friday brought a trip to Memorial Sloan Kettering Cancer Center. I remember asking my mom, "Why do you have such a large backpack on?" She said, "I brought changes of clothes for all of us because we have to stay the night in the hospital." They were prepared for the worst. I wasn't.

> Life throws curveballs. You better
> learn how to hit.

The next few months were a blur. Shortly after that first trip to Memorial Sloan Kettering, I underwent a biopsy. There my mom was, all suited up in surgical-wear, in the operating room with me until I fell asleep. I didn't know then, but that initial biopsy came back negative. Our family's prayers answered? Not quite. The surgeon told my parents, "I know this is cancer. I just know it is. But, the pathology report is negative."

Being treated at Memorial Sloan Kettering requires having cancer. Plain and simple. Because my initial pathology report came up negative for cancer, I was sent to a hospital near my home to treat the infection that they thought was causing all of my symptoms. However, what they didn't know is that I had bone cancer *and* a bone infection. The cancer I had is so rare to begin with that also having a bone infection is usually never even considered an option. It's just a ridiculous idea. Regardless, they had to give me a PICC line in my arm to infuse antibiotics. They kept changing the antibiotics to cover different strains and types of bacteria. Doctors even went in surgically and tried scraping the bone attempting to clear it and rid it of the infection. Each treatment approach failed. The monster inside of me kept growing. The doctors told my parents it looked like something was gnawing and eating away at my bone.

I continued antibiotics during my general cancer treatment including chemo. The infection played a major factor with me getting a device called a Broviac to receive my chemo instead of a Mediport. The biggest and most devastating difference between the two is that a Broviac cannot, under any circumstance, get wet. If it does, you must admit yourself to the hospital because you'll get an infection in the device. I actually had an infection in my Broviac once, causing my chemo regimen to be bumped back a week. I needed that Broviac so my mom could administer antibiotics every 6 hours. She had to set alarms in the middle of the night. I continued antibiotic treatment for nearly a year, even after they threw out my rotted bone.

The Broviac was one of the most difficult things psychologically I had to deal with during my cancer treatment—only second to losing all my hair. In the dead heat of the summer, I had to sit on the edge and dip my toes in the pool while my friends did backflips off the diving board. It may sound like no big deal. But, to me, it was. I didn't need another reminder of what I was dealing with.

Though I was originally turned away from Memorial Sloan Kettering, we were told to make an appointment in June just in case nothing resolved. This appointment came, and it was like déjà vu. But, this time, with a different outcome. Most kids have absolutely no idea what that six letter word means. But, not me. Watching my older cousin undergo treatment for brain cancer just a year prior, I knew what it meant. It changes lives. Forever.[63]

> I never knew how much I loved life
> until I had to fight for it.

No one tells you what it feels like to be an 8-year-old girl losing all your hair. How you'll be jumping on the trampoline with your friends and have to run inside to your mom because a chunk of your hair is falling out. Or that you'll have your parents turn around or cover all the mirrors in the house because you cannot bear to see your bald reflection staring back at you. Or how you'll have to beg your parents to not cut off the last strands left of your hair. Or how you'll be so psychologically attached to wearing bandanas on your bald head trying to mask the fact that you're an 8-year-old girl with no hair.

---

63 Mairead's cousin, Tommy, started battling brain cancer at 16. Thank God, Tommy also defeated the Hydra. He's now 31. Warriors are in their bloodline.

No one tells you what it feels like to miss out on every event with family and friends. Or the envy you'll feel for your friends who can attend each other's birthday parties. Or how while you never quite thought you'd do this, but you'd beg, plead, and bargain to go to school for some sense of normalcy—knowing you can't because your immune system was too weak.

No one tells you what it feels like to spend Thanksgiving in the hospital with your family. To have your meal catered. To eat in the hospital playroom. To not even be able to cut your own damn turkey.

No one tells you what it feels like to constantly feel nauseous. And, how it almost feels abnormal to not feel like you're going to vomit. Or that you'll throw up every single time you receive chemo. Or that you'll make your mom eat her lunch outside your chemo treatment room because even the smell makes you nauseous. Or the one day when you had enough energy to go to the playroom and you had to leave because they were making brownies, and the smell made you throw up everywhere. Or how you have no appetite, but then suddenly you need to eat an entire pizza pie because of the steroids.

No one tells you what it feels like to have a backpack of fluids strapped to your back between days of treatment. How making the car ride home without having to stop to use the bathroom is itself a victory and mini miracle. Or how you have to get up every 3 hours during the night to pee, lugging the backpack behind you.

No one tells you what it feels like to be left with the aftermath of treatment. How you're covered with scars criss-crossing your body. Or how people stop, stare, and ask questions about what happened to you. Or how your hair never quite grows back the same and how your skin is ultra-sensitive to light.

You know what else *no one tells you?* You know what you'll be so thankful to have discovered on your own? It's something you never thought you'd think. It's something that unless you go through this you'd never understand. What is it? You can't imagine your life without battling cancer. Nor would you ever want to.

> *Painful times are valuable*
> *because through them we learn*
> *who we really are.*

Wow. That's powerful. I appreciate your honesty and authenticity. What type of cancer were you diagnosed with? And, can you please expand on your treatments?

I was diagnosed with a rare form of bone cancer in my left forearm called Ewing's Sarcoma. It was odd that it was located in the radius because most often it's in bigger bones such as in your legs and pelvis. The bone infection I mentioned before made my diagnosis even rarer and harder to pinpoint. My surgeon had only heard of one other such case.

After receiving my final diagnosis of cancer, I almost immediately started the process to begin treatment. I underwent a procedure to have the Broviac implanted in my chest to receive chemotherapy treatments. I also had location markers tattooed on my left arm for radiation. After eight rounds of grueling chemotherapy and radiation, I underwent a limb-sparing bone transplant because my bone was too decayed to be viable. To avoid amputating my left arm, a team of surgeons removed my left fibula in my leg and, along with several tendons and skin, used it to replace the left radius in my arm.

How old were you when you finished treatment? How long have you been in remission?

I was 8 years old when I finished treatment. I started chemo in June 2006 and had my bone transplant in November 2006. Thankfully, treatment for Ewing's Sarcoma is usually shorter, though way more aggressive, compared to other cancers such as leukemia.

On November 18, 2019, I will be in remission for 13 years. I sometimes can't believe this. It's truly a miracle. People say they don't believe in miracles. Survive cancer. You'll believe.

Congratulations! What role did the medical staff play in your recovery?

I refer to Memorial Sloan Kettering Cancer Center as "Disney World." It's filled with angels performing miracles. I truly believe in my heart that if that original orthopedist didn't tell my parents that if I was his kid he would take me to Memorial Sloan Kettering, I might not have ended up there. Frankly, I don't know if I would even be alive. Do you know how scary that is?

Do you also know how grateful that makes me for every second that I'm alive?

Everyone in that hospital played a huge part in my recovery. The woman who used to change the garbage every morning and sit down and chitchat with my family and me while we were waiting for our morning chemo appointments. The vital signs technician who came back to my room to play cards with my mom and me. My original orthopedic surgeon who never gave up on me and listened to her gut. My orthopedic hand surgeon who saved my arm and prevented amputation. My nurse practitioner who called me, "My Mairead," and, "Cookie," and who shaped me into the woman I am today. My primary nurse who you might think I would despise because she was the one pumping toxins into my body. But, I adored and worshipped her because she always knew what to do, what to say, and when to say it. Literally, everyone helped me recover. They pushed me and knew exactly how to make me take that med, endure that needle stick, or walk one more lap at PT (sometimes even holding my hand while doing it).

How specifically did the medical staff help you cope and recover physically, mentally, emotionally, and spiritually?

Physically, the medical staff put the pieces together for my treatment plan and guided me through the necessary steps to physically recover. Even getting me back to my maximum potential. Whether it was my dedicated PT and OT staff who helped me through hundreds and hundreds of hours of therapy, the hospital professionals implementing individualized care, or my amazing surgical team who performed limb-sparing surgery…everyone helped me cope and recover physically.

Because my cancer was an orthopedic cancer, the physical component of coping was huge. I had to mourn the loss of my previous capabilities and learn new ones. I had a chunky cast in a sling on my left arm with two drains sticking out of the sides. And, once given the okay, I had to relearn how to walk with one less bone in my leg. It was draining. For weeks, I endured 2 hours of grueling therapy. Keeping it together was so hard when I would then waddle to the car. I often sobbed in pain. However, I think the medical staff being there alongside me at every point—through the funny and the painful times—really helped me push through the initial physical struggles and stay committed to years of therapy.

> I truly think the greatest thing you can give someone to help them cope with adversity is yourself.

I'm left with physical limitations in my arm. Yet, never for one second did anyone let me think this was something I should be embarrassed by or ashamed of. Instead, they convinced me I should be proud of my story. I am. Extremely so. They also never let me use it as an excuse to get out of working as hard as possible to recover. They were with me every step of the way. From when I was bedbound to when I was ready to go back to playing sports. I'm so blessed to have met and worked with these incredible people. Words can never express how grateful I am for them.

Mentally and emotionally, the medical staff helped support me in ways I didn't even know I needed. I'm a huge believer in the power of the mind, and the medical staff helped me develop that. When the mind is strong and sound, the body can do anything. Cancer takes so much psychological healing. So much personal searching. So much vulnerability. It's just as much a mental battle as it's a physical one.

What really helped me cope was how aware they were of my needs. They knew when I needed to be hugged. They knew when I needed to be told that it was going to be okay. They also knew when I needed tough love. When I needed to suck it up and face the issue head on. They allowed me to scream, to cry, to express my feelings. They validated my pain, and they also used it to help me understand who I am through my emotions. I think this stems from the medical staff getting to know me for me. By taking the time to sit with me. It made me feel at ease knowing someone was always there. It makes me wonder what the world would be like if we all extended ourselves to each other.

> Sitting with someone and really listening to them is one of the most loving things we can do.

The biggest struggle I grapple with spiritually is how I'm now left with the effects of cancer treatment. Facing this is really hard. I never thought that after going through cancer and all of the hardships that I'd now still have to think about the effects on my heart muscles. Nor did I know I'd have to worry about preserving my fertility so I can have a family of my own. I almost think, "Why do I have to deal with this if I already put in my time? If I already survived hell? Why, God, can't I just be left alone?" My faith was at a crossroads.

What I never knew possible was how the medical team and staff at Memorial Sloan Kettering would help me cope with this spiritual conflict through acceptance and gratitude. Healing this spiritual wound first required accepting that this was something God gave me to deal with and work through. This is my cross to bear.

I had to make my gratitude and thankfulness for life-saving medical treatment bigger than the nasty side effects of treatment.

That's incredible. Those people are amazing. You mention gratitude. How else did gratitude help you recover?

I often tell people how grateful I am to have had cancer. Most people laugh and think I'm joking. However, I could not be more serious or feel more passionate about something. It sounds so cliché. I know. But, each day I'm truly grateful for the lessons I learned throughout my battle with cancer. You know what I'm really grateful for? God's love. I'm alive because of Him.

I'm also insanely grateful for my mom. Imagine your mom having to learn how to maintain a sterile field and change your port dressing. Or, like I said, your mom having to set alarms every 6 hours so she can get up and hang you a new bag of intravenous antibiotics. Gratitude for my mother during my recovery and while I had cancer was so integral to why I kept fighting, why I kept going. I was so thankful that my mother gave up her life to be my sole caretaker. She made all of my appointments, drove me to all of my treatments, bathed me, dressed me, and spoon-fed me. Talk about being vulnerable and humbled. It was so hard. Seriously. Whenever I thought about giving up, about calling it quits, I just kept thinking about how thankful I was to be surrounded by someone as amazing as my mother. Thanks to my mother's love, I kept fighting.

Gratitude for everyone in my family also played a huge part in my recovery. As mentioned before, my family spent Thanksgiving Day in the hospital. They gave up everything to trek into the city to sit at a folded table in the hospital playroom while we ate a catered and gross Thanksgiving meal (not like the gourmet meals my mom always made). My younger 5-year-old sister had to be raised by my neighbor. My dad was practically a single working father. And, my older brother and sister had to grow up way faster than most kids their age. My family sacrificed so much for me to have a chance at living.

I could never even think about giving up when I had such an amazing support system to be thankful for.

Gratitude for the medical treatments also had a major impact on my recovery. Like I said, this helped heal my spiritual wound. However, it went deeper. An 8-year-old would probably never think about losing a limb. I had to. When I was told amputation was on the table, I freaked out. Here I am, 8 years old with cancer, and they may have to saw my arm off so I can live. You see this stuff in movies. And, here it was happening to me. It was crazy. When my doctors constructed a surgical plan to throw out my rotted radius, take the fibula from my leg and use it to replace that radius so I could still have an arm, I was ecstatic. This gratitude helped me through my occupational and physical therapy treatments. I spent 10 hours a week with therapists, crying and sobbing in pain, while also doing hours of exercises at home. But, none of this mattered to me. I was just so overwhelmed by gratitude to have my arm that I would do anything to keep it. Thanks to God, I did.

How can I ever repay God? I guess by being the best "Mairead" possible.

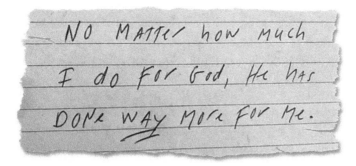

NO MATTer how much
I do For God, He has
DONe WAy More for Me.

I know you want to be a pediatric oncology nurse. How did your experience battling and defeating cancer influence this choice?

During my experience with cancer, I was shown how profound an impact someone can have on your life trajectory. All it takes is one person opening the door for you. Or a nurse staying 5 minutes after the end of her shift to hold your hand. Or a doctor coming in on a day off to care for you. These kind acts can seriously change your life. Forever! It wasn't the people who invented these amazing drugs or the CEOs of the hospital who shaped me into the person I am today. Yes, I'm grateful to them. I always will be. I wouldn't be here without them. But, it was the actions of those who I interacted with every day who inspired me to pursue an occupation in nursing.

Cancer brought me many hardships. I'd be lying if I said it didn't. I can never get back my childhood. However, it was through this experience that my passion and gratitude for life was recognized. Thanks to cancer, I know what I want to dedicate my life to: helping other pediatric oncology patients. So many people I know have no idea what they want to do with their lives. They're miserable. It stinks. And, here I am knowing for sure that this is what God wants me to do. Yes, I had to battle cancer to find it. But, although it sounds crazy, it was worth it.

> Finding your purpose in life is worth
> the pain while finding it.

I met a very special woman who influenced my life forever. One of my nurse practitioners at Memorial Sloan Kettering Cancer Center completely took me under her wing. I was a shy and quiet kid, scared of the beeping machines and miles of wires attached to me. She knew exactly how to make me feel like I was the most important person in the hospital. She got me through my darkest moments by being my biggest cheerleader through the bad—and good—times. In this process, she unintentionally helped spark a desire in me to pursue an occupation in pediatric oncology nursing. I aspire to one day be a beacon of hope to other children with cancer by sharing my own battle and struggles with this horrible disease. This is all because of one person taking an interest in and caring for me.

One person really can make all the difference in your life.

All of the medical staff, but specifically the nurses, knew exactly how to get me pushing forward. They knew my fears and pushed me to face them. They texted me good luck on my big exams. They called me each year to say, "HAPPY BIRTHDAY!" They even attended my graduations. I can't describe how much these actions meant to me. I knew I wanted to be "that person" for other kids battling cancer. I knew in my heart that nursing was my calling and purpose in life. This is why I went through and endured what I did. I'm meant to be a nurse. I *have* to be a nurse. Love really is the best medicine.

What about being a pediatric oncology nurse are you most passionate about?

Childhood cancer accounts for less than 1% of all cancer cases in the U.S. each year. That's extremely rare. I think this motivates me even more to dedicate my life to this. Because it's so rare, I'm sure most people barely think about it. But, I do. Every day.

I couldn't be more certain that I want to dedicate my life to working with these kids and families. I *have* to. I just *have* to.

I'm most passionate about being there for the kids and helping them through the most vulnerable point of their life. I'd be so privileged being there from start to finish with a kid who's dying and being deprived of their childhood to face the monster inside of them. I'd be so privileged holding that basin while they throw up. Or, holding their hand through that needle stick. Then seeing them grow up and get back to their life. I'm tearing up just saying this. Doing something like this for someone is the most humbling and fulfilling thing I can do with my life.

> What better life to live than to make my life and actions really matter to someone else?

One of my largest complaints when going through treatments was when people would say, "I understand." No, you don't. You don't understand what it means to be 8 and to have cancer, to be bald, to be robbed of your childhood. No, you simply don't "understand." But, I do.

I'm very passionate about incorporating my story into my nursing care. I'll use it to be more understanding and empathic. I want to be a role model for other kids. I want to help them to keep pushing, to keep fighting, to show them that it's worth it. And, if they're lucky enough like me, maybe their life will be positively changed forever. Who knows, maybe they'll also find their mission? Can you imagine? That would be awesome!

Please describe the training you've already received for becoming a nurse.

I'm a traditional student in the BSN (Bachelor of Science in Nursing) program at the M. Louise Fitzpatrick College of Nursing at Villanova University. I'm the type of person who once they have an idea in their head, I become obsessed with it. This is how I am with pediatric oncology nursing. Ever since I set my eyes on my dream of being a nurse to kids with cancer, I did everything and anything to achieve this dream.

In the summer of 2017, I did one of the most spiritually fulfilling things I've ever done: I became a cabin counselor at *Happiness Is Camping*. This is a sleepaway camp for children with cancer and their siblings. The nurse practitioner who inspired me to become a nurse is on the board there. She told me, "If you want a career in pediatric oncology, you just *have* to do this." To say this was one of the best summers of my life doesn't even scratch the surface of what my experience was like and how much it meant to me. These kids…they're the most inspirational group of people I've ever met. I'm tearing up again now just thinking about them.

Here they are, with prosthetic legs, glass eyes, receiving chemo at camp, in wheelchairs, amputees, and everything in between. And, what are they doing at camp? They're shooting arrows in archery, doing belly flops off the deep end, and zip lining through the woods. Despite all they're going through and all they've lost, they live life to the fullest. And, they're some of the most grateful people I've ever met. These kids taught me to never let myself use excuses for anything. Never! I cried the entire 3-hour drive home after the 5th and final week of camp. Working with those kids changed me. Forever.

> If you're looking to find purpose and joy
> in life, look no further than life itself.

I then worked at a local hospital on the pediatric and pediatric ICU floor as a patient care associate. Here, I crafted my nursing skills, both technically and relationally. I built such intimate relationships with these patients, most of whom were from low socio-economic backgrounds. I made mistakes. I learned about working with different types of people. I learned how to problem-solve. However, my eye was still on the prize: Memorial Sloan Kettering Cancer Center.

Between your junior and senior year of nursing school you go on externship. Just hearing "externship" triggers crazy anxiety in most upper level nursing students. Since I decided on nursing school, one of my primary nurses told me about the *Clinical Assistant Program* at Memorial Sloan Kettering. This is a mentorship program where nursing students are paired with a seasoned nurse preceptor who they shadow and learn from. In typical "Mairead" fashion, I repeatedly called HR, stalked the job website, and applied the first day it opened. After two rounds of interviews, all I wanted was this program. This was the first taste of my dream. I then realized why I went to nursing school and why I wake up at 5 am. Over 500 people applied. Only 35 get in.

On April 4, 2019, I "got the call." I woke up to an email saying, "You've been accepted into the program." I instantly sobbed. Everything I worked so hard for was starting to pay off. I could see my dream in sight. Actually, I was LIVING my dream! I called my dad immediately. He originally missed the call because he was at Mass. I now know that wasn't a coincidence. When I told my dad, he cried. Everyone knew how much this meant to me. God was steering me toward realizing my dream.

> And, by living my dream, I was living God's dream for me.

I grew so much during the summer of 2019. It felt almost surreal to be called an "employee" instead of a "patient" at a place that I call "home." My position was on the Women's Oncology floor. Obviously, it wasn't pediatrics. But, I seriously mean this when I say I would've taken a janitor's job there. I truly think God needed me to work on that floor because, man, did I learn so much. I learned how to deal with difficult patients. I learned how to deliver family-centered care. I learned how to *really* be a nurse.

I'm forever thankful for the nurses who quizzed me, taught me, brought me into rooms, and who I became very close with. And, man oh man, am I thankful for my preceptor. The nurse who I shadowed taught me not only so much about nursing, but so much about myself. She told me when I needed to pick it up. When I did a superb job. When I made a mistake. We just "clicked." My preceptor and I still talk often and plan on taking a "girls' trip" with other nurses on the floor in the near future.

Not only did I confirm my purpose at Memorial Sloan Kettering, I found friends. For life.

Oncology is a field filled with a lot of death. You need to know this going into it. But, geez, was I surrounded by death. More so than any other floor in that hospital. I was there when a patient and their loved ones were told they were out of options—and death was inevitable. I was there when a patient told me how at peace she was, how she felt so connected to God, and that she was ready to be embraced by Him in Heaven. I was there performing end-of-life care, giving oral swabs to a patient begging to die. I was there performing post-life-care. I was there while a patient took her last breath, surrounded by family and friends.

> If you've never felt God present in your life, hold someone's hand as they take their last breath. You'll feel Him holding your other hand.

How did gratitude for defeating cancer help determine your career path?

My experience with cancer taught me that gratitude is way more powerful and deeper than many people think. Gratitude means being thankful for experiences or actions. Gratitude, however, is only genuine when we give the compassion we received to others. I'm nothing but grateful for my experience with cancer, and I really mean this very seriously and humbly. I've learned so much about life and myself in what seems like the most horrifying and miserable experience that one could ever endure. Being thankful for battling cancer has had such a large impact on my future career plans. Of course, I didn't think like this when I was an 8-year-old.

But, sometimes we learn the most about ourselves when we least expect it.

To what degree has your experience with battling and defeating cancer influenced your view that life is a gift?

Cancer taught me so much about myself. It taught me how to be strong. How to have pride in my experiences. How to push myself further than I thought possible. How to be grateful for the many opportunities I have. And, most importantly, how to view life as a gift. Every day that I wake up, I'm so beyond grateful to be alive. I have the opportunity to attend a university I love. I have the opportunity to be surrounded by people I love. I have the opportunity to pursue an occupation I love. How lucky am I?!

I think that coming close to death taught me how quickly and easily the carpet can be taken out from underneath you. One day, I was a typical second-grader. The next day, I received a hospital sentence (and almost a death sentence). I lost my hair and missed out on a lot of normal experiences a second and third-grader has. Sports practices turned into physical and occupational therapy appointments.

Classes in school turned into tutoring sessions at the hospital. My
bed at home turned into an uncomfortable hospital bed.

To be living your life and to have everything instantly taken away
from you teaches you an important lesson: life is fragile.

Thirteen years is a long time to reflect on how cancer affected me.
Every day I try to be thankful that God gave me one more day to go
to school, to make a difference in others—to live. Nothing is guaranteed in life. Everyone learns this differently. I sometimes think there
are people who never learn this. Over the years, I have lost two class-
mates to cancer, both who I battled cancer alongside with. It's crazy
to think that two people out of my small Catholic elementary school
of about 250 students lost their battle to cancer. Absolutely crazy.
It's easy to feel guilty thinking, "Why am I here, and why are they
not?" I'm not going to lie. Sometimes I really feel like this. But, what
I've learned and try to incorporate into my life is how I need to see
each day as a new beginning, a new opportunity.

> Life is too short, too fragile, and too
> valuable to treat it as anything less
> than a divine gift.

**Now that you more than ever see life as a gift, how has this view influ-
enced your desire and passion to become a pediatric oncology nurse?**

After my experience with cancer and understanding firsthand that
life is truly a gift—something God gave me because He loves me—I
wanted my life to have meaning. I wanted to figure out what I was
supposed to do—and who I was *supposed to be*—while on Earth.[64] I literally had to fight to be alive. I have, therefore, made it my life's mission to make a difference in people's lives. Every day. My life was in

---

64 Clearly, Mairead enjoys listening to Kermit the Frog sing on a lily pad, strumming his banjo (see
Commandment X).

jeopardy of being taken from me. This is something so terrifying. Yet, it's so liberating. I soon realized that because no day is guaranteed, I had to make each day count. To me, this is by giving back to a community that is so close and personal to me: kids battling cancer.

Am I saying everyone needs to be a pediatric oncology nurse to treat life as a gift? Of course not. But, I think everyone needs to find their purpose so they can pay back this gift. So many people I know don't have a purpose in life. They kind of go about their days. One day leads to the next. Yet, nothing really gets done. Nothing happens. But, when people find their purpose…wow! That really changes things. They know why they're getting up every morning. I know so many people my age who struggle with depression. They're in a funk that they can't shake. I feel so bad for them. Some of them eventually find a passion. Something that brings life to their life. Many, though, don't. I pray for them.

> How will you live your life and not take it for granted and make a difference? That's the question I think people must answer.

How has your experience with cancer influenced your relationship with God?

I've attended Catholic school my entire life. I started in nursery school and kept going through high school. I grew up a devout Catholic. I, therefore, developed an intimate relationship with God. Every Sunday my family would attend Mass. I also participated in activities within the Church such as vacation bible school.

I think attending a small, tightknit Catholic elementary school had the largest effect on my cancer journey and relationship with God. Maybe it was because I was in elementary school during the toughest times. It's so easy to sit there and think, "God, why me?" However, I feel that I became closer with God through my experience with cancer. Maybe that's why I got cancer. Who knows?

I'm not angry at God for giving me cancer. And, I don't think He was being "unfair." I truly and honestly believe God gave me this experience so I can go through a personal and spiritual awakening to find out more about my inner strength and myself so I can do what He destined me to do—become a nurse. He gave me this opportunity and life experience to find meaning by helping and serving others during their own battles. Something so many did for me. I now have more trust in His plan for me and for the world. This helps me accept those things that I cannot control. It's somewhat freeing, actually. Through my experience, I learned that God will always be there for me no matter what the situation is or what hardship I may face.

> **Ultimately, acceptance and gratitude kept me close to God. It even made me closer to Him.**

Is there anything else you want to tell me? Now's the time to inspire the world with your story—like you've inspired me!

I'm nothing but grateful for my life and my experience with cancer. I have the opportunity to go to a school I've wanted to go to my entire life, and I get the chance to pursue nursing; something I'm so passionate about and have dreamed of doing since I was 8 and going through cancer. Talk about lucky! I understand what it feels like to have life crashing down on you. This makes me even more appreciative of life's opportunities. I can never get back the time I lost in my childhood. I know that. I never got the chance to make memories that a typical third-grader did. I lost my hair, received chemotherapy and radiation, and underwent a 12-hour bone transplant. I still have to battle the effects of cancer every day. But, I've accepted this.

And, like I've said, I'm grateful for it, too. Life is way too precious to "sweat the small stuff." I had two options: sit, sulk, and dwell on how unfair life was to me; or, I could try and figure out how to make a bad and unfortunate situation work in my favor. With God's help, I picked the latter.

A picture says a thousand words. Mairead's smile says millions.[65]

Like Jonah, resist as some might, everyone lands where God intended. Mairead did. I did. You will, too. But, like Mairead, you'll only reach your destination and master your mission if you know that life is a divine gift—and act accordingly. "Do not be deceived, my beloved brothers: all good giving and every perfect gift is from above, coming down from the Father of lights, with whom there is no alteration or shadow caused by change. He willed to give us birth by the word of truth that we may be a kind of firstfruits of his creatures" (James, 1:16-18). Think your life is accidental, and nihilism awaits. Give thanks to God for life, and meaning awaits. Gratitude helps you find your place in the cosmic puzzle. Corner pieces are prized. But, every 🧩 matters.

---

65 See Keara's letter in ~~Deleted~~ Scenes. Like Mairead, gratitude fueled her success. Though Mairead more explicitly articulates gratitude for life itself than Keara, Keara's gratitude for her physical capabilities, training, and social support is nonetheless inspiring.

10%'ers

"You formed my inmost being; you knit me in my mother's womb...My very self you knew; my bones were not hidden from you, When I was being made in secret, fashioned as in the depths of the earth. Your eyes foresaw my actions; in your book all are written down; my days were shaped, before one came to be." — Psalm 139:13-16

Giving thanks requires acknowledging our blessings and recognizing the transcendent source. It also requires remembering the **3 Gs to Give Thanks: grace, gift,** and **God.**[66] Yes, you contributed to your welfare. Perhaps year-round enrollment expedited graduation. Perhaps wowing investors ensured promotion. Perhaps good credit secured a mortgage. But, we only influence earthly matters. God alone controls divine matters. The greater our realization that God gave us life, the greater our drive to thrive. Dicyanoacetylene burns hot like the sun. A grateful heart, however, burns hot like the Son.

Entering a village, ten lepers approached Jesus and asked Him for pity. After cleansing them, only one leper returned. He glorified God, fell at His feet, and thanked Him. Jesus said, "Ten were cleansed, were they not? Where are the other nine? Has none but this foreigner returned to give thanks to God?" (Luke, 17:17-18). Before leaving the thankful leper, Jesus said: "Stand up and go; your faith has saved you" (Luke, 17:19). Thanking God for blessings—especially life—reflects our faith in Him. It reflects our dependence on and indebtedness to Him. It also reflects our acknowledgment of His holiness, divinity, and love. Giving thanks to God, therefore, requires prayers of thanksgiving. Gratitude absent action, however, is shallow gratitude. While God likes hearing that we're grateful to Him for life, He prefers seeing that we're grateful to Him for life. Sometimes, even God wants to see to believe.

---

66 Mairead's middle name is *Grace*. "Weird."

Emulate the grateful leper, and return to God. Praise Him. Thank Him. Then, glorify Him with your life. Let your deeds demonstrate that like the stars above, God's blessings are also countless. Let your gratitude toward the supreme benefactor radiate, attract others, and fuel your drive to master your mission. Be a 10%'er.

Life is a loan from God. Repay it with interest.

A grateful heart asks,
"How can I pay you
back, Lord?"

Thou Shalt
Give Thanks

1. When you start forgetting that life is God's gift, read these bible verses: "God created man in his image; in the divine image he created him; male and female he created them" (Genesis, 1:27), "Before I formed you in the womb I knew you" (Jeremiah, 1:5), and "For you created all things; because of your will they came to be and were created" (Revelation, 4:11). Memorize the verse that most stirs your heart. Ponder it. Pray on it. Personify it.

2. Be more grateful for life by "thinking gratefully." There are three components to this cognitive processing: 1) *Intent:* "God purposely created me. With deliberate care and extreme conscientiousness, He paid attention to my details." 2) *Cost:* "God expended considerable time and widgets creating me. Yes, He's God. He's omnipotent. But, still. He could've created someone else instead." 3) *Benefit:* "Without God's love, I'd never have experienced joy, connection, or life. I owe everything to God." Consider God's grace and love using this "blessing filter." You'll be grateful you did.

3. For 5 minutes, close your eyes and think of who loved you into being. Then, think of who loved them into being. Do this until you can no longer expand your "love tree." Afterward, think about who loved everyone in your tree into being. You'll then realize that God is love—and the creator of the cosmic love tree.

4. Recall Mairead, the Hydra-killing warrior. Internalize her wisdom, and let it inspire you: *"Finding your purpose in life is worth the pain while finding it," "If you're looking to find purpose and joy in life, look no further than life itself,"* and *"Life is too short, too fragile, and too valuable to treat it as anything less than a divine gift."* Make Mairead's words dwell in your heart. Make them guide your behaviors. Make them strengthen your faith.

5. Start and end every day with prayer. Acknowledge your blessings and recognize the transcendent source. To help remember that God gave you life, structure your prayer using the 3 **Gs to Give Thanks: grace, gift,** and **God.** Emulate the grateful leper, and return to God. Praise Him. Thank Him. Then, glorify Him with your life. Let your gratitude toward the supreme benefactor radiate, attract others, and fuel your drive to master your mission. Be a 10%'er.

X

Thou Shalt

MASTER
MISSION

Though a descendent of royalty, Joseph swung a hammer. He lived simply and loved his fiancée and God. Devout Jews, Joseph and his fiancée remained sexually abstinent before marrying. Thus, he was dismayed when he discovered she was pregnant. To spare his fiancée public disgrace, Joseph intended to end their relationship quietly—until God spoke to him. A righteous man, Joseph listened. He stayed engaged. Soon after, Joseph and his now wife welcomed their son. Though they didn't yet mail the birth announcements, people visited bearing gifts. Apparently, others heard the good news.

A dedicated family man, Joseph always helped and protected his wife and son. One night while sleeping, he stirred. Tossing, turning, and sweating profusely, Joseph abruptly awoke. God warned him of imminent danger. So, while still nighttime, Joseph and his family left the life they started. After trudging nearly 90 miles in the desert, they settled in a safe city. They met neighbors. They made friends. Life was good, stable. Until about a year later when God warned Joseph of more danger. They again packed their belongings and traveled about 130 miles to their hometown. Though weary, Joseph kept walking. He kept leading his family. He kept following God.

Over the years, Joseph's little boy became his own man. During one trip to Jerusalem for Passover, his son disappeared. After frantically searching, Joseph and his wife finally found him in the temple, enlightening teachers about God. He astonished everyone with his wisdom, particularly because he was only 12. Though Joseph knew his son was special, this was his first time seeing it displayed publically. In that moment, Joseph thanked God for his wife and son and for guiding him toward—and helping him master—his mission of being a family man. May we all thank God for St. Joseph, our Father's father.

CLEAN YOUR TEMPLE

"God creates out of nothing. Wonderful you say. Yes, to be sure, but he does what is still more wonderful: he makes saints out of sinners." — *Søren Kierkegaard*

Extra weight limits our potential. Another 3.4 lbs. can decrease an athlete's vertical jump by 2 inches and increase their 40-yard dash by .26 seconds. Another 2-5 lbs. can decrease a race horse's lap time by .20 seconds. These differences, while seemingly trivial, can cost an athlete the contract and a horse the race. Sin, much like weight, also limits our potential. But, the stakes are higher. It hardens our heart. It burdens our soul. It weakens our spirit. We then struggle walking with Jesus, climbing toward Heaven, and running to God. If you've indulged a bit, consider shedding some "pounds."[67]

We clean our car. We clean our home. But, we often neglect our soul, not cleaning the temple within us housing God. To illustrate, about 66% of Americans get their car washed 1-2 times monthly, and within several years, the U.S. Department of Commerce expects 80% of two-income households to pay for housecleaning. Yet, only 2% of Catholics regularly attend confession. Jesus denounced polishing our exterior and ignoring our interior, while St. Paul warned about its impact on mastering our mission.

> Jesus said: ...*You cleanse the outside of cup and dish, but inside they are full of plunder and self-indulgence. Blind Pharisee, cleanse first the inside of the cup, so that the outside may also be clean...You are like whitewashed tombs, which appear beautiful on the outside, but inside are full of dead men's bones and every kind of filth. Even so, on the outside you appear righteous, but inside you are filled with hypocrisy and evildoing.* (Matthew, 23:25-28)

> St. Paul further cautioned people, saying: *Watch carefully then how you live, not as foolish persons but as wise, making the most of the opportunity, because the days are evil. Therefore, do not continue in ignorance, but try to understand what*

---

67 Sin is an offense against God that contradicts reason, truth, and right conscience. It's a morally reprehensible act that hurts you, others, and God. If you adopt moral relativism (i.e., the idea that there's no universal or absolute set of moral principles) and I adopt moral absolutism (i.e., the idea that actions are inherently moral or immoral), then we'll disagree about objective morality. You might think that adultery only breaks a marital contract. I, however, would think that adultery also breaks a divine contract. So, if you consider morality a "virtuous ideal" and not a divine law (akin to a natural law like gravity), let's minimally agree that eradicating certain thoughts and behaviors will purify your heart and soul—helping you thrive and master your mission. Handshake?

*is the will of the Lord...be filled with the Spirit, addressing one
another [in] psalms and hymns and spiritual songs, singing
and playing to the Lord in your hearts, giving thanks always
and for everything....* (Ephesians, 5:15-20)

Living your best-life-possible requires elbow grease and deep scrub-
bing. So, clear the cobwebs, vacuum the dust bunnies, and remove the
gunk. Make your soul sparkle. Make it shine. Then, make the world glow.

Clean your temple. Not your room.

Good-Bye

Pig-Pen is always grubby. He attracts a permanent cloud of filth and
bugs, and his friends joke that he's the only person who gets dirty in a
snowstorm. Despite his best efforts, Pig-Pen remains grimy. Us, too. Our
flesh often overpowers our will. We say the next time is the last. It's not.
We compare our trespasses to our neighbor's trespasses. Guilt then sub-
sides. Pain, however, remains—and mediocrity endures. We then flirt
with wasting our life. We roll the dice. I'm the last person to ask about
gambling. But, I can tell you this: if you keep sinning, you have the best
odds of suffering.

Some sins perpetuate languishing more than others. For the past decade, one choked my soul. God freed me numerous times. But, I was a
recidivist. I then condemned and cursed myself. I understood Job's anguish. "For sighing comes more readily to me than food, and my groans
well forth like water. For what I fear overtakes me, and what I shrink
from comes upon me. I have no peace nor ease; I have no rest, for trouble comes!" (Job, 3:24-26). Enough was enough. I begged God for the
strength to deny my desires, to align my suffering to Jesus' suffering, and
to relieve my pain with His love—not pleasure. Easy, right? Try it.

Two years ago, I planned my sin's burial. It was the weekend my wife
and I celebrated our 15-year anniversary in Montauk. Knowing I love
churches, she suggested we attend a local Mass. Arriving early, I people
watched. Several pews away, an older gentleman sat with his family. He

had a huge incision along his head covered in scabs and closed with staples. He looked around, smiled, and kept his hands in a prayer position. People from all directions ran over to hug him, children nestling their heads into his chest. Jesus was clearly present. Tears trickled down the man's face. Mine, too. The opening hymn then made me cry. *"Amazing Grace, How sweet the sound; That saved a wretch like me; I once was lost, but now am found; T'was blind but now I see."* God had my attention. I straightened my back. I cleared my throat. I wiped my eyes. The priest then preached about the prodigal son. I wept. God knew about the burial.

Leaving Mass, my wife asked about my reaction. After telling her my plan and how God spoke to me during Mass, she hugged me. We cried. She then said, "When I pray at night, I always thank God for bringing you into my life." That confirmed my decision. We held hands walking to the cemetery. After lowering the casket, I grabbed the shovel. The priest then spoke, and we lit a candle. Driving home, I looked in my rearview mirror. The sun disappeared beyond the horizon—along with my sin. It was an Oscar-worthy ending to my drama. The credits appeared, and I gave a standing ovation. Then, the screen went dark...until my drama started. Again. This time, though, it began with the doorbell ringing. I wasn't expecting anyone. I carefully peeked through the curtain. There my sin stood—covered in dirt and dried blood. I opened the door.

My sin was a horrible guest. He was a nightmare. He made me late to important events, kept me in the shadows, and distracted me from mastering my mission. So, after 2 months of hell, I dragged him to the curb. While walking away, he clasped my ankle. I stomped him. The next day was a father-daughter day. A perfect celebration for my freedom. A perfect reminder of my values. But, that evening, **"DING-DONG!"** He needed a room. He promised it was just for the night. He was cold, wet, and hungry. I felt bad. Moments later, I felt terrible. After 6 weeks, I again dragged him to the curb. This time, I threw him in the garbage and slammed the lid. The sanitation worker waved, "Hello." I waved, "Good-Bye."

Cleaning my temple was arduous. I frequently stumbled walking toward "Calvary." Eventually, I collapsed. I needed someone to carry my cross. I humbled myself and sought God. Everything then changed. St. Francis of Assisi reminds us, "Start by doing what's necessary; then do what's possible; and suddenly you are doing the impossible." Sorry, Tom Cruise. With God, no mission is impossible!

Lighten your load. Lift your spirit. Live your destiny.

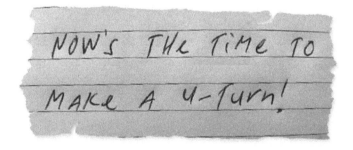

COLORFUL COVENANT

"Courage is not simply one of the virtues but the form of every virtue at the testing point, which means at the point of highest reality." — C. S. Lewis

Small elements can create massive explosions. Assume there was a pond about 165 feet wide. If an atom were the size of this pond, the nucleus would be like a pencil eraser. If two atomic nuclei combine to form a single heavier atom, the nuclear reaction (i.e., fusion) could create an explosion equivalent to 50 million tons of TNT. The spirit within us is more powerful than a nuclear bomb. Follow it, and you'll realize your potential and facilitate humanity's potential. Ignore it, and you'll bring chaos into your life and everyone else's. A nuclear war could destroy the world. Following the spirit within you and mastering your mission, however, could save it.

A loving parent, God guides us. He gives green lights. He tells us when to yield and stop. He identifies school zones, sharp turns, and deadly cliffs. Like Dorothy Day, we must look for His signs (see Commandment IX). Then, we must have the courage to follow them. Are you that bold? I'm not. For inspiration, consider the disciples.

> *As he passed by the Sea of Galilee, he saw Simon and his brother Andrew casting their nets into the sea; they were fishermen. Jesus said to them, "Come after me, and I will make you fishers of men." Then they left their nets and followed him. He walked along a little farther and saw James, the son of Zebedee, and his brother John. They too were in a boat mending their nets. Then he called to them. So they left their father Zebedee in the boat along with the hired men and followed him.*
>
> *–Mark, 1:16-20*

Dropping our "net" to follow God sounds great—for someone else. We have leaky roofs, endless bills, and small nest eggs. Our children's sick days often exceed ours. Hand-me-downs are done being handed down. Tomorrow's leftovers are sometimes eaten today. These are real, practical matters. But, I think fear often exaggerates their magnitude and significance. This creates tunnel vision and extinguishes our courage. We then pray for hump day and cheer "TGIF!" Regret builds. Pain festers. Emptiness knocks.[68]

Pursuing your mission is risky. So is ignoring it.

Our fear of pursuing our mission also fosters amnesia. We often forget about God's promise to us. After the flood, God said to Noah, "As the [rain]bow appears in the clouds, I will see it and recall the everlasting covenant that I have established between God and all living beings" (Genesis, 9:16). God promised to never again flood the earth and destroy humanity. This is realized in Jesus' death and resurrection whereby God pays for our sin, sparing us a debt we could never pay and giving us eternal life. The rainbow, therefore, reminds us of God's grace and love, reassuring us that there will always be two sets of adjacent footprints leading to our mission—except when He's carrying us.

Music can inspire us to find and follow our mission. It stirs our souls. It gives our heart a voice and makes us ponder life. Consider the *Rainbow Connection*. Please listen to it now (seriously, please). Follow along with the lyrics below. For maximum effect, listen to Kermit the Frog's version. If you're like me, you'll feel confused, anxious, and uncomfortable. This happens when we realize that the "weird" voice in our head is God.

---

68 Do you now fully understand and appreciate the sequential and systematic nature of keeping the 10 commandments to thrive (see *The Skeleton*)? Consider the issue of practical vs. spiritual matters when trying to master your mission. Taking a pay cut, spending less, and downsizing would provide more time, widgets, clarity, and focus to pursue your destiny. Thus, keeping Commandment III (*Thou Shalt* **LIVE SIMPLY**) facilitates keeping Commandment X (*Thou Shalt* **MASTER MISSION**). Unfortunately, I'm still too scared to drop my "net." Our mortgage and other endless bills are hindering my mission. Hopefully, you're braver—and less encumbered.

Rainbow Connection

Why are there so many
Songs about rainbows
And what's on the other side?
Rainbows are visions
But only illusions
And rainbows have nothing to hide.
So we've been told and some choose to believe it,
I know they're wrong, wait and see.

Someday we'll find it,
The *Rainbow Connection,*
The lovers, the dreamers, and me.

Who said that every wish
Would be heard and answered
When wished on the morning star?
Somebody thought of that,
And someone believed it,
Look what it's done so far.
What's so amazing
That keeps us stargazing,
And what do we think we might see?

Someday we'll find it,
The *Rainbow Connection,*
The lovers, the dreamers, and me.

All of us under its spell,
We know that it's probably magic.

Have you been half asleep,
And have you heard voices?
I've heard them calling my name.
Is this the sweet sound that calls the young sailors?
The voice might be one and the same.
I've heard it too many times to ignore it,
It's something that I'm supposed to be.

Someday we'll find it,
The *Rainbow Connection,*
The lovers, the dreamers, and me.

We've all *"been half asleep."* We've all *"heard voices."* And we're all terrified of pursuing and becoming what we're *"supposed to be."* We should, instead, be more terrified of letting our souls wither and die. Of following the compass of comfort—not courage. Levers and zippers realized their potential and changed the world because they knew what they could do. They knew their mission. They also heeded their creator. Do likewise.

You're not crazy for hearing things. But, you're crazy for not listening.

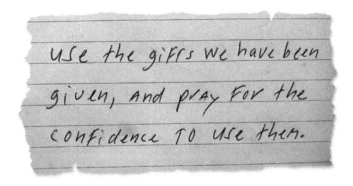

SEEK, SERVE, SURRENDER

"Some are dining in our ears that we...are intellectual dwarfs compared with the ancients, or even the Elizabethan men. But what is that to the purpose? A living dog is better than a dead lion. Shall a man go and hang himself because he belongs to the race of pygmies, and not be the biggest pygmy that he can? Let everyone mind his own business, and endeavor to be what he was made." — Henry David Thoreau

Gangs recently roamed Kruger National Park. The once-endangered African elephants were now too numerous and needed relocation. The adult bull elephants were too large to transport. Thus, the juveniles went alone, leaving them fatherless. Chaos ensued. Never learning how to be gentlemen, the young male elephants began terrorizing other animals— even murdering white rhinos. Teaching pachyderm protocol required the bulls. Therefore, the fathers were eventually transported to show their children proper etiquette. Within weeks, order was restored. Boys became men.

Like the young male elephants, my father taught me many life lessons. Old pants can become new shorts. Remove your glove before shaking hands. Tie new blood knots and replace your line before a fishing trip. Campbell's soup deserves saying grace. Use the checkout with the person—not the machine. Barbers are sages. Listening to rain is like listening to a symphony. Order little; tip big. Never turn your back on the ocean. Let the other person walk on the inside of the road. In my early 30s, I reflected on my superhero's influence. I thought, "Imagine if I could help build a legion of superheroes. Imagine the love we'd spread and the evil we'd destroy. Imagine if we made God our leader." My destiny was crystallizing.[69]

---

69 I recently ordered new wheels for my car. I accidentally entered my father's zip code for the shipping address, rerouting my order back to Texas. Because of our tumultuous relationship, I haven't mailed my father anything in over 10 years. Why, then, would I enter his zip code? Similar to what happened with my mother (see Commandment IV), I last spoke to my father over 1 year ago. Since then, his health plummeted. I, therefore, thought the shipping faux pas was God telling me, "Jeff, call your father. It's time to forgive him, as I've forgiven you." I ignored God. Four days later, my father

THRIVE

Over the following years, the spirit continued stirring my soul. Now 44, I no longer question my mission. I know what I'm supposed to do. I <u>must</u> help men pursue their spousal and paternal potential. I <u>must</u> help men create thriving families and communities. I <u>must</u> help men embody St. Joseph. You can see my mission reflected in my value system: *faith, family, fitness, work,* and *friends.* You can see it in the note I gave my wife with the Winnie the Pooh doll: *"...my ultimate aim is love—love for you and the kids."* In Commandment II, I wrote, *"Nothing happens when we let things 'just' happen."* I forgot the asterisk. After surrendering to God, our mission "just" happens.

Though I went from an apprentice to a journeyman, I'm far from a master. I still ignore God's whispers. I still succumb to fear. I still pursue my personal mission—not my divine mission. But, I'm trying. Fulfilling your destiny requires following the **3 Ss to Master Mission**: **seek, serve,** and **surrender.** God will guide you. He'll leave breadcrumbs. Or, as with me, He'll send bread truck deliveries.

Paternal Purpose

Puzzle Pieces

I had my last first date July 19, 2000. My now wife, Cara, and I had dinner at *Ristorante Orlando.* I loved that she ate a 10-ounce steak. I loved that she thought me trying to pay at the hostess station was endearing. I loved that she, too, enjoyed a latte nightcap. After dinner, we sat on storefront steps, talking another 4 hours. I learned about her love affair with books, her desire to travel, and how much she bench pressed. She was classy, cool. Wife material. Before Cara, my longest relationship lasted 6 weeks. I knew this would be different. She was different. She still is today.

---

died. If you still question God's existence after considering the numbers in the "Weird" Science *Easter egg,* please consider 11772. Rest in peace, Dad. I miss you. I love you. I forgive you. Hopefully, you forgive me, too.

While dating, we frequently discussed our dream of starting a family together. Of creating future snuggle bugs. I knew I was destined to be a father. And, I knew Cara had to be the mother. She's affectionate, generous, and loving. She anticipates everyone's needs. She knows that ginger ale, toast, and kisses cures nausea. To me, Cara embodied Mary. God told me to make it official. On a dreary autumn day, at the end of a pier overlooking Northport Harbor, I got on bended knee. A nerdy scientist, I collected pre-post data. Thankfully, she said, "Yes." I hate failed experiments.

Earth Angels

Love underlies commitment. I realized this when I became a father. The nurse had to teach me how to swaddle our hours-old son, James. At first, I struggled. By nightfall, I made "Burrito Baby." Because of complications, James was admitted to the neonatal intensive care unit (NICU). "Game on, Dad," whispered God. "Much will be required of the person entrusted with much, and still more will be demanded of the person entrusted with more" (Luke, 12:48). James needed his terry cloth monkey. Therefore, while holding him, I read James his first book. When tears blurred the words, God read for me. Five years later, James needed finger surgery. Unfortunately, only one parent was allowed in his room afterward. He chose me. I remember thinking, "Wow. I guess children can also bond with their fathers. Do men know this?" Slowly, God was directing me toward my mission.

Fathers have different relationships with sons and daughters. I learned this after the doctor said, "It's a…GIRL!" Energy surged throughout my body, shooting from head to toe. I was scared. It was surreal, spooky. The thought, "I will protect her," spontaneously emerged.[70] Eleven years later, I'm still trying to protect my daughter. Before going to bed, I always kiss my family and ensure they're swaddled. This morning, Julianne said to me, "Daddy, I was still awake last night when you turned off *Dreamland*. Before doing that, you looked at me and made the sign of the cross. Why?" Welling with tears, I said, "It's my way of blessing you like God has blessed me with you." She smiled. Then asked me to get a spoon for her Cocoa Krispies. I've been called many bitter names. But, the sweetest name I've ever been called is, "Daddy."

Serving others creates meaning—and sanctifies life.

Holy Orders

Married with children, I had the basics for ministering to men. For being able to understand their struggles and dreams. I still, however, had a void. Without a religious affiliation, I felt lost, like a spiritual orphan.

---

70 I'm not chauvinistic or sexist. Women are strong, and they don't need men for protection. I can't explain my experience and response. I can only report that it happened and that overwhelming love, not fear that she's weak, created it. Trust me, my daughter can handle her own. She's a lioness—and forever "my girl" (see Commandment I).

I needed a home. I needed a family. And considering my nascent mission, I had to bond with my heavenly father. I also had to surrender to Him. So, in 2010, I was received into the Catholic Church. My family then grew exponentially. I gained brothers and sisters, while my children gained aunts, uncles, and many grandparents. Over time, my new family saw my strengths, proclivities, and love for Jesus. With a nudge here, and a kind word there, they gently steered me further toward God—and my mission.

Whenever possible, I participate in bible study. I love learning about Jesus, Lectio Divina, and the Holy Family. About Christian persecution and the gospels. About St. Paul and his endless letters. Eight years ago, our group leader, Lorraine, loaned me a book. It was Matthew Kelly's, *Rediscover Catholicism*. I finished it within 1 week. The next week, I read his book, *The Rhythm of Life*. I felt connected to his writing and his message. He encouraged faith without proselytizing. That's tough. I recall thinking, "I'd love to write like that. To teach people about God's love using passion—not persuasion." Though I doubted my ability, God made me wonder. I didn't then connect this to my paternal purpose. But, I now realize that God wants me helping men by writing books.

Like a savory Sunday sauce, mastering our mission takes time.

> After our talk yesterday and rereading chapter 4 I really do believe that there's some greater plan for you. You were meant to write and people were meant to hear your words. I mean it when I say that. I'm soooo excited for you and what's to come, please keep me posted.

It also requires listening to God's messengers. Several months ago, Phyllis, a parish matriarch, ambushed me in our church parking lot. Panting from running, she put her hand on my shoulder. "Jeff, I've been hoping to see you for months," she said. "I have to tell you something. You're supposed to be a deacon. I see how you contribute here. I see how you live your secular life. I see how you're raising your family. You have to help other men do this. You just have to." We then hugged. Like Father Peter (see Commandment I), Phyllis didn't know I felt called to be a deacon ministering to men. My children asked, "Daddy, what was that about?" Still shocked, I said, "I guess God is trying to tell me something." He's trying to tell you something, too.

God's most recent bread truck delivery happened while writing this section. I called the *New York Catholic Worker* seeking copyright permission for the Dorothy Day photograph in Commandment IX. After helping me, a kind gentleman took my contact information to mail me the current edition of *The Catholic Worker* newspaper. After opening the package, I froze. My chest tightened and tingled. In neon lights, God used an image pushing me further toward my mission. "Of all the possible images," I thought, "why did you have to put that one on the front page? You know I'm confused. You know I'm scared." God replied, "I know. Hence my reassurance." I immediately shared this story with my friend, Matt. "Guy, that's crazy," he said. "Remember, you also attended St. Joseph's College." So much for me creating my destiny.

Mastering your mission is gratifying. And, terrifying. We must be bold, heed God, and trust Him. "Ask and it will be given to you; seek and you will find; knock and the door will be opened to you. For everyone who asks, receives; and the one who seeks, finds; and to the one who knocks, the door will be opened" (Matthew, 7:7-8). Use the doorknocker. Ring the bell. Tap the window. Like God, make your presence known.

Care less about your living will. Care more about God's divine will.

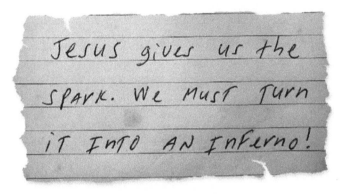

Jesus gives us the spark. We must turn it into an inferno!

THE 4TH CUP

"The soul which has no fixed purpose in life is lost; to be everywhere, is to be nowhere." — Michel de Montaigne

We're made for worship. It gives us direction, focus, and meaning. Our heart knows that we should honor God. That we should offer Him our life as a living sacrifice. But, like the Israelites, we get impatient with God. We drum our fingers awaiting His instruction, until becoming too fidgety and pursuing pleasure—not purpose. We then create false Gods. We worship a golden calf. We eat, drink, and cry in revelry instead of sacrificing, surrendering, and crying in joy. Jesus worshipped God. He obeyed Him—until His last breath. We should, too.

The Passover meal consists of four parts. Each one includes drinking a cup of wine. The Last Supper assumed the Passover meal's structure.

Notably, the cup blessed and shared by Jesus is considered the third cup (i.e., the "cup of blessing"). But, deviating from the meal's structure, Jesus and His disciples didn't drink the fourth cup of wine. This is like a priest omitting the words of consecration at Mass. Instead, after singing the "Great Hallel," which happens at the Passover's climax, they went to the Mount of Olives. Did Jesus forget about the fourth cup? No. It wasn't time. "Amen, I say to you, I shall not drink again the fruit of the vine until the day when I drink it new in the kingdom of God" (Mark, 14:25). Jesus knew the Passover meal must end at Calvary. The lamb still required slaughtering.

Jesus was determined to complete His mission. Thus, during His crucifixion, though He was obviously thirsty, Jesus initially declined something to drink. "They gave him wine drugged with myrrh, but he did not take it" (Mark, 15:23). After realizing everything was done, to fulfill the Scripture, Jesus said, "I thirst" (John, 19:28). The soldiers then "put a sponge soaked in wine on a sprig of hyssop and put it up to his mouth" (John, 19:29).[71] Having now drank the fourth cup of wine, Jesus consummated the Passover meal started in the Upper Room. He transformed the Passover sacrifice of the Old Covenant (i.e., the Law of Moses) into the Eucharistic sacrifice of the New Covenant (i.e., the Law of the Gospel). He accomplished His mission. He mastered it. So, before bowing His head and surrendering His spirit, Jesus said, "It is finished" (John, 19:30).[72]

---

71 Isaiah predicted Jesus would initially refuse the wine. "Though he was harshly treated, he submitted and opened not his mouth; Like a lamb led to the slaughter or a sheep before the shearers, he was silent and opened not his mouth" (Isaiah, 53:7). Further, the soldiers using a hyssop branch to give Jesus the wine seems trivial. It's not. Moses instructed the Israelites to "Go and procure lambs for your families, and slaughter them as Passover victims. Then take a bunch of hyssop, and dipping it in the blood that is in the basin, sprinkle the lintel and the two doorposts with this blood" (Exodus, 12:21-22). Thus, Jesus' Eucharistic sacrifice as the Passover lamb was completed with His crucifixion at Calvary, making Him the Lamb of God. Prophets knew Jesus would master His mission. Jesus knows you can, too.

72 Dr. Scott Hahn's book, *The Fourth Cup: Unveiling the Mystery of the Last Supper and the Cross*, provided the basis for this section. Dr. Hahn was instrumental in me finding and deepening my faith. He's considered one of the greatest theologians ever. Read *The Fourth Cup*, and you'll understand why.

God created you for your mission. Every detail matters. Only you, therefore, can complete your mission. You need you, humanity needs you, and God needs you. It will be arduous. You'll fall, you'll wail, and you'll bleed. But, it's worth it. Stop asking, *"What do I want from life?"* Start asking, *"What does life want from me?"* Fulfill your scripture. Complete your story. Master your mission. Before taking your last breath, like Jesus, you can then say:

"It is finished."

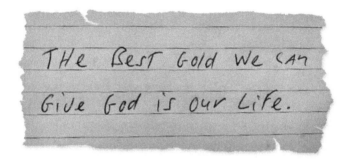

THe BesT Gold We CAn Give God is our Life.

COMMANDMENT X TIPS

Thou Shalt
Master Mission

1. Review childhood photos. What did you want to be when you grew up? Before money's influence. Before worldly propaganda. Recall praise from your family and friends. What did they say were your gifts? Playing music? Painting or writing? Listening to others? Fixing or building things? Teaching? Sharing your faith? Visualize these interactions. Feel the warmth in your heart. God might have been—and probably was—whispering to you your mission. Consider how you could now use your gifts to help others. You might rediscover your destiny.

2. Sit in silence, be alone, and close your eyes. Conduct a ruthless self-inventory. Identify your sins, the thoughts and behaviors interfering with you mastering your mission. Give yourself the permission to be human; judgment and guilt worsen matters. Then, confess your struggles to someone trustworthy. A parent, friend, spouse, or God. Be thorough, detailed, and honest. Free your mind, soothe your heart, and feel the peace. Clean your temple.

3. God promised to love us, forever. That means helping us discover and master our mission. When doubtful, and everyone is occasionally, listen to Kermit the Frog sing, *"Rainbow Connection."* Sing along with the lyrics. Wake your neighbors! Let the words arouse your spirit. Let them stir your soul. Let them remind you of God's colorful covenant.

4. Mastering your mission requires traveling new lands, discovering new territory, and staking your claim. You must be bold, heed God, and trust Him. To increase your spiritual strength, pray more frequently and sincerely. Ask others to pray for you, too. Leaving Mass, request an additional blessing. Building a spiritual army will help you accomplish the *3 Ss to Master Mission:* **seek, serve,** and **surrender.** You can then add your piece to the cosmic puzzle.

5. Recognize why God created you. Write it down, and review it. Record it on your phone, and listen to it. Then, share it with others. Make a contract. Sign it, date it, and get it notarized. Stop asking, *"What do I want from life?"* Start asking, *"What does life want from me?"* Fulfill your scripture. Complete your story. Master your mission. Before taking your last breath, like Jesus, you can then say, *"It is finished."*

Epilogue

When he saw the crowds, he went up the mountain, and after he sat down, his disciples came to him. He began to teach them, saying:

> *"Blessed are the poor in spirit,*
> *for theirs is the kingdom of heaven.*
> *Blessed are they who mourn,*
> *for they will be comforted.*
> *Blessed are the meek,*
> *for they will inherit the land.*
> *Blessed are they who hunger and thirst for righteousness,*
> *for they will be satisfied.*
> *Blessed are the merciful,*
> *for they will be shown mercy.*
> *Blessed are the clean of heart,*
> *for they will see God.*
> *Blessed are the peacemakers,*
> *for they will be called children of God.*
> *Blessed are they who are persecuted for the sake of righteousness,*
> *for theirs is the kingdom of heaven.*
> *Blessed are you when they insult you and utter every kind of evil*
> *against you [falsely] because of me.*
> *Rejoice and be glad, for your reward will be great in heaven."*

–Matthew, 5:1-12

Ventilating my heart in this book was tough. Sometimes, I cried. Other times, I panicked, fearing judgment, ridicule, and rejection. I pray my pain wasn't in vain. I pray you and others learn from it. I pray you're inspired to share your story, too. But, only to those who are worthy. Sharing your story will likely elicit someone else's story; vulnerability begets vulnerability. If you receive this gift, bring it to your casket. Hear-

ing someone's story is a privilege. Honor it. Respect it. Protect it. As C.
S. Lewis writes, "Friendship…is born at the moment when one [person]
says to another, 'What! You too? I thought that no one but myself…'" Suffering unites.

People are typically shocked when my vault is slightly ajar. Many cry,
all gasp. In class, I sometimes share a personal story with my students
to humanize dull data. Before that, however, I often discuss my current
functioning, hoping to model best practices to thrive. Someone usually
says, "Your life is amazing. Your family seems awesome. And your relationships are great. I assume it has always been this way." After reading
this book, you know the truth. Dreams were rare. Nightmares were common.

My childhood, however, had fine moments: fishing in Montauk with
my father, skateboarding with friends, and playing football with my
Golden Retriever, Odie. My early trauma, however, created long, jagged
scars that still bleed. I'll forever protect myself with anger. I'll forever
avoid chitchat because it reminds me of failed attempts at connection. I'll
forever struggle with abandonment, insecurity, and trust. Our world tells
people like me that it's hopeless. That I'm fragile and defective. But, the
human spirit is dogged. Suffering transforms. The best among us suffer.
And, no one suffered more than Jesus.

Brokenness is a blessing.

Having tried keeping the 10 commandments to thrive for nearly 25
years, and with God's enduring grace, I've prevailed. "Do not be afraid of
anything that you are going to suffer. Indeed, the Devil will throw some
of you into prison, that you may be tested, and you will face an ordeal
for ten days. Remain faithful until death, and I will give you the crown
of life" (Revelation, 2:10). Do I still struggle? Hell yeah. Daily. My past,
however, will never determine my present or my future. If you learn anything from me or this book, please learn this: *You can thrive.* It takes
heeding your heart's counsel—not the world's counsel. It takes embracing your uniqueness and finding *real* connection. It takes accepting and

bravely pursuing your mission. Above all, it takes surrendering to God. You don't need Dumbo's magic feather. The spirit within you is greater. I did it. You can, too.

I'm finally starting to understand my story. The characters. The setting. The plot. The conflict. The resolution. I'm starting to understand how life works, how I work, and how God works. Yet, I'm still confused. I'm still lost. I recently wrote some insights in my journal. While roaming around backstage (see *Behind the Scenes*), remember that I've been trying to thrive since I was about 20. I had to awaken. I had to retire my self-hatred. I had to make Jesus my North Star. Thriving is daunting; you'll fail, repeatedly. As I have, as I still do. But, anything worth anything is hard. "Life is a journey to be experienced, not a problem to be solved," said Winnie the Pooh. Wise old bear.

I pray that this book helps you realize your potential. I pray that it helps you find your adjoining puzzle piece. I pray that the words stir your soul and transcend your life, beautifying our world's tapestry. With a loving heart and generous spirit, show others how to thrive. Your reward

will be great in Heaven. Play differently. Work differently. Love differently.

Be different.

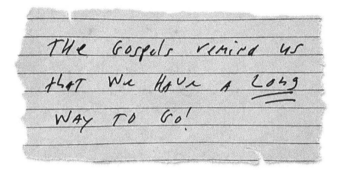

The Gospels remind us that we have a long way to go!

BEHIND THE SCENES

- My family is the best! I love them so much.
- Every time I simplify my life, I'm happier, more focused, and more energized.
- Having a consistent sleep schedule, 7 days a week, is a game-changer.
- I need more time resting with Jesus. He brings me peace, clarity, compassion, and love.
- I need to spend more time with my family hiking, biking, swimming, fishing, and stargazing.
- I love long walks in quiet places.
- I love and value silence and solitude. I need more quiet and alone time to rejuvenate and reflect.
- Cultivating character and virtue is a priority. This helps me become all God created me to be.

- Cell phones, email, and the internet are MAJOR distractions. I Love Focus. My mind, soul, heart, relationships, and body need me to stay unplugged— For extended periods of time.
- I Love praying. I Love the rosary. I Love reading the bible.
- God is with me 24/7.
- I'm supposed to be a deacon, ministering to husbands and fathers.
- "I LOVE YOU" is my favorite saying. "NO" is my favorite word.
- My family and I must spend more time in state and national parks.
- Reading daily is central to growth, insight, and understanding.
- Function over fashion. ALWAYS!
- I'm done managing other people's expectations of me.
- Live for an audience of ONE!

- I'm an outsider. And, I LOVE IT!
- Being real is very important
  to me.
- Blankets should be used
  whenever possible.
- Candles are peaceful.
- Darkness is calming.
- I TALK TOO Much.
- I judge too much.
- I'm NOT intense. I'M PASSIONATE!
- I will NOT OWN any relationship.
- I will NO Longer be Anyone's
  energy source.
- I will only Ask/Tell people
  something once, Maybe twice.
  I'm fine letting the balls drop.
- I LOVE writing books.
- Thinking, deep thinking, is A
  deliberate Act. I Must MAKE
  More time To Think — really think.
- I Like waking up NATURALLY.
- I Love sprinting on A
  field. I Feel like A Kid.
- I Must Drive in Silence More.

- Nature provides a much better playground than a playground.
- Listening to Julianne play piano warms my heart and calms my mind.
- I love attending Mass with my family.
- Call people. DON'T TEXT. DON'T email. Even better, go for a WALK.
- I love the rain.
- I hate shopping.
- I love being home.
- Background Noise is just that — NOISE!
- My phone will stay home as much as possible. Especially when I'm out with my family. And, I'll NEVER take it on vacation.
- I AM NOT my physique.
- I LOVE shooting hoops with James.
- I'm in Major trouble if the ordinary fails to be EXTRAORDINARY!

God's Library

Behe, M. J. (2007). *The edge of evolution: The search for the limits of Darwinism.* Free Press.

Boyer, P. (2001). *Religion explained: The evolutionary origins of religious thought.* Basic Books.

Chesterton, G.K. (1908). *Orthodoxy.* Ignatius Press.

Collins, F. (2006). *The language of God: A scientist presents evidence for belief.* Free Press.

Dawkins, R. (2006). *The God delusion.* Houghton Mifflin Company.

Gingerich, O. (2006). *God's universe.* Harvard University Press.

Lewis, C. S. (1952). *Mere Christianity.* HarperCollins Publishers.

Newberg, A., D'Aquili, E., & Rouse, V. (2002). *Why God won't go away: Brain science and the biology of belief.* Ballantine Books.

Peck, S. M. (1978). *The road less traveled: A new psychology of love, traditional values, and spiritual growth.* Simon & Schuster.

Strobel, L. (1998). *The case for Christ: A journalist's personal investigation of the evidence for Jesus.* Zondervan.

Strobel, L. (2000). *The case for faith: A journalist investigates the toughest objections to Christianity.* Zondervan.

Strobel, L. (2004). *The case for a creator: A journalist investigates scientific evidence that points toward God.* Zondervan.

Warren, R. (2002). *The purpose driven life.* Zondervan.

Note: I read these books the summer I realized that *it takes more faith to be an atheist than a theist* (see Commandment I). Since then, I've read many more on the interface of science and religion. One, however, stands out. It's Scott Hahn and Benjamin Wiker's book, *Answering the New Atheism: Dismantling Dawkins' Case Against God.* Read it if you're ready for "weird" to become God.

"Weird" Science

✟ The beginning of our universe is so incalculable that it's as precise as throwing a dart from space and hitting a bullseye just a trillionth of a trillionth of an inch in diameter on Earth.

✟ The Cambrian explosion was a geological period that likely began a little over 540 million years ago. It's called the "Biological Big Bang" because that's when the majority, if not all, of the world's forty phyla (i.e., the highest category in the animal kingdom) virtually and abruptly appeared with unique body plans. This change would've required massive amounts of new biological information far beyond what any Darwinian mechanism can produce. Therefore, design is a better explanation. Dr. Stephen Meyer, director of the Discovery Institute's Center for Science and Culture and founder of the intelligent design movement, maintains that, "Information is the hallmark of mind. And purely from the evidence of genetics and biology, we can infer the existence of a mind that's far greater than our own—a conscious, purposeful, rational, intelligent designer who's amazingly creative."

✟ Natural, biological causes fail to explain how DNA code influences behavior. Instruction and precise information like this must have been intentionally constructed.

✟ Based on only one of the hundreds of parameters of the physical universe, Sir Roger Penrose, mathematical physicist, calculated that the probability of a life-giving cosmos emerging was 1 divided by 10, raised to the power 10, and again raised to the power of 123. This is as close to zero as imaginable. You have better odds of winning the Mega Millions jackpot more times than days the universe has existed!

✟ Gravity is fine-tuned to one part in a hundred million billion billion billion billion billion. (This isn't a typo.)

✟ If the constants of nature—unchanging numbers like the strength of gravity, the charge of an electron, and the mass of a proton—were even the tiniest bit different, then atoms wouldn't bond, stars wouldn't burn, and life wouldn't exist.

✟ Biochemist, Dr. Arthur Peacocke, became a priest in the Church of England in 1971. Yet, he believes in evolution. He finds in it signs of God's nature. He infers, from evolution, that the appearance of chance mutations, and the Darwinian laws of natural selection acting on this "variation," brings about the diversity of life on Earth. Creation and evolution, thus, are compatible. As author, Dan Brown, writes in his book, *Angels & Demons*, "Science and religion were not enemies, but rather allies—two different languages telling the same story, a story of symmetry and balance...Heaven and Hell, night and day, hot and cold, God and Satan. Both science and religion rejoiced in God's symmetry...the endless contest of light and dark."

✟ The flagellum, a biological machine that propels cells, is only several microns big (a micron is about 1/20,000 of an inch) and spins at 10,000 revolutions per minute (rpm). It can also stop spinning within a quarter turn and reverse direction at 10,000 rpm. The Porsche 911 GT3 RS, a technological marvel, however, can only hit 9,000 rpm. Moreover, if you stop the pistons mid travel, you'll bend the connecting rods, shatter the pistons, break the valves, and destroy the crankshaft. Biochemist, Dr. Michael Behe, asserts that the flagellum is "a coherent, complex, cellular system [that] did not arise by random mutation and natural selection, any more than the Hoover Dam was built by the random accumulation of twigs, leaves, and mud."

✟ Physicists discovered that entities thought of as particles, like electrons, can also act as waves. And light, considered a wave, can act like a barrage of particles. Thus, light is simultaneously wave and particle. Physicist, Dr. F. Russell Stannard, thinks that this helps explain how Jesus was fully divine and fully human. According to theoretical physicist, Dr. John Polkinghorne, such parallels show "that this is not just some deeply weird Christian idea."

Note: These are some of the fun facts I've learned studying the relation between science and religion. Hundreds of other jelly beans exist. Go on an egg hunt. Bring a basket. Bring friends. Bring an open mind. You might find more than your favorite flavor—you might find God.

~~Deleted~~ Scenes

COMMANDMENT III: *Thou Shalt* LIVE SIMPLY

A Philosophical Dilemma

A "philosophical dilemma",in my case a dilemma with a pedological and emotional perspective as well.

It appears that our society is rushing full bore to make every social institution known to personkind as technological as possible.Each day brings with it a new dimension to the computer age.At the same time we are told how critical it is not to lose the "human touch".My problem is that I subscribe to the latter, to the degree that I am an Olympic class technophobe and have neither the desire or will to change.In my case as a teacher and a professional the problem is rather acute.My record speaks for itself.I am effective in the classroom and I make a difference.My tools are love for teaching,enthusiasm,creativity,preparation, relevancy to life and a love for people.My physical tools are very basic, a piece of chalk and a blackboard.

I "live to teach" not the reverse,but as each day goes by I get the horrible feeling that my day has come.I find it very difficult to show my students and and my colleagues that "I care" utilizing the computer,E mail,websites,and answering machines. I am searching for a teaching environment that will recognize my " people" skills as opposed to my "computer" skills.

I do not know if I can function not going into a classroom each day,sadly, if I do it has to be on my terms.

William B. Thisban
4/30/04

High Tech Blues (Wm. B. Thieben)

(Key of "A" capo 3rd fret)

Re:
{ Like to talk to a person
{ Don't want that to fail
Give me a real man to talk to
Don't need that old "E Mail"

Re
{ When I talk on the phone
{ I think that's mighty keen
What kind of a human
Wants to talk to a machine

Re
{ Let me write a letter
{ That's as good as it will get
Don't need no computer
Don't need that Internet

Re
{ Got me an address
{ I think that it's right
Got me a mail man
Don't need me a web site

Re
{ Gonna write you a letter
{ When I am out of town
My pen always works
The computer aint down

MANIPULATED MINDS

"What information consumes is rather obvious: it consumes the attention of its recipients. Hence, a wealth of information creates a poverty of attention, and a need to allocate that attention efficiently among the overabundance of information sources that might consume it." — Herbert A. Simon

Per Greek mythology, sirens shipwrecked sailors with their alluring song. In Homer's *Odyssey*, Odysseus escaped such peril by stuffing his crewmember's ears with wax, making them deaf to the sirens' call. Odysseus himself was desperate to hear their songs. Therefore, he tied himself to the mast so he wouldn't steer the ship astray, killing everyone. Most beings sometimes crumble to tempting, dangerous calls. Consider a male widow spider and praying mantis. I'm sure they wished they knew that mating ended with being devoured. The come-hither, however, is too enticing. We, too, often succumb to such calls. And we, too, are being devoured—but without foreplay.

Consumer culture and materialistic propaganda are today's siren songs. We hear them calling our name. Seducing us, daily. We must plug our ears. We must close our eyes. We must tie ourselves to the mast. If not, like many seafarers before, we'll shipwreck....

LONGITUDE, LATITUDE, & LANGUISHING

"A nation's culture resides in the hearts and in the souls of its people." — Mahatma Gandhi

In America, we often worship money...we can thrive by rejecting materialism and living simply...the U.S. Declaration of Independence gives us the right to pursue happiness—it doesn't guarantee it.

Culture shapes our values and, thus, our level of materialism. For example, Denmark rejects the American "occupational caste system" allowing a sanitation worker to be revered like a physician. Danes, compared to Americans, also work less hours per week (37.2 vs. 41.5) and have more (government-funded) vacation weeks (5 vs. 0). Thus, Danish culture promotes balance—not burnout. Considering the low crime rate, Danish children frequently walk to school. In America, let your child walk to school, and you'll be judged. Maybe even visited by CPS. Further, Danish families have easy access to nature and beaches, whereas American families have easy access to parkways and parking lots. Danish families also often live in green, bicycle-friendly cities, whereas American families often live in concrete jungles. Sure, Danes endure dreary weather (and higher taxes). But, Americans endure dreary lifestyles.

Compared to America, Bhutan is a fairytale when considering materialism. To illustrate, America uses gross domestic product (GDP) to measure society's functioning. Bhutan, however, uses gross national happiness (GNH) to measure society's functioning. Mandated by its constitution, Bhutan always preserves 60% of its land under forest cover. Though upholding this mandate limits economic development, the Bhutanese maintain their position. Why? They value cultural resilience, protecting their environment, and helping families live simply. Adopting healthy values also lets wildlife—like Bengal tigers, snow leopards, black cranes, and elephants—roam free in the country's 5 million-acre network of protected areas. The GNH philosophy helps the Bhutanese maintain a fundamental birthright: thriving. As the Cree Indian proverb says, "Only when the last tree has died and the last river been poisoned and the last fish been caught will we realize we cannot eat money." Start rationing your food. A shortage is looming.[73]

Living simply is challenging in a superficial, complex world. "Simple" is "boring." And boring is, well, boring. Complicating matters, our cul-

---

73 Please don't interpret these country comparisons as me "hating on" America. No way! I love our country. I love our freedom. I love our people. I just wish that our culture promoted a healthier work-life balance and the development of our whole being. I'll keep fighting the good fight—after I nap.

ture is obsessed with having "fun." Need evidence? Consider the t-shirt emblazoned with, *"I Don't Feel Like Adulting Today."* Some of the greatest minds in history lived simply. Think Gandhi. Think Lao Tzu. Think Jesus. I'm sure they had good times. I'm sure they laughed. But, I'm sure they also studied instead of shopped, worked instead of schmoozed, and invested in others instead of the market. If only more people were "boring"....

Hulk Hogan Wannabe

Because of values osmosis, living in certain countries (and, thus, cultures) can affect our mental health. Eating disorders, for example, are sometimes called "culture-bound syndromes" because societal values facilitate their development. Can you imagine someone from an impoverished country, struggling with disease, drought, and death, understanding that people starve themselves to be thin? Unfortunately, because of influential socio-cultural factors, many people from western countries do understand.

In America, pop culture and the fashion industry largely dictate our beauty standards. Females aged 15-24 are the most at-risk group for absorbing materialistic propaganda. For example, compared to same-age peers, young women with anorexia have 10 times the mortality risk. Further, an ongoing study of adolescent and emerging adult females found anorexia's incidence steadily increasing over the last 50 years. The incidence, however, remained stable in other age groups and in males. Working with hundreds of emerging adult women, I've met many who struggle with an eating disorder (see Gianna's story in Commandment IV). Even by 3rd grade, girls often believe that their appearance dictates their worth. Having a daughter in 5th grade, this resonates with me. Thanks to our culture, many females unfortunately spend more time looking into their mirror than into their soul.

Men are now also becoming heavily influenced by similar media messages. In their lifetime, approximately 10 million American boys and men will have an eating disorder. Like women, they're also learning how they "should" look. Magazine covers are littered with chiseled men resembling the Greek god, Adonis. What Barbie did to girls, action figures and video game characters are now doing to boys. Thus, more than ever, men are excessively exercising, using steroids, and developing body dysmorphic disorder. Men like to think they're powerful. But, they'll never overpower culture. I know. I lost the fight, and I can prove it with my scars.

Experiencing child abuse made me insecure (see Commandment VI). Afraid someone would hurt me again, my young mind found a solution: get jacked. If I intimidated you, good. You'd leave me alone. As a child, I loved watching WWF (now WWE). I idolized Hulk Hogan, and I was a Hulkamaniac. I had to resemble him and have 22-inch "pythons." Therefore, at 12, I bought a Hulkamania weight set. I became obsessed with bodybuilding. Peer approval and compliments felt good. Like when I walked by the "Ring the Bell" game at a carnival, and the worker called to me, "Hey, big guy. You got this!" But, I still remained insecure. So, I lifted harder and more frequently. I punished my body, triggering a cascade of injuries. By 16, I had to tape the reminder "ICE SHOULDERS" on my speaker because of burning bicep tendonitis. Did child-abuse fuel self-abuse? Probably.

In my late teens and early 20s, my undiagnosed body dysmorphic disorder was full-blown. Concerned I was too small (218 lbs. at 5'9" with visible abs is far from small), when my friends visited unexpectedly I'd run into my room for a sweatshirt to cover my "tiny" forearms. This is also why I always trained in a sweatshirt—even in heatwaves. One day, my friend Jeremy and I were lifting in a gym with no air conditioning when the "feel like" temperature was 103 degrees. He convinced me to remove my sweatshirt. "Guy, it's a sauna in here. Lose that thing," he urged. Feeling a panic attack brewing, I reluctantly listened. "Dude, your forearms are friggin' huge!", he said. News to me.

Fast forward 20 years. January 7, 2019 I had pec reconstruction surgery and shoulder debridement surgery. Pushing myself for too long,
with excessive volume and intensity, I tore my pec in half. The injury
was so severe that my world-class surgeon, who works with professional
athletes, remarked, "Jeff, this is crazy. I've never seen anything like this.
No one tears a muscle in half. What the hell were you doing?" (Hiding
my insecurities, duh!) As I type these words, 15 months from surgery,
it feels like a hot knife is slowly cutting my flesh. I still can't fully raise
my left arm, I can't hold a gallon of milk, and sleeping is miserable. To
numb the pain, I sleep with ice on my chest. Horrible, right? Yes, and no.
This injury changed my life—for the better. I learned that trauma will
always co-author my story. I learned that I'm not my physique. I learned
that materialism is a master puppeteer. You know what else I learned? I
learned that if Pinocchio could eventually pull his own strings, you can,
too.

COMMANDMENT IV: *Thou Shalt* ACCEPT THYSELF

We owe people honest, direct feedback. This helps them gauge their
growth and develop their being. Take Allison, for example. When she
met with me to discuss getting her Ph.D. in clinical psychology, I first
asked about her grades. "My overall GPA is a 2.7, and my psych GPA is
3.1," Allison said. After hearing Allison's story, I said, "Getting your Ph.D.
in clinical psychology is a wonderful goal. But, given your GPA and poor
research experience, I suggest applying to master's programs first. Prove
yourself there. Aim for a 4.0, do serious research, and try getting published. Then, apply for your Ph.D."

Allison was stunned, speechless. Tears welling in her eyes, she re-
sponded, "Wow, so you really don't think I can get into a Ph.D. program?" "With your current grades, no," I said. "If you step up your game,"
I continued, "then I think you have a better chance. But, in your current
position, it won't happen. Put your time, energy, and money into first ap-

plying for a master's degree. Getting your Ph.D. would be awesome. But, given your grades and minimal research experience, I think you're setting yourself up for needless rejection and wasted application fees if you apply to Ph.D. programs now."

Allison processed this for a bit. She clutched my tissue box and ended our meeting saying, "Though hearing I shouldn't apply to Ph.D. programs now really hurt, I appreciate you being straight with me. No one has ever been so honest before. I've always been told I could do anything. That I was great. So, while I'm really upset about being in this position, I'll be okay. I'll figure it out. Thank you for giving me the truth—as brutal as it was hearing it."

Honesty is often a dangerous, shaky element. It's simultaneously desired and despised. People have a love-hate relationship with the truth. But, there's no love for lying—only hate.

We shoot our messengers and crucify our truth tellers....

PAINFUL GIFTS

"You, me or nobody is gonna hit as hard as life. But, it ain't about how hard you hit. It's about how hard you can get hit and keep moving forward." — Rocky Balboa

You've heard about post-traumatic stress disorder (PTSD). You've probably, however, never heard about the flipside of this psychological coin: post-traumatic growth (PTG). Developed by clinical psychologists, Dr. Richard Tedeschi and Dr. Lawrence Calhoun in the mid-1990s, PTG brings truth to Friedrich Nietzsche's insight, "That which does not kill us, makes us stronger." Surprising many, a major life crisis or traumatic event can actually help us thrive. Adversity typically facilitates growth by: 1) bolstering **gratitude**, 2) attracting **love**, 3) awakening **resilience**, 4) igniting **optimism**, and 5) strengthening **spirituality**....

Gianna, 25, experienced PTG. Her struggle? Gianna thought she *needed* people's approval—especially for her appearance—to feel worthy. Her letter below perfectly demonstrates how adversity can promote thriving. Prepare to be inspired. Prepare to learn that pain is a gift—wrapped in heartache.

Dear Dr. Flett,   12/20/17

In life, you meet so many people who come & go, but very few have the ability to truly make an impact on your life. It shocks me that a lot of individuals (teachers, therapists, etc.) are underappreciated for all of the work that they do & are not properly thanked. Each & every day they work hard to change people's lives. People like yourself deserve to be acknowledged & to know that you're truly making a difference. Although you may not know it, you certainly did in mine & will always have such a special place in my heart because of it.

Last year this time, I was battling severe anorexia & went into inpatient for treatment & then residential for three months during the spring. I had drastically dropped from 140 lbs to 80 lbs within several months, & had to take a medical leave from college in order to get better. Deep in the throes of my eating disorder, I was certain that my life had absolutely no meaning. I was depressed & anxious the majority of the time. I hated who I was—both inside & out, & my will to live was shrinking with each passing day. I spent most of my time religiously restricting my food intake & constantly exercising to burn off the calories that I consumed. Looking back, this is what my life consisted of every single day, repulsed with who I was & struggling to get out of bed every morning. This certainly was no way to live. Why am I sharing my story with you exactly? Because, I want you to know that what you do for a living is truly inspiring others to better themselves, & how much you've made an impact in my life in such a short period of time.

This semester was actually my first semester back on campus since my medical leave. It's also my last, as I'm graduating this December. I've been working really hard with my outpatient team to continue the recovery process & stay on track. All of them have noticed a complete turn-around from where I was a couple of months prior to taking your positive psychology class. Yes, part of my transformation was because of treatment, but part of it was also because of you. Everyday I come to your class, eager to learn how I could become a better version of myself & improve my quality of life.

In my therapy sessions, I would always bring up what we spoke about in class & how I could apply it to my own life. I'm actually teaching my therapist about positive psych - go figure! From learning about savoring life's experiences, gratitude, & the importance of spending our time & energy on the things in life that really matter, I've learned that life is so short, & we should make the most of what we have. In your lectures, you reminded me that my life was important & worth it. That life is good & I should live it to the fullest. My fight has not been easy—there are still days in my recovery where I do slip up, but your class has taught me that I shouldn't give up the fight, no matter how hard it gets.

I never thought that I had any reason to be here on this earth, but only until recently with the help of what I learned from your class, have I realized that my life does have meaning, & that I was put on this earth for a reason. After I graduate, I will be attending an accelerated nursing program. I made the conscious decision to chose a career path in nursing to be able to help others the way that nurses helped me &

to change people's lives. I want to be able to empower others & give them the hope that they need during a time when things look bleak. I want to share my gifts of love, kindness, & humility that God gave me with others. Not only to help individuals mend their bodies, but their hearts as well. I feel that this was meant to be, & that this is my higher calling. I can truly say that now, I am flourishing. I went from getting B's & C's last semester while I was in treatment to getting straight A's this semester. I am able to be more mindful now, & I realize how much beauty & joy there is in the world we live in. When I was sick, I wasn't able to see or enjoy any of it.

    I'm very happy with where I am right now in life & who I am becoming. The struggles & obstacles I've faced have shaped me into the person I am today & have prepared me for the road that lies ahead.

    And for that, I am grateful.

I am also truly grateful for the people that I've met along the way, including you. An infinity of "thank you's" would never be enough, but a simple thank you for now - for empowering me, for inspiring me, & for guiding me into becoming & being the better, happier, healthier person I am today - will have to do. I am so happy that I was able to end my last semester at Hofstra with such a meaningful class, & such an amazing professor.

                          Sincerely,
                          Gianna

PTG oozes from Gianna's letter. She captures every facet of it: **gratitude** (*"The struggles & obstacles I've faced have shaped me into the person I am today & have prepared me for the road that lies ahead. And for that, I am grateful."*), **love** (*"I am also truly grateful for the people that I've met along the way, including you."*), **resilience** (*"My fight has not been easy—there are still days in my recovery where I do slip* *up. But your class has taught me that I shouldn't give up the fight, no matter how hard it gets."),* **optimism** *("I want to share my gifts of love, kindness, & humility that God gave me with others. Not only to help individuals mend their bodies, but their hearts as well."),* and **spirituality** *("...I realized that my life does have meaning, & that I was put on this Earth for a reason.... I feel like this was meant to be, & that* <u>this</u> *is my higher calling.").* Gianna even went one step further. Did you catch it? She said, *"I'm* <u>very</u> *happy with where I am right now in life & who I am becoming."* Sound familiar? Gianna achieved a linchpin for thriving: unconditional self-acceptance (U.S.A.). Her suffering brings truth to Professor Dumbledore's wisdom: "Happiness can be found, even in the darkest of times, if one only remembers to turn on the light."

Through adversity, Gianna became more grateful, reconnected with loving people, awakened her fighting spirit, ignited optimism, and found her mission. It also gave her the confidence and peace created by U.S.A....

COMMANDMENT VI: *Thou Shalt* LOVE DEEPLY THE LONELIEST GENERATION

"We are all so much together, but we are all dying of loneliness." — Albert Schweitzer

While Americans born between 1901-1924 are the *Greatest Generation,* Americans born between 1990-2001 may be the *Loneliest Generation.* A recent poll conducted by YouGov found that 30% of emerging adults report "always" or "often" feeling lonely. The loneliest are 18-22 year-olds, with 23-37 year-olds immediately behind. Further, 25% of emerging adults report having no acquaintances, and 22% report being friendless. Loneliness increases our risk of heart disease and stroke. It also gets us closer to meeting St. Peter at Heaven's gates. Therefore, while solitude draws us nearer to God, too much solitude draws us nearer to death.

Aside from using the wrong roadmap to love deeply, other factors have fostered loneliness in emerging adults. One is *radical individualism*. In American books published between 1990-2008, the phrase *"Make yourself happy"* more than tripled, *"Never compromise"* doubled, and *"I love me"* skyrocketed, while between 1970-2008, *"Don't need anyone"* quadrupled.[74] Promoting this message of narcissism, Kim Kardashian's book, *Selfish*, contains 300 selfies. Per the *New York Daily News*, it includes 115 pics of her breasts, 23 of her butt, 10 of her naked body, and only 1 of her baby bump. No wonder numerous emerging adults think egotism—not altruism—creates the best-life-possible.

Another factor that has fostered loneliness in emerging adults is *technology*. Emerging adults seemingly prefer electronic communication to verbal communication. This helps explain why alone time has replaced "alone time." On a typical day, 18-24 year-olds send and receive 110 texts, and 25-34 year-olds send and receive 42 texts. Yet, only 53% of Americans report having meaningful conversations. These statistics are likely related; observe any restaurant, coffee shop, or kitchen table. Minding your phone during a conversation isn't just rude; it also decreases your biological capacity for connection. Muscles atrophy when they're neglected. So do our social and emotional "muscles." Keeping these "muscles" strong requires face time—not FaceTime.

Let your phone die. Not your relationships.

Unfortunately, some people even use technology hoping to cure their loneliness. For example, Gatebox developed an Anime-inspired VR companion for people preferring a virtual—not human—partner. If simulated connection isn't enough, no worries. Softbank Robotics invented the Pepper robot, a humanoid made for companionship. If the void still remains, there's always Sony's robot dogs. These dogs apparently forge such strong relationships that some people hold funerals when Fido short-circuits and flatlines. Again, I'm reminded of Professor Thieben. After each meeting, while placing his hand on my shoulder, he'd say, "Jeffrey, don't

---

74 These data are discussed in Dr. Jean Twenge's book, *iGen: Why Today's Super-Connected Kids are Growing Up Less Rebellious, More Tolerant, Less Happy—and Completely Unprepared for Adulthood—and What That Means for the Rest of Us*. Read her book, and you may then want to join "Flip Phone Fanatics." If so, I'll waive your membership fee.

let the human touch die." I'm trying. (Notice the name and logo I chose for my publishing imprint.)

Emotions aren't facts. Sometimes, they reflect our insecurities and traumas—not reality. I know. This often happens with loneliness. But, while no one might be home, we're not alone. God is always nearby. You can friend Him, though He's not on Facebook. You can message Him, though He's not on Twitter. You can follow Him, though He's not on Instagram.

Loneliness is sometimes in our head. God is always in our heart....

"I Do"

Many emerging adults are still exchanging vows. According to the 2018 U.S. Census Bureau, 29% of 18-34 year-olds are married (though that's down 30% since 1978). Few decisions will affect your ability to thrive like who you marry. So, choose your spouse wisely. If they have a dark past, proceed with caution. But, be compassionate, encouraging, and hopeful. People can prevail. The essential question you must answer is this: *Would I want my son becoming this man? Would I want my daughter becoming this woman?* It will happen. Trust me. "What you do speaks so loudly that I cannot hear what you say," says Ralph Waldo Emerson. Heed his advice. The ultimate litmus test? Hang Christmas tree lights together. Tangled wires, blown bulbs, and piercing pine needles reveal our "best."

If you decide to tie the knot, and God gives you an earth angel, take it seriously. Give thanks, cherish the blessing, and sanctify parenthood. At naptime, while holding your partner, watch your child's chest rise and fall. When reading bedtime stories, don't skip pages. Your child will know and realize that your head is elsewhere (even if it's only dreaming about your pillow). Tub time rocks. Get wet. Laugh. Enjoy. When your child crouches to investigate an inchworm, crouch beside him; you can be late to the party. Diapers leak, markers stain, and juice spills. Don't yell. Deal. When your child builds a nativity scene from random Legos and you see the spark for creation, fan the flame. She might be a future engineer. Atheists beware: parenthood makes the invisible visible. Give hugs. Give kisses. Give love. Disney didn't patent fairytales....

Courtship is under siege. Commitment is under siege. The family is under siege. We must fight and protect our homes. We can do this by teaching our children to love deeply. How? Love your spouse, and love your children. Your children will then love themselves—and others. Love begets love.

Sow love. Grow love.

COMMANDMENT IX: *Thou Shalt* GIVE THANKS

Tuesday April 23rd 2019

DR. FROH,

Your class came into my life at the most perfect time. I have always considered myself a happy person, but your class goes so far beyond that. When I took the VIA survey during week 1, it was not surprising that gratitude was my top strength. I am very expressive about how grateful I am for all of the blessings in my life; I have an unusually close family, extending out to my aunts, uncles, and cousins, whom all share my most treasured core values and beliefs; I have been dating the most loving, kind, and thoughtful boyfriend for over 8 years (since I was 13 years old); I have a few close friends whom I cherish so dearly. How could taking this class make my life even greater? I have been Irish Dancing since I was 3 years old. I took my first trip to scotland to compete when I was 4. I have grown up with a passion for Irish Dancing like many others, but a drive and determination like no other. Irish Dancing turned me into a perfectionist because it is subjective in nature. You work and work to go to a competition and be at the mercy of a panel of judges. Unlike sports such as gymnastics, there is no starting value for difficulty or guidelines for deductions. There are a few understood technical requirements such as crossing and turning out your feet and keeping your arms down, but other than that it's up to the judge's opinion. For years I have danced one way in the studio and not as well on stage because I was terrified of being so vulnerable as to give everything I had and the judges to say that's not enough. Here is

where your class comes in. i have been sitting in class
for 85 minutes twice a week soaking up every word.
i tried to internalize everything you've said. i've read
and re-read the books by Fredrickson and Lyubomirsky to
reinforce that i have control over my thoughts and feelings
and how i approach situations. i started to use my top
strength of gratitude and take in the journey to the
competition more than the results. It's the time i get
to spend with people i love and doing what i love
day in and day out that has formed my love of Irish
Dancing. i came home every night thinking about how i
worked as hard as i could that day and i am blessed to
be able to put my body through what i do. i have
grown up dancing for the best school in the world; my
teachers have produced more world champions, top 5 placers,
top 10 placers, and world medal holders than any other
school in history. The best part? They have always believed
in me and told me i should shoot for the stars. They
don't say that to very many people. So i went into
the world championships this year completely
vulnerable. i happened to be wearing a USA sweatshirt
the night before i danced and i smiled to myself
and thought of unconditional self acceptance. No
matter what happened the next day i knew i had given
everything to my training and the rest was out of
my hands. if the result didn't come back in my favor,
i would survive. But that didn't mean i wasn't going to
try. Thanks to you and your class, i am now Third In The World

I can barely write that without tears coming to my eyes. It is beyond even my wildest dream to think I am Ranked the third best Irish Dancer in the entire world. Your class bridged the gap between what I did dancing in class and what I did dancing on stage. Who I am and who I wanna be could finally connect. Yes, that NF line was on purpose. I've been listening to NF on my way to dance for months to get myself in the right head space. Your class has changed my life forever, and not just in Irish Dancing. I will never turn back to who I was before positive psychology came into my life.

All of my gratitude,
Keara

The Commission

Jesus and twelve disciples changed the world. Walking across continents and preaching on hillsides, all while facing persecution, the disciples spread God's message of love. Two millennia later, 31% of people now follow Jesus. Such conversion occurs when a message transforms our being. I hope you experienced even a fraction of such transformation after reading **Thrive**. If so, I give you a commission: please give a copy of **Thrive** to someone, like you and me, limping along life's dusty road and encourage him or her to do likewise. For added effect, attach a paperclip to one of the pages. Ten percent of profits from all book (and merch) sales will go to St. Jude Children's Research Hospital (see website for details). Thus, your gift will create a ripple effect in the lake of love.

Giving **Thrive** to someone might not change the world. It might not make 31% of people flourish. It might not start a movement (though I hope it does). But, it will help you follow God's Commandment to "love your neighbor as yourself" (Matthew, 22:39). And, as you've learned, following commandments provides freedom—and promotes thriving! Everything that exists, including individual and societal change, was caused to exist. Sometimes, by something. Other times, by someone. Let that "someone" be you.

thrive10commandments.com

Timeless Wisdom

PROLOGUE

Matthew, 13:3-8

"A sower went out to sow. And as he sowed, some seed fell on the path, and birds came and ate it up. Some fell on rocky ground, where it had little soil. It sprang up at once because the soil was not deep, and when the sun rose it was scorched, and it withered for lack of roots. Some seed fell among thorns, and the thorns grew up and choked it. But some seed fell on rich soil, and produced fruit, a hundred or sixty or thirtyfold."

Matthew, 22:37

"You shall love the Lord, your God, with all your heart, with all your soul, and with all your mind."

1 Peter, 2:11

"Beloved, I urge you as aliens and sojourners to keep away from worldly desires that wage war against the soul."

Matthew, 6:27-29

"Can any of you by worrying add a single moment to your life-span? Why are you anxious about clothes? Learn from the way the wild flowers grow. They do not work or spin. But I tell you that not even Solomon in all his splendor was clothed like one of them."

Philippians, 2:9

[Jesus' name]…is above every name….

Psalm 139:14

I praise you, so wonderfully you made me; wonderful are your works!

Proverbs, 12:22

Lying lips are an abomination to the Lord, but those who are truthful are his delight.

1 Corinthians, 13:4-7

Love is patient, love is kind. It is not jealous, [love] is not pompous, it is not inflated, it is not rude, it does not seek its own interests, it is not quick-tempered, it does not brood over injury, it does not rejoice over wrongdoing but rejoices with the truth. It bears all things, believes all things, hopes all things, endures all things.

Matthew, 11:28

"Come to me, all you who labor and are burdened, and I will give you rest."

1 Timothy, 4:4

For everything created by God is good, and nothing is to be rejected when received with thanksgiving....

2 Colossians, 1:16

For in him were created all things in heaven and on earth, the visible and the invisible...all things were created through him and for him.

Proverbs, 3:5-6

Trust in the Lord with all your heart, on your own intelligence rely not; In all your ways be mindful of Him, and He will make straight your paths.

Exodus, 31:18

When the Lord had finished speaking to Moses on Mount Sinai, He gave him the two tablets of the commandments, the stone tablets inscribed by God's own finger.

Deuteronomy, 9:9-10

"Meanwhile I stayed on the mountain forty days and forty nights without eating or drinking, till the Lord gave me the two tablets of stone inscribed by God's own finger...."

Proverbs, 4:25

Let your eyes look directly forward, and your gaze be straight before you.

Mark, 6:50

"Take courage, it is I, do not be afraid!"

Jeremiah, 29:13-14

When you look for me, you will find me. Yes, when you seek me with all your heart, you will find me with you....

John, 20:25

"Unless I see the mark of the nails in his hands and put my finger into the nail marks and put my hand into his side, I will not believe."

1 Corinthians, 10:13

No trial has come to you but what is human. God is faithful and will not let you be tried beyond your strength; but with the trial he will also provide a way out, so that you may be able to bear it.

Matthew, 4:9-10

[The Devil said to Him], "All these I shall give you, if you will prostrate yourself and worship me." [Jesus replied], "Get away, Satan! It is written: 'The Lord, your God, shall you worship and Him alone shall you serve.'"

2 Timothy, 1:7

For God has not given us a spirit of timidity, but of power and love and discipline.

Mark, 14:34

"My soul is sorrowful even to death. Remain here and keep watch."

Mark, 14:36

"Abba, Father, all things are possible to you. Take this cup away from me, but not what I will but what you will."

Mark, 8:15

"Watch out, guard against the leaven of the Pharisees and the leaven of Herod."

Matthew, 6:26

"Look at the birds in the sky; they do not sow or reap, they gather nothing into barns, yet your heavenly Father feeds them. Are not you more important than they?"

James, 5:1-6

Come now, you rich, weep and wail over your impending miseries. Your wealth has rotted away, your clothes have become moth-eaten, your gold and silver have corroded, and that corrosion will be a testimony against you; it will devour your flesh like a fire. You have stored up treasure for the last days. Behold, the wages you withheld from the workers who harvested your fields are crying aloud, and the cries of the harvesters have reached the ears of the Lord of hosts. You have lived on earth in luxury and pleasure; you have fattened your hearts for the day of slaughter. You have condemned; you have murdered the righteous one; He offers you no resistance.

Matthew, 11:29-30

"Take my yoke upon you and learn from me, for I am meek and humble of heart; and you will find rest for yourselves. For my yoke is easy, and my burden light."

Mark, 6:8-9

He instructed them to take nothing for the journey but a walking stick— no food, no sack, no money in their belts. They were, however, to wear sandals but not a second tunic.

Matthew, 6:24

"No one can serve two masters. He will either hate one and love the other, or be devoted to one and despise the other. You cannot serve God and mammon."

Mark, 8:36

"What profit is there for one to gain the whole world and forfeit his life?"

1 John, 3:1

See what love the Father has bestowed on us that we may be called the children of God. Yet so we are....

Matthew, 5:37

Let your "Yes" mean "Yes," and your "No" mean "No."

1 John, 3:13

Do not be amazed...if the world hates you.

Luke, 12:7

"Even the hairs of your head have all been counted. Do not be afraid. You are worth more than many sparrows."

1 John, 4:19

We love because he first loved us.

Luke, 15:29-30

"Look, all these years I served you and not once did I disobey your orders; yet, you never gave me even a young goat to feast on with my friends. But when your son returns who swallowed up your property with prostitutes, for him you slaughtered the fattened calf."

Luke, 15:31-32

"My son, you are here with me always...But now we must celebrate and rejoice, because your brother...was lost and has been found."

1 Peter, 5:8

Be sober and vigilant. Your opponent the Devil is prowling around like a roaring lion looking for [someone] to devour.

Psalm 27:1

The Lord is my light and my salvation; whom do I fear? The Lord is my life's refuge; of whom am I afraid?

Matthew, 26:61

This man said, "I can destroy the temple of God and within three days rebuild it."

Mark, 14:62

"I am."

Matthew, 27:19

"Have nothing to do with that righteous man. I suffered much in a dream today because of him."

Genesis, 3:10

"I was afraid, because I was naked…."

John, 13:34

"I give you a new commandment: love one another. As I have loved you, so you also should love one another."

Matthew, 22:39

"You shall love your neighbor as yourself."

Luke, 23:34

"Father, forgive them, they know not what they do…."

Luke, 23:43

"Amen, I say to you, today you will be with me in Paradise."

John, 14:6

"I am the way and the truth and the life…."

Jeremiah, 33:3

Call to me, and I will answer you; I will tell you things great beyond reach of your knowledge.

Mark, 6:31

"Come away by yourselves to a deserted place and rest a while...."

Zechariah, 8:5

The city shall be filled with boys and girls playing in her streets.

John, 12:24

"Unless a grain of wheat falls to the ground and dies, it remains just a grain of wheat; but if it dies, it produces much fruit."

Acts, 9:4-6

"Saul, Saul, why are you persecuting me?... I am Jesus...get up and go into the city and you will be told what you must do."

Acts, 9:17

"Saul, my brother, the Lord has sent me...that you may regain your sight and be filled with the Holy Spirit."

Acts, 13:47

"[He became] an instrument of salvation to the ends of the earth."

Acts, 20:23-24

"The Holy Spirit has been warning me that imprisonment and hardships await me. Yet I consider life of no importance to me, if only I may finish my course and the ministry that I received from the Lord Jesus, to bear witness to the gospel of God's grace."

Acts, 21:13-14

"What are you doing, weeping and breaking my heart? I am prepared not only to be bound but even to die in Jerusalem for the name of the Lord Jesus…The Lord's will be done."

1 Corinthians, 6:19

Do you not know that your body is a temple of the Holy Spirit within you…?

John, 1:3

All things came to be through him, and without him nothing came to be.

Romans, 12:4-5

For as in one body we have many parts, and all the parts do not have the same function, so we, though many, are one body in Christ and individually parts of one another.

Psalm 118:24

This is the day the Lord has made; let us rejoice in it and be glad.

Isaiah, 9:1

The people who walked in darkness have seen a great light; upon those who dwelt in the land of gloom a light has shown.

Luke, 1:35, 37

"The Holy Spirit will come upon you, and the power of the Most High will overshadow you. Therefore the child to be born will be called holy, the Son of God…for nothing will be impossible for God."

Luke, 1:38

"Behold, I am the handmaid of the Lord. May it be done to me according to your word…."

Romans, 12:2

Do not conform yourselves to this age but be transformed by the renewal of your mind, that you may discern what is the will of God, what is good and pleasing and perfect.

Psalm 118:29

Give thanks to the Lord, who is good, whose love endures forever.

Genesis, 1:27

God created man in his image; in the divine image he created him; male and female he created them.

Jeremiah, 1:5
Before I formed you in the womb I knew you....

Revelation, 4:11
"For you created all things; because of your will they came to be and were created."

James, 1:16-18
Do not be deceived, my beloved brothers: all good giving and every perfect gift is from above, coming down from the Father of lights, with whom there is no alteration or shadow caused by change. He willed to give us birth by the word of truth that we may be a kind of firstfruits of his creatures.

Psalm 139:13-16
> You formed my inmost being;
> you knit me in my mother's womb...
> My very self you knew;
> my bones were not hidden from you,
> When I was being made in secret,
> fashioned as in the depths of the earth.
> Your eyes foresaw my actions;
> in your book all are written down;
> my days were shaped, before one came to be.

Luke, 17:17-18
"Ten were cleansed, were they not? Where are the other nine? Has none but this foreigner returned to give thanks to God?"

Luke, 17:19
"Stand up and go; your faith has saved you."

Matthew, 23:25-28

"You cleanse the outside of cup and dish, but inside they are full of plunder and self-indulgence. Blind Pharisee, cleanse first the inside of the cup, so that the outside may also be clean…You are like whitewashed tombs, which appear beautiful on the outside, but inside are full of dead men's bones and every kind of filth. Even so, on the outside you appear righteous, but inside you are filled with hypocrisy and evildoing."

Ephesians, 5:15-20

"Watch carefully then how you live, not as foolish persons but as wise, making the most of the opportunity, because the days are evil. Therefore, do not continue in ignorance, but try to understand what is the will of the Lord…be filled with the Spirit, addressing one another [in] psalms and hymns and spiritual songs, singing and playing to the Lord in your hearts, giving thanks always and for everything…."

Job, 3:24-26

For sighing comes more readily to me than food, and my groans well forth like water. For what I fear overtakes me, and what I shrink from comes upon me. I have no peace nor ease; I have no rest, for trouble comes!

Mark, 1:16-20

As he passed by the Sea of Galilee, he saw Simon and his brother Andrew casting their nets into the sea; they were fishermen. Jesus said to them, "Come after me, and I will make you fishers of men." Then they left their nets and followed him. He walked along a little farther and saw James, the son of Zebedee, and his brother John. They too were in a boat mending their nets. Then he called to them. So they left their father Zebedee in the boat along with the hired men and followed him.

Genesis, 9:16

"As the [rain]bow appears in the clouds, I will see it and recall the everlasting covenant that I have established between God and all living beings...."

Luke, 12:48

"Much will be required of the person entrusted with much, and still more will be demanded of the person entrusted with more."

Matthew, 7:7-8

"Ask and it will be given to you; seek and you will find; knock and the door will be opened to you. For everyone who asks, receives; and the one who seeks, finds; and to the one who knocks, the door will be opened."

Mark, 14:25

"Amen, I say to you, I shall not drink again the fruit of the vine until the day when I drink it new in the kingdom of God."

Mark, 15:23

They gave him wine drugged with myrrh, but he did not take it.

John, 19:28

"I thirst."

John, 19:29

[They] put a sponge soaked in wine on a sprig of hyssop and put it up to his mouth.

Isaiah, 53:7

Though he was harshly treated, he submitted and opened not his mouth; Like a lamb led to the slaughter or a sheep before the shearers, he was silent and opened not his mouth.

Exodus, 12:21-22

"Go and procure lambs for your families, and slaughter them as Passover victims. Then take a bunch of hyssop, and dipping it in the blood that is in the basin, sprinkle the lintel and the two doorposts with this blood...."

John, 19:30

"It is finished...."

EPILOGUE

Matthew, 5:1-12

When he saw the crowds, he went up the mountain, and after he sat down, his disciples came to him. He began to teach them, saying:

> "Blessed are the poor in spirit,
> for theirs is the kingdom of heaven.
> Blessed are they who mourn,
> for they will be comforted.
> Blessed are the meek,
> for they will inherit the land.
> Blessed are they who hunger and thirst for righteousness,
> for they will be satisfied.
> Blessed are the merciful,
> for they will be shown mercy.
> Blessed are the clean of heart,
> for they will see God.
> Blessed are the peacemakers,
> for they will be called children of God.

Blessed are they who are persecuted for the sake of righteousness,
for theirs is the kingdom of heaven.
Blessed are you when they insult you and utter every kind of evil
against you [falsely] because of me.
Rejoice and be glad, for your reward will be great in heaven...."

Revelation, 2:10

"Do not be afraid of anything that you are going to suffer. Indeed, the
Devil will throw some of you into prison, that you may be tested, and
you will face an ordeal for ten days. Remain faithful until death, and I
will give you the crown of life."

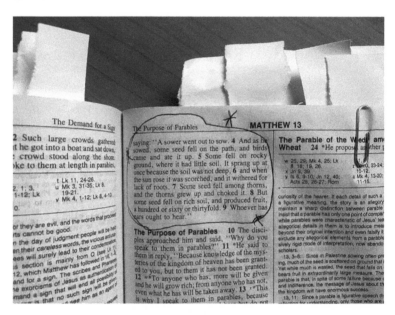

✟   Scripture quotations are from the *New American Bible (2003): Catholic Reader's Edition NABRE.* St. Jerome Press.

ACKNOWLEDGMENTS

Parental support and warmth is critical to thrive. Loving parents look for monsters under our bed. They pack an extra cookie when we have an exam. They meet us by the tree after practice. If we're really blessed, they help us write our story and find our mission. Thank you, God, for loving me. Thank you for making me return to your pasture. The grass actually is greener.

Belle kissed me before the last rose petal fell. Nonetheless, I'm still sometimes a beast. Thank you, Cara, for loving me anyway. Thank you for helping me protect my time and widgets to read, think, and write. Thank you for helping me polish my thoughts and tolerating my OCD by reading consecutive drafts—even when only one word changed or when I was trying to trim a syllable. Thank you for taking notes while I was driving and giving me the last Twizzler. Thank you for keeping my Acadia and Shenandoah mugs clean and bearing with my bear pants. "Overwhelming feelings of love." Good news, hun. The laundry fairy returned.

Life is better with good travel companions. They make life exciting, joyous, and worth living. To my children, James and Julianne, you continue doing more for me than I do for you. Thank you for dragging me out of my office to braille the world. You replenished my widgets and released me from pride's prison. James, thank you for giving me Commandment VIII and helping me conceptualize and create The Skeleton. Thank you also for making me pause to stargaze, watch meteors, and play dominoes. You soar like an Eagle. I love you, buddy. "Always and forever." Julianne, thank you for drawing and teaching me about the roadmap to love deeply. Thank you for taking me to pet dogs. Thank you for asking me to brush your hair. I'm excited about our adventure with Harper. "I love you to the moon—and back, and back, and back."

God blessed me with a loving family and support system. John and Kathy, thank you for deeming me "stocking worthy." You gave an orphan a home. Kevin, thank you for always asking questions and letting me crash at your pad to write. I'm good at making predictions. But, I never predicted that the crazy little brother and quiet boyfriend would become partners on the quest to thrive. Love ya, man! Colleen, thank you for giving me nasty looks. I love how we always keep it *real*. The Ryan family, thank you for remembering pretzels and accepting defeat in Kan Jam and Cornhole. You inspire others to be generous and humble. Professor William Thieben, thank you for seeing God's gifts within me. I was lost, but now I'm found. "You made my day." Father Peter, Father Francois, Deacons Allan, Dave (R.I.P.), Jean, and Jim, and my church brothers and sisters—Anita M., Barbara C., Celeste B., Diane Y., Lorraine L., Mike K., Mike. M., Neil C. and family, Phyllis P., and Rose C.—thank you for helping me discover my mission. Much love. Dr. Dan Boyle and Dr. Spiro Theoharakis, thank you for keeping my brain healthy. I hope to never again meet the Lizard King. Karen, thank you for calling me "Doll," "Babe," and "Sweetie." You make me feel special, "Sugar."

As stated in Commandment VI, *"If friends are life's treasure, I'm rich like King Solomon."* Sal, thank you for reading everything and making our monthly meetings a big rock. Thank you also for helping me find and follow Jesus. Without your encouragement and love, I'd still be worshipping science. Matt, thank you for nurturing my creativity and suggesting I provide practical tips to thrive. Thank you also for wiping my tears after I read you the lead to *Thou Shalt Love Deeply*. You're a Care Bear. Keith, thank you for family dinners and always calling at the right time. Imagine if we never had potato sack races. Todd, thank you for almost pushing me to mania. Thank you also for encouraging me to leave academia and become a rapper. I'll dedicate to you my first sold out stadium. Joe and Martha, thank you for being adventurous. I look forward to snowshoeing with Sasquatch. Helen and Andrew, thank you for listening—*really* listening. You make me feel understood, valued, and loved. Matt and Erin, thank you for being silly. "I don't even wanna know you're here!"

If you're lucky like me, your work buddies are also your buddies. Norm, thank you for nudging me to work with emerging adults and covering the clinic during my sabbatical. Thank you even more for always ending our meetings with a hug. Bill, thank you for our "*Walk 'n Talks*," though our joints need oil like the Tin Man. You inspire me to live as if I'm dying. To my Hofstra campus crew, thank you for supporting me. Bob, thank you for checking if I was alive; Carol, thank you for keeping your seat warm; Eugene, thank you for cracking jokes; Kim, thank you for always asking about my family; Lola, thank you for suggesting that I change "my" commandments to "these" commandments; Paul, thank you for working more so I could write more; Sergei, thank you for covering my classes and encouraging me to leave my closet.

We rise and fall to our team's functioning. Thankfully, I only play with all-stars. Tom, thank you for teaching me about character development, screenwriting, and producing. Thank you for teaching me about leads and closings. Thank you for tolerating migraines while helping me trim the fat—even when all that remained was bones. Thank you also for treating this book like your own. I look forward to reciprocating. Most importantly, thank you for your friendship. Leah, thank you for your digital magic. Amidst your own chaos, you always prioritized my work. Thanks, soul sister. Jess, thank you for researching material for my book and solving every mystery. You must be related to Sherlock Holmes. Anthony, thank you for editing earlier drafts. To the revolution! Brian Cirillo, thank you for helping me share my struggles using my tattoos. Shout out to *NY360 Tours & Digital Media*! Ashleigh, Gianna, Joe, and Mairead, thank you for sharing your story. You'll inspire others to be courageous and vulnerable—as you've inspired me.

This is my first book as an indie author. The learning curve was steep, and I got pummeled. Eventually, I figured it out with help from some amazing, talented people. Laura Antonioli, thank you for your crisp typesetting, beautiful interior design, and care. You bring new meaning to the saying, "You can't judge a book by its cover." Actually, you also created a fabulous cover. So, I guess you can judge a book by its cover! Kit Brookman, thank you for your masterful proofreading. There are levels to the game—and you're King of the Hill! Robin Phillips at *Author Help*, thank you for uploading my book and teaching me about self-publishing. You pulled my book from the wreckage and helped give it life. Guy Haines from *Haines Creative*, thank you for your wizardry with building my website and designing my merch. People will now know the power of the paperclip!

Finally, to my readers. Writing this book was cathartic and therapeutic. Thank you for listening. You've earned your co-pay. Also, by purchasing this book, you donated to St. Jude Children's Research Hospital. Now, we're no longer strangers. We're forever bonded by compassion, generosity, and love. Nice meeting you. Hopefully, I'll see you again.

CONTACT

To contact me, send a note to the address below via USPS, the Pony Express, or hawk. If you'd like a response, please include a self-addressed stamped envelope. I'm excited to read about your story.

```
          Jeffrey Froh
   1 Hewitt Square, Suite 163
  East Northport, NY 11731-2519
```

BELIEVE

Cornling Publishers   1/15/21

Hey there, Jeffrey

My company, Cornling Publishers, heard that you have a book
called "Thrive." My company is interested in your book. We do
understand that you do not have a big "platform." My company
tries to give "low-platformed people" a chance. If we can't work
something out I wish you luck on finding publishers.

Sincerely,

Frank Rasse and Cornling Publishers

NOTES

Prologue

8   *Envy and avarice are covetous desires...*Libreria Editrice Vaticana. (1994). *Catechism of the Catholic Church.*

14 *God believes sexual desire for someone besides your spouse...*Libreria Editrice Vaticana. (1994). *Catechism of the Catholic Church.*

Commandment I: *Thou Shalt Have Direction*

21 *A recent survey of 1,700...*Ekins, E. (2019, September 24). *What Americans think about poverty, wealth, and work.* Cato Institute. https://www.cato.org/publications/survey-reports/what-americans-think-about-poverty-wealth-work#who-finds-most-meaning-purpose

21 *Imagine there's a large empty container...*Covey, S. R. (2020). *The 7 habits of highly effective people.* Simon & Schuster.

26 *According to a recent Pew Research Center survey...Religion in America: U.S. religious data, demographics and statistics.* Pew Research Center's Religion & Public Life Project. (2020, September 9). https://www.pewforum.org/religious-landscape-study/religious-family/atheist/age-distribution/18-29/#demographic-information

26 *per the American Freshman Survey* (as cited in)*...*Twenge, J. M. (2017). *iGen: Why today's super-connected kids are growing up less rebellious, more tolerant, less happy—and completely unprepared for adulthood—and what that means for the rest of us.* Atria Books.

29 *two main obstacles to being grateful...*Emmons, R. A. (2007). *THANKS! How practicing gratitude can make you happier.* Houghton Mifflin.

31 *The number seven is biblically significant...*Larkin, Rev. C. (1919). *The book of Revelation.* Pantianos Classics.

Commandment II: *Thou Shalt Stay Focused*

39 *Almost 80% of New Year's resolutions...*Norcross, J. C., & Vangarelli, D. J. (1988). The resolution solution: Longitudinal examination of New Year's change attempts. *Journal of Substance Abuse, 1*(2), 127-134.

43   *Contrast this to scrolling social media daily...*Perrin, A. (2020, May 30). *Social media usage: 2005-2015.* Pew Research Center: Internet, Science & Tech.   https://www.pewresearch.org/internet/2015/10/08/social-network-ing-usage-2005-2015/

43   *the average time spent is 3 hours...GlobalWebIndex's flagship report on the latest trends in social media.* globalwebindex. (2018). https://www.global-webindex.com/hubfs/Downloads/Social-H2-2018-report.pdf

43   *gaming 2-12 hours weekly...*Limelight Networks. (2019, March 15). *Market research: The state of online GAMING – 2019.* Market Research: The State of Online Gaming – 2019. https://www.limelight.com/resources/white-paper/state-of-online-gaming-2019/

43   *binge-watching shows at least several times monthly...*Morning Consult Poll & The Hollywood Reporter . (2018). https://morningconsult.com/wp-con-tent/uploads/2018/11/181049_crosstabs_HOLLYWOOD_REPORTER_Adults-TV-Watchers_FINAL-1.pdf

44   *Challenging our mind and body builds...*Thuret, S. (2019). *You can grow new brain cells: Here's how. TED.* https://www.ted.com/talks/sandrine_thuret_you_can_grow_new_brain_cells_here_s_how?language=en

44   *whereas excessive screen time fosters depression...*Madhav, K. C., Sherchand, S. P., & Sherchan, S. (2017). Association between screen time and depres-sion among U.S. adults. *Preventive Medicine Reports, 8,* 67-71. https://doi.org/10.1016/j.pmedr.2017.08.005

44   *consider Benjamin Franklin's daily schedule...*Franklin, B. (1886). *The auto-biography of Benjamin Franklin.* Cassell.

44   *Neurogenesis occurs when new brain cells...Adult neurogenesis.* Queensland Brain Institute. (2018, March 14). https://qbi.uq.edu.au/brain-basics/brain-physiology/adult-neurogenesis.

44   *Exercise, sex, and creative and novel pursuits foster hippocampal neurogene-sis...*Blackmore, D. G., Vukovic, J., Waters, M. J., & Bartlett, P. F. (2012). GH mediates exercise-dependent activation of SVZ neural precursor cells in aged mice. *PLoS ONE, 7*(11). https://doi.org/10.1371/journal.pone.0049912
Thuret, S. (2019). *You can grow new brain cells: Here's how. TED.* https://www.ted.com/talks/sandrine_thuret_you_can_grow_new_brain_cells_here_s_how?language=en

44 *whereas binge-watching shows...*Fancourt, D., & Steptoe, A. (2019). Television viewing and cognitive decline in older age: Findings from the English Longitudinal Study of Ageing. *Scientific Reports, 9*, 2851. https://doi.org/10.1038/s41598-019-39354-4

Hoang, T. D., Reis, J., Zhu, N., Jacobs, Jr., D. R., Launer, L. J., Whitmer, R. A., Sidney, S., & Yaffe, K. (2016). Effect of early adult patterns of physical activity and television viewing on midlife cognitive function. *JAMA Psychiatry, 73*(1), 73-79. https://doi.org/10.1001/jamapsychiatry.2015.2468

44 *even shrinking the hippocampus by 10%...*Ahdidan, J., Hviid, L. B., Chakravarty, M. M., Ravnkilde, B., Rosenberg, R., Rodell, A., Stødkilde-Jørgensen, A., & Videbech, P. (2011). Longitudinal MR study of brain structure and hippocampus volume in major depressive disorder. *Acta Psychiatrica Scandinavica, 123*(3), 211-219. https://doi.org/10.1111/j.1600-0447.2010.01644.x

46 *Task-switching, like responding to a text...*Madore, K. P., & Wagner, A. D. (2019). Multicosts of multitasking. *Cerebrum*, PMID: 32206165

46 *Even if we're only distracted for several tenths of a second...*American Psychological Association. (2006, March 20). *Multitasking: Switching costs.* American Psychological Association. https://www.apa.org/research/action/multitask

Meyer, D. E., & Kieras, D. E. (1997a). A computational theory of executive cognitive processes and multiple-task performance: Part 1. Basic mechanisms. *Psychological Review, 104*, 3-65. https://doi.org/10.1037/0033-295x.104.1.3

Meyer, D. E., & Kieras, D. E. (1997b). A computational theory of executive cognitive processes and multiple-task performance: Part 2. Accounts of psychological refractory-period phenomena. *Psychological Review, 104*, 749-791. https://doi.org/10.1037/0033-295X.104.4.749

Rubinstein, J. S., Meyer, D. E., & Evans, J. E. (2001). Executive control of cognitive processes in task switching. *Journal of Experimental Psychology: Human Perception and Performance, 27*, 763-797. https://doi.org/10.1037//0096-1523.27.4.763

50 *what psychologist, Dr. Mihaly Csikszentmihalyi, called "flow"...*Csikszentmihalyi, M. (1997). *Flow: The psychology of optimal experience.* Harper Perennial.

52 *Benjamin Franklin thought similarly...*Franklin, B. (1886). *The autobiography of Benjamin Franklin.* Cassell.

Commandment III: *Thou Shalt Live Simply*

59 *In the 1970s, people saw about 500 ads daily*...Caitlin, C. (2007, February 01). *Cutting through advertising clutter.* Retrieved from https://www.cbsnews.com/news/cutting-through-advertising-clutter/

59 *Now, we see about 4,000-10,000 ads daily*...Simpson, J. (2017, August 25). *Council post: Finding brand success in the digital world.* Forbes. https://www.forbes.com/sites/forbesagencycouncil/2017/08/25/finding-brand-success-in-the-digital-world/?sh=7e8c9b42626e

59 *Our culture even influences eating disorder prevalence*...Markey, C. N. (2004). Culture and the development of eating disorders: A tripartite model. *Eating Disorders, 12*(2), 139-156. https://doi.org/10.1080/10640260490445041

60 *people in wealthier neighborhoods*...Zhang, J. W., Howell, R. T., & Howell, C. J. (2016). Living in wealthy neighborhoods increases material desires and maladaptive consumption. *Journal of Consumer Culture, 16*(1), 297-316. https://doi.org/10.1177/1469540514521085

61 *The average American household income*...Easterbrook, G. (2004). *The progress paradox: How life gets better while people feel worse.* Random House.

Myers, D. G. (2000). *The American paradox: Spiritual hunger in an age of plenty.* Yale University Press.

61 *per a USA Today article from 2016*...Gardner, G. (2016, March 4). *Report: More new cars leased than ever.* USA Today. https://www.usatoday.com/story/money/cars/2016/03/03/report-more-new-cars-leased-than-ever/81286732/

61 *between 2011 and 2014*...Pratt, L., Brody, D., & Gu, Q. (2017). *Antidepressant use among persons aged 12 and over: United States, 2011–2014.* https://www.cdc.gov/nchs/data/databriefs/db283.pdf

62 *Materialistic people have struggles beyond depression*...Dittmar, H., Bond, R., Hurst, M., & Kasser, T. (2014). The relationship between materialism and personal well-being: A meta-analysis. *Journal of Personality and Social Psychology, 107*(5), 879–924. https://doi.org/10.1037/a0037409

Kasser, T. (2002). *The high price of materialism.* MIT Press.

Kasser, T. (2016). Materialistic values and goals. *Annual Review of Psychology, 67,* 489-514. https://www.annualreviews.org/doi/10.1146/annurev-psych-122414-033344

62 *increasing their loneliness and affecting their health...*Holt-Lunstad, J., Smith, T. B., Baker, M., Harris, T., & Stephenson, D. (2015). Loneliness and social isolation as risk factors for mortality: A meta-analytic review. *Perspectives on Psychological Science, 10*(2), 227-237. https://doi.org/10.1177/1745691614568352

64 *Unless you prolonged your newfound happiness...*Brickman, P., Coates, D., & Janoff-Bulman, R. (1978). Lottery winners and accident victims: Is happiness relative? *Journal of Personality and Social Psychology, 36*(8), 917–927. https://doi.org/10.1037/0022-3514.36.8.917

Diener, E., Lucas, R. E., Scollon, C. N. (2006). Beyond the hedonic treadmill: Revising the adaptation theory of well-being. *American Psychologist, 61*(4), 305–314. https://doi.org/10.1037/0003-066X.61.4.305

64 *The hedonic treadmill serves...*Lyubomirsky, S. (2012). Hedonic adaptation to positive and negative experiences. In S. Folkman (Ed.), *The Oxford Handbook of Stress, Health, and Coping* (pp. 200-226). Oxford University Press. https://doi.org/10.1093/oxfordhb/9780195375343.013.0011

64 *In a posthumous tribute featured in Time magazine...*Barr, A., & Gupta, P. (2011, October 9). *Steve Jobs on biography: 'I wanted my kids to know me'.* The Sydney Morning Herald. https://www.smh.com.au/technology/steve-jobs-on-biography-i-wanted-my-kids-to-know-me-20111010-1lgef.html.

65 *beyond leaving our basic human needs...*Kasser, T. (2016). Materialistic values and goals. *Annual Review of Psychology, 67*, 489-514. https://www.annualreviews.org/doi/10.1146/annurev-psych-122414-033344

65 *The dopamine flooding our brain...*Tomkins, D. M., Sellers, E. M. (2001). Addiction and the brain: The role of neurotransmitters in the cause and treatment of drug dependence. *Canadian Medical Association Journal, 164*(6), 817-821. PMID: 11276551

65 *Appreciation is the strongest antidote...*Lyubomirsky, S. (2012). Hedonic adaptation to positive and negative experiences. In S. Folkman (Ed.), *The Oxford handbook of stress, health, and coping* (pp. 200-226). Oxford University Press. https://doi.org/10.1093/oxfordhb/9780195375343.013.0011

65 *Self-Determination Theory (SDT) maintains...*Ryan, R. M., & Deci, E. L. (2000). Self-determination theory and the facilitation of intrinsic motivation, social development, and well-being. *American psychologist, 55*(1), 68-78. https://doi.org/10.1037/0003-066X.55.1.68

66   *Living simply gives us more time and widgets*...Elgin, D. (1993). *Voluntary simplicity: Toward a way of life that is outwardly simple, inwardly rich.* HarperCollins Publishers.

Commandment IV: *Thou Shalt Accept Thyself*

78   *Rejection stings*...Cawley, R., Pontin, E. E., Touhey, J., Sheehy, K., & Taylor, P. J. (2019). What is the relationship between rejection and self-harm or suicidality in adulthood? *Journal of Affective Disorders, 242*(1), 123-134. https://doi.org/10.1016/j.jad.2018.08.082

78   *Many factors contribute to how we cope with rejection*...DeWall, C. N., & Bushman, B. J. (2011). Social acceptance and rejection: The sweet and the bitter. *Psychological Science, 20*(4), 256-260. https://doi.org/10.1177/0963721411417545

78   *Something thought to foster greater educational attainment*...Baumeister, R. F., Campbell, J. D., Krueger, J. I., & Vohs, K. D. (2003). Does high self-esteem cause better performance, interpersonal success, happiness, or healthier lifestyles? *Psychological Science in the Public Interest, 4,* 1–44. https://doi.org/10.1111/1529-1006.01431

Harris, M. A., & Orth, U. (2020). The link between self-esteem and social relationships: A meta-analysis of longitudinal studies. *Journal of Personality and Social Psychology, 119*(6), 1459-1477. http://dx.doi.org/10.1037/pspp0000265

78   *Instead, it fosters earlier sex and substance use*...Baumeister, R. F., Smart, L., & Boden, J. M. (1996). Relation of threatened egotism to violence and aggression: The dark side of high self-esteem. *Psychological Review, 103,* 5–33. https://doi.org/10.1037/0033-295x.103.1.5

78   *Society convinced your parents*...Twenge, J. M., & Campbell, W. K. (2009). *The narcissism epidemic: Living in the age of entitlement.* Atria Paperback.

79   *Consider the 2019 college admissions scandal*...Medina, J., Benner, K., & Taylor, K. (2019, March 12). *Actresses, business leaders and other wealthy parents charged in U.S. college entry fraud.* The New York Times. https://www.nytimes.com/2019/03/12/us/college-admissions-cheating-scandal.html

79   *Self-esteem—counterfeit or authentic—creates needless pain*...Baumeister, R. F., Smart, L., & Boden, J. M. (1996). Relation of threatened egotism to violence and aggression: The dark side of high self-esteem. *Psychological Review, 103,* 5–33. https://doi.org/10.1037/0033-295x.103.1.5

79 *self-esteem is tenuous, outcome dependent*...Hauck, P. A. (1991). *Overcoming the rating game: Beyond self-love—beyond self-esteem.* Westminster/John Knox Press.

95 *Listen for your "if...then" beliefs*...For a scholarly account, read: Ellis, A. (1994). *Reason and emotion in psychotherapy: A comprehensive method of treating human disturbances.* Birch Lane Press.

For a lay account, read: Ellis, A., & Harper, R. A. (1961). *A guide to rational living.* Wilshire Books.

95 *Do shame attacks*...Ellis, A. (1991). *How to control your anxiety before it controls you.* Kensington Publishing Corp.

Commandment V: *Thou Shalt Be Real*

97 *Nathan grew up in Gladwin, Michigan*...NF. (2015). *Mansion.* Capitol Christian Music Group.

NF. (2016). *Therapy session.* Capitol Christian Music Group.

NF. (2017). *Perception.* NF Real Music.

NF. (2019). *The search.* NF Real Music.

97 *Nathan's friends supported him during these dark times*...NF. (2015). *Mansion.* Capitol Christian Music Group.

97 *Eventually, he lost focus at work and was fired*...NME. (2020). NF in Conversation. *YouTube.* https://www.youtube.com/watch?v=3Nvclo48GPI

98 *Sheep are social*...Cobb, R. (1999, January 22). *An introduction to sheep behavior.* http://livestocktrail.illinois.edu/sheepnet/paperDisplay.cfm?ContentID=1

99 *Dr. Carl Rogers, psychologist and leader*...Rogers, C. R. (1961). *On becoming a person: A therapist's view of psychotherapy.* Houghton Mifflin Company.

99 *Everyone struggles being real*...Brown, B. (2010). *The power of vulnerability.* TEDxHouston. https://www.ted.com/talks/brene_brown_on_vulnerability

100 *Authentic people are typically calm*...Goldman, B. M., & Kernis, M. H. (2002). The role of authenticity in healthy psychological functioning and subjective well-being. *Annals of the American Psychotherapy Association, 5*(6), 18-20.

Wood, A. M., Linley, P. A., Maltby, J., Baliousis, M., & Joseph, S. (2008). The authentic personality: A theoretical and empirical conceptualization and the development of the Authenticity Scale. *Journal of Counseling Psychology, 55*(3), 385-399. https://doi.org/10.1037/0022-0167.55.3.385

100 *synchronous traits, behaviors, and emotions...*Hayes, S. C. (2020). *A liberated mind: How to pivot toward what matters.* Avery Publishing.

Ryan, R. M., & Deci, E. L. (2000). Self-determination theory and the facilitation of intrinsic motivation, social development, and well-being. *American Psychologist, 55*(1), 68-78. https://doi.org/10.1037//0003-066x.55.1.68

100 *When we're real, so are our relationships...*Brown, B. (2010). *The gifts of imperfection: Let go of who you think you're supposed to be and embrace who you are.* Hazelden Publishing.

100 *Longitudinal research...*Boyraz, G., Waits, J. B., & Felix, V. A. (2014). Authenticity, life satisfaction, and distress: A longitudinal analysis. *Journal of Counseling Psychology, 61*(3), 498-505. https://doi.org/10.1037/cou0000031

101 *courage is telling our story from our heart's abyss...*Brown, B. (2012). *Daring greatly: How the courage to be vulnerable transforms the way we live, love, parent and lead.* Gotham Books.

101 *Originals are priceless, while replicas have little value...*USA Art News. (2021, January 31). *The most expensive artworks ever sold at auction.* https://usaartnews.com/art-market/the-most-expensive-artworks-ever-sold-at-auction

124 *for people truly desperate for connection, it's worth death...*Brighton, E. (2020). *True crime stories: Deadly love triangles.*

Love, H. A., Nalbone, D. P., Hecker, L. L., Sweeney, K. A., & Dharnidharka, P. (2018). Suicidal risk following the termination of romantic relationships. *Crisis, 39*(3), 166–174. https://doi.org/10.1027/0227-5910/a000484

124 *Pilate, therefore, ordered Jesus' scourging...*Mansfield, S. (2013). *Killing Jesus: The unknown conspiracy behind the world's most famous execution.* Worthy Publishing.

Commandment VI: *Thou Shalt Love Deeply*

131 *In the 1960s, psychologist, Dr. Harry Harlow...*Harlow, H. F., Dodsworth, R. O., & Harlow, M. K. (1965). Total social isolation in monkeys. *Proceedings of the National Academy of Sciences of the United States of America.* Retrieved from https://www.ncbi.nlm.nih.gov/pmc/articles/PMC285801/pdf/pnas00159-0105.pdf

Harlow's classic studies revealed the importance of maternal contact. Association for Psychological Science - APS. (2018, June 20). https://www.psychologicalscience.org/publications/observer/obsonline/harlows-classic-studies-revealed-the-importance-of-maternal-contact.html

131 *Elephants hug each other, play together...*Moss, C. J., & Poole, J. H. (1983). Relationships and social structure in African elephants. In R. A. Hinde (Ed.), *Primate social relationships: An integrated approach* (pp. 315–325). Blackwell Scientific Publications.

131 *Birds, like the Brewer's sparrows...*Halley, M. R., Holmes, A. L., & Robinson, W. D. (2015). Biparental incubation and allofeeding at nests of sagebrush Brewer's sparrows. *Journal of Field Ornithology, 86*(2), 153–162. https://doi.org/10.1111/jofo.12098

131 *and chinstrap penguins...*Mori, Y., Kokubun, N., Shin, H.-C., & Takahashi, A. (2010). An observation of between-mates feeding behaviour in chick-guarding chinstrap penguins. *Polar Biology, 33*(10), 1437–1438. https://doi.org/10.1007/s00300-010-0842-8

131 *Mother-baby blue whale pairs caress one another...*Fothergill, A. (2012). *Planet earth as you've never seen it before: The complete series* [Film; DVD]. BBC Video.

131 *Spindle neurons are brain cells...*Chen, I. (2009, June 1). Brain cells for socializing. Smithsonian.com. https://www.smithsonianmag.com/science-nature/brain-cells-for-socializing-133855450/

132 *we, too, learn how to love from our parents...*Levine, A., & Heller, R. (2010). *Attached: The new science of adult attachment and how it can help you find—and keep—love.* TarcherPerigee.

Peck, M. S. (1978). *The road less traveled: A new psychology of love, traditional values and spiritual growth.* Simon & Schuster.

135 *Thriving relationships require people to have similar values...*Gottman, J., & Silver, N. (1999). *The seven principles for making marriage work: A practical guide from the country's foremost relationship expert.* Harmony Books.

136 *Romantic BFFs report more teamwork...*Grote, N. K., & Frieze, I. H. (1994). The measurement of friendship-based love in intimate relationships. *Personal Relationships, 1*(3), 275–300. https://doi.org/10.1111/j.1475-6811.1994.tb00066.x

Hecht, M. L., Marston, P. J., & Larkey, L. K. (1994). Love ways and relationship quality in heterosexual relationships. *Journal of Social and Personal Relationships, 11*(1), 25–43. https://doi.org/10.1177/0265407594111002

Sheets, V. L. (2013). Passion for life. *Journal of Social and Personal Relationships, 31*(7), 958–974. https://doi.org/10.1177/0265407513515618

Sprecher, S., & Regan, P. C. (1998). Passionate and companionate love in courting and young married couples. *Sociological Inquiry, 68*(2), 163–185. https://doi.org/10.1111/j.1475-682x.1998.tb00459.x

VanderDrift, L. E., Wilson, J. E., & Agnew, C. R. (2012). On the benefits of valuing being friends for nonmarital romantic partners. *Journal of Social and Personal Relationships, 30*(1), 115–131. https://doi.org/10.1177/0265407512453009

136 *Loving relationships take considerable time...*Hall, J. A. (2018). How many hours does it take to make a friend? *Journal of Social and Personal Relationships, 36*(4), 1278–1296. https://doi.org/10.1177/0265407518761225

138 *People are only listening to each other...*Gottman, J. M. (2011). *The science of trust: Emotional attunement for couples.* W.W. Norton & Company.

138 *our response to good news better predicts relationship satisfaction...*Gable, S. L., Reis, H. T., Impett, E. A., & Asher, E. R. (2004). What do you do when things go right? The intrapersonal and interpersonal benefits of sharing positive events. *Journal of Personality and Social Psychology, 87*(2), 228–245. https://doi.org/10.1037/0022-3514.87.2.228

138 *Trust is the biggest stress buster in relationships...*Gottman, J. M. (2011). *The science of trust: Emotional attunement for couples.* W.W. Norton & Company.

139 *The average American has $38,000 in personal debt...*Northwestern Mutual. (2018). *2018 Planning & Progress Study: Deep dive into debt.* https://filecache.mediaroom.com/mr5mr_nwmutual/178219/Debt%20deck%208.3.pdf

140 *if you keep taking your partner for granted...*Algoe, S. B. (2012). Find, remind, and bind: The functions of gratitude in everyday relationships. *Social and Personality Psychology Compass, 6*(6), 455–469. https://doi.org/10.1111/j.1751-9004.2012.00439.x

140 *Languishing relationships have a 1:1 ratio...*Gottman, J. M., Coan, J., Carrere, S., & Swanson, C. (1998). Predicting marital happiness and stability from newlywed interactions. *Journal of Marriage and the Family, 60*(1), 5. https://doi.org/10.2307/353438

141 *Touch is powerful...*Dobson, R. (2011, October 23). *How the power of touch reduces pain and even fights disease.* The Independent. https://www.independent.co.uk/life-style/health-and-families/health-news/how-the-power-of-touch-reduces-pain-and-even-fights-disease-419462.html

142 *even 1-second touches to the forearm...*Hertenstein, M. J., Keltner, D., App, B., Bulleit, B. A., & Jaskolka, A. R. (2006). Touch communicates distinct emotions. *Emotion, 6*(3), 528–533. https://doi.org/10.1037/1528-3542.6.3.528

142 *If, however, they committed to one person...*Lydon, J. E., Meana, M., Sepinwall, D., Richards, N., & Mayman, S. (1999). The commitment calibration hypothesis: When do people devalue attractive alternatives? *Personality and Social Psychology Bulletin, 25*(2), 152–161. https://doi.org/10.1177/0146167299025002002

145 *Dying and suffering—6-inch spikes driven into His extremities...*Mansfield, S. (2013). *Killing Jesus: The unknown conspiracy behind the world's most famous execution.* Worthy Publishing.

Commandment VII: *Thou Shalt Slow Down*

151 *Henry grew up just outside Boston...*Walls, L. D. (2018). *Henry David Thoreau: A life.* The University of Chicago Press.

153 *Per a recent stress survey...*American Psychological Association. (2017, November 1). *Stress in America: The state of our nation.* https://www.apa.org/news/press/releases/stress/2017/state-nation.pdf

153 *Chronic stress accelerates aging by shortening our telomeres...*Epel, E. S., Blackburn, E. H., Lin, J., Dhabhar, F. S., Adler, N. E., Morrow, J. D., & Cawthon, R. M. (2004). Accelerated telomere shortening in response to life stress. *Proceedings of the National Academy of Sciences, 101*(49), 17312–17315. https://doi.org/10.1073/pnas.0407162101

153 *It's also linked to suppressed thyroid function...*Scott, E. (2021, January 5). *What you need to know about the stress hormone.* Verywell Mind. https://www.verywellmind.com/cortisol-and-stress-how-to-stay-healthy-3145080

154 *Chronic stress also increases our risk for liver cirrhosis*...Bieliauskas, L. A. (2020). *Stress and its relationship to health and illness.* Routledge.

154 *undue stress hormones (e.g., cortisol) facilitates autoimmune*...Soares, N. M., Pereira, G. M., Altmann, V., de Almeida, R. M., & Rieder, C. R. (2018). Cortisol levels, motor, cognitive and behavioral symptoms in Parkinson's disease: A systematic review. *Journal of Neural Transmission, 126*(3), 219–232. https://doi.org/10.1007/s00702-018-1947-4

154 *It impairs basic biological functions*...Walker, M. (2017). *Why we sleep: Unlocking the power of sleep and dreams.* Scribner.

154 *people kept awake for 24 hours*...Alhola, P., & Polo-Kantola, P. (2007). *Sleep deprivation: Impact on cognitive performance.* Neuropsychiatric disease and treatment. https://www.ncbi.nlm.nih.gov/pubmed/19300585

154 *Sleep deprivation has also contributed*...Belenky, G., Penetar, D. M., Thorne, D., Popp, K., Leu, J., Thomas, M., Sing, H., Balkin, T., Wesensten, N., & Redmond, D. (1994, January 1). *The effects of sleep deprivation on performance during continuous combat operations.* https://www.ncbi.nlm.nih.gov/books/NBK209071/

154 *Nearly 90% of Americans*...American Psychological Association. (2017, February 23). *Stress in America: Coping with change.* https://www.apa.org/news/press/releases/stress/2017/technology-social-media.pdf

154 *People generally engage with their phone*...Winnick, M. (2016, June 16). *Putting a finger on our phone obsession.* Resources for remote, qualitative and in-context research. https://blog.dscout.com/mobile-touches

154 *67% of men and 25% of women*...Wilson, T. D., Reinhard, D. A., Westgate, E. C., Gilbert, D. T., Ellerbeck, N., Hahn, C., Brown, C. L., & Shaked, A. (2014). Just think: The challenges of the disengaged mind. *Science, 345*(6192), 75–77. https://doi.org/10.1126/science.1250830

154 *Days later, I read about "text neck"*...Al-Hadidi, F., Bsisu, I., AlRyalat, S. A., Al-Zu'bi, B., Bsisu, R., Hamdan, M., Kanaan, T., Yasin, M., & Samarah, O. (2019). Association between mobile phone use and neck pain in university students: A cross-sectional study using numeric rating scale for evaluation of neck pain. *PloS ONE, 14*(5). https://doi.org/10.1371/journal.pone.0217231

154 *Per the Centers for Disease Control*...Centers for Disease Control and Prevention. (2017, March 21). *Drowsy Driving.* Centers for Disease Control and Prevention. https://www.cdc.gov/sleep/about_sleep/drowsy_driving.html

155 *People with internet addiction have shown brain atrophy*...Chen, C., Yen, J., Wang, P. Liu, G., Yen, C., & Ko, C. (2016). Altered functional connectivity of the insula and nucleus accumbens in internet gaming disorder: A resting state fmri study. *European Addiction Research, 22*(4), 192–200. https://doi.org/10.1159/000440716

Lin, X., Dong, G., Wang, Q., & Du, X. (2015). Abnormal gray matter and white matter volume in 'internet gaming addicts.' *Addictive Behaviors, 40,* 137–143. https://doi.org/10.1016/j.addbeh.2014.09.010

Yuan, K., Cheng, P., Dong, T., Bi, Y., Xing, L., Yu, D., Zhao, L., Dong, M., von Deneen, K. M., Liu, Y., Qin, W., & Tian, J. (2013). Cortical thickness abnormalities in late adolescence with online gaming addiction. *PLoS ONE, 8*(1). https://doi.org/10.1371/journal.pone.0053055

Zhou, Y., Lin, F., Du, Y., Qin, L., Zhao, Z., Xu, J., & Lei, H. (2011). Gray matter abnormalities in internet addiction: A voxel-based morphometry study. *European Journal of Radiology, 79*(1), 92–95. https://doi.org/10.1016/j.ejrad.2009.10.025

155 *Further, every buzz jolts our nervous system*...Price, C. (2019, April 24). Putting down your phone may help you live longer. *New York Times.* https://www.nytimes.com/2019/04/24/well/mind/putting-down-your-phone-may-help-you-live-longer.html

157 *We rarely play*...Schor, J. B. (1992). *The overworked American: The unexpected decline of leisure.* Basic Books.

157 *Play teaches us teamwork*...Elkind, D. E. (2007). *The power of play: Learning what comes naturally.* Da Capo Press.

157 *Negative emotions—like those facilitated by stress*...Fredrickson, B. L. (2001). The role of positive emotions in positive psychology: The broaden-and-build theory of positive emotions. *American Psychologist, 56*(3), 218–226. https://doi.org/10.1037/0003-066x.56.3.218

157 *Play also increases our happiness*...Yogman, M., Garner, A., Hutchinson, J., Hirsh-Pasek, K., & Golinkoff, R. M. (2018). The power of play: A pediatric role in enhancing development in young children. *Pediatrics, 142*(3). https://doi.org/10.1542/peds.2018-2058

160 *Insecurity creates needless suffering*...Young, J. E., & Klosko, J. S. (1994). *Reinventing your life: How to break free from negative life patterns and feel good again.* Plume.

175   *Between 1993-2017, maximum speed limit increases...*Farmer, C. M. (2019, April). *The effects of higher speed limits on traffic fatalities in the United States, 1993–2017.* https://www.iihs.org/api/datastoredocument/bibliography/2188#:~:text=Traffic%20fatalities%20in%20the%20U.S.,speed%20limits%20had%20not%20increased.&text=Each%205%20mph%20increase%20in%20the%20maximum%20speed%20limit%20for,2.8%25%20increase%20on%20other%20roads

177   *doing what we* <u>*must*</u> *do...*Palmer, P. J. (2000). *Let your life speak: Listening for the voice of vocation.* Jossey-Bass.

Commandment VIII: *Thou Shalt Befriend Nature*

181   *John and his family emigrated from Scotland...*Worster, D. (2008). *A passion for nature: The life of John Muir.* Oxford University Press.

182   *Through all the wonderful, eventful centuries...*Muir, J. (2020). *Our national parks: Historic explorations of priceless American treasures.* Doublebit Press.

182   *Ralph Waldo Emerson, Henry David Thoreau, and John Muir...*Nichols, A. (2006). *Emerson, Thoreau, and the transcendentalist movement.* The Great Courses.

182   *When Emerson offered Muir a job...*Tallmadge, J. (1997). *Meeting the tree of life: A teacher's path.* University of Utah Press.

183   *According to a national survey from 2016...*U.S. Department of Health and Human Services. (2016, June 22). *Americans spent $30.2 billion out-of-pocket on complementary health approaches.* National Center for Complementary and Integrative Health. https://www.nccih.nih.gov/news/press-releases/americans-spent-302-billion-outofpocket-on-complementary-health-approaches

183   *people typically only experience nature...*The Nature of Americans. (2017). *The Nature of Americans National Report: Disconnection and recommendations for reconnection.* https://natureofamericans.org/

White, M. P., Alcock, I., Grellier, J., Wheeler, B. W., Hartig, T., Warber, S. L., Bone, A., Depledge, M. H., & Fleming, L. E. (2019). Spending at least 120 minutes a week in nature is associated with good health and wellbeing. *Scientific Reports, 9*(1). https://doi.org/10.1038/s41598-019-44097-3

183   *Like ecosystems, our bodies have four...*Covey, S. R. (2020). *The 7 habits of highly effective people.* Simon & Schuster.

184 *83% of dog owners visit their vet annually...*American Veterinary Medical Association. (2017). *AVMA Pet ownership and demographics sourcebook.* https://www.avma.org/sites/default/files/resources/AVMA-Pet-Demographics-Executive-Summary.pdf

184 *30% of people visit their doctor annually...*Michas, F. (2018, September 26). *Frequency U.S. adults visited or consulted a primary care physician as of 2018.* Statista. https://www.statista.com/statistics/916781/primary-care-physician-visit-frequency-among-adults-us/

184 *Noise creates stress...*Münzel, T., Sørensen, M., Schmidt, F., Schmidt, E., Steven, S., Kröller-Schön, S., & Daiber, A. (2018). The adverse effects of environmental noise exposure on oxidative stress and cardiovascular risk. *Antioxidants & Redox Signaling, 28*(9), 873–908. https://doi.org/10.1089/ars.2017.7118

184 *people who listened to aircraft noise...*Halperin, D. (2014). Environmental noise and sleep disturbances: A threat to health? *Sleep Science, 7*(4), 209–212. https://doi.org/10.1016/j.slsci.2014.11.003

184 *Spending two nights in the forest...*Miyazaki, Y., Lee, J., Park, B.-J., Tsunetsugu, Y., & Matsunaga, K. (2011). Preventive medical effects of nature therapy. *Nippon Eiseigaku Zasshi (Japanese Journal of Hygiene), 66*(4), 651–656. https://doi.org/10.1265/jjh.66.651

Song, C., Ikei, H., & Miyazaki, Y. (2016). Physiological effects of nature therapy: A review of the research in Japan. *International Journal of Environmental Research and Public Health, 13*(8), 781. https://doi.org/10.3390/ijerph13080781

184 *Data across 20 studies...*Ideno, Y., Hayashi, K., Abe, Y., Ueda, K., Iso, H., Noda, M., Lee, J.-S., & Suzuki, S. (2017). Blood pressure-lowering effect of Shinrin-yoku (Forest bathing): A systematic review and meta-analysis. *BMC Complementary and Alternative Medicine, 17*(1). https://doi.org/10.1186/s12906-017-1912-z

185 *walking in a forest, compared to walking in a city...*Lanki, T., Siponen, T., Ojala, A., Korpela, K., Pennanen, A., Tiittanen, P., Tsunetsugu, Y., Kagawa, T., & Tyrväinen, L. (2017). Acute effects of visits to urban green environments on cardiovascular physiology in women: A field experiment. *Environmental Research, 159,* 176–185. https://doi.org/10.1016/j.envres.2017.07.039

185 *Professional athletes have RHRs in the 40s...*Baggish, A. L., & Wood, M. J. (2011). Athlete's heart and cardiovascular care of the athlete. *Circulation, 123*(23), 2723–2735. https://doi.org/10.1161/circulationaha.110.981571

185 *patients who recently had their gallbladders removed...*Ulrich, R. (1984). View through a window may influence recovery from surgery. *Science, 224*(4647), 420–421. https://doi.org/10.1126/science.6143402

186 *Aristotle walked around...*Athensliving. (2015, May 8). *Aristotle's Lyceum.* Athens Living Diaries. https://athensliving.wordpress.com/2015/04/09/aristotles-lyceum/

186 *Dr. Edward Jenner...*Dewees, W. B. (1896). Eulogy on Jenner. *The Journal of the American Medical Association, XXVII*(22), 1128–1130. https://doi.org/10.1001/jama.1896.02431000004001a

186 *St. Thomas Aquinas created the "Five Ways"...*Barron, B. (2011). *Catholicism: A journey to the heart of faith.* Image.

186 *Aristotle founded the Peripatetic school at the Lyceum...*Athensliving. (2015, May 8). *Aristotle's Lyceum.* Athens Living Diaries. https://athensliving.wordpress.com/2015/04/09/aristotles-lyceum/

187 *a 10-decibel increase in aircraft noise...*Floud, S., Vigna-Taglianti, F., Hansell, A., Blangiardo, M., Houthuijs, D., Breugelmans, O., Cadum, E., Babisch, W., Selander, J., Pershagen, G., Antoniotti, M. C., Pisani, S., Dimakopoulou, K., Haralabidis, A. S., Velonakis, V., & Jarup, L. (2010). Medication use in relation to noise from aircraft and road traffic in six European countries: Results of the HYENA study. *Occupational and Environmental Medicine, 68*(7), 518–524. https://doi.org/10.1136/oem.2010.058586

187 *people living near noisy streets...*Orban, E., McDonald, K., Sutcliffe, R., Hoffmann, B., Fuks, K. B., Dragano, N., Viehmann, A., Erbel, R., Jöckel, K.-H., Pundt, N., & Moebus, S. (2016). Residential road traffic noise and high depressive symptoms after five years of follow-up: Results from the Heinz Nixdorf Recall Study. *Environmental Health Perspectives, 124*(5), 578–585. https://doi.org/10.1289/ehp.1409400

188 *Walking in the woods for 50 minutes...*Bratman, G. N., Daily, G. C., Levy, B. J., & Gross, J. J. (2015). The benefits of nature experience: Improved affect and cognition. *Landscape and Urban Planning, 138*, 41–50. https://doi.org/10.1016/j.landurbplan.2015.02.005

201   *the first words spoken by angels*...Hamstra, B. (2012, January 13). *Why does the angel keep saying that?* Sabbath School Net Bible Study and Discussion. https://ssnet.org/blog/why-does-the-angel-keep-saying-that/

Commandment IX: *Thou Shalt Give Thanks*

205   *Growing up, Dorothy's parents rarely discussed God*...Loughery, J., & Randolph, B. (2020). *Dorothy Day: Dissenting voice of the American century.* Simon & Schuster.

207   *Physician, Dr. Ali Binazir, calculated*...Binazir, A. (2011, August 16). *Why you are a miracle.* HuffPost. https://www.huffpost.com/entry/probability-being-born_b_877853

207   *you must have sex five consecutive days*...Mayo Foundation for Medical Education and Research. (2019, October 5). *How to get pregnant.* Mayo Clinic. https://www.mayoclinic.org/healthy-lifestyle/getting-pregnant/in-depth/how-to-get-pregnant/art-20047611

208   *Only 26% of married couples have sex weekly*...Montgomery, H. (2018, June 11). *How often do 'normal' couples have sex?* Healthline. https://www.healthline.com/health/baby/how-often-do-normal-couples-have-sex

208   *About 30% of women have irregular ovulation*...WebMD. (2020, June 21). *Irregular periods, getting pregnant, and infertility.* WebMD. https://www.webmd.com/infertility-and-reproduction/irregular-periods-and-getting-pregnant

208   *200 million sperm are released*...Chertoff, J. (2018, August 29). *Normal sperm count: Understanding your semen analysis.* Healthline. https://www.healthline.com/health/mens-health/normal-sperm-count

208   *If the sperm is strong and healthy*...Helo, S. (2020, June 12). *Abnormal sperm morphology: What does it mean?* Mayo Clinic. https://www.mayoclinic.org/diseases-conditions/male-infertility/expert-answers/sperm-morphology/faq-20057760

208   *Of the approximately 10,000 sperm*...Suarez, S. S., & Pacey, A. A. (2005). Sperm transport in the female reproductive tract. *Human Reproduction Update, 12*(1), 23–37. https://doi.org/10.1093/humupd/dmi047

208   *around 200 get to the egg*...Alberts, B. (2008). *Molecular biology of the cell.* Garland Science.

208 *Almost 15% of couples are infertile...*Agarwal, A., Mulgund, A., Hamada, A., & Chyatte, M. R. (2015). A unique view on male infertility around the globe. *Reproductive Biology and Endocrinology, 13*(1). https://doi.org/10.1186/s12958-015-0032-1

208 *more than two cups of coffee daily can decrease fertility...*Mayo Foundation for Medical Education and Research. (2020, April 25). *Can lifestyle choices boost my chance of getting pregnant?* Mayo Clinic. https://www.mayoclinic.org/healthy-lifestyle/getting-pregnant/in-depth/female-fertility/art-20045887

208 *as can certain medications...*ScienceDaily. (2015, June 11). *Non-steroidal anti-inflammatory drugs inhibit ovulation after just 10 days.* ScienceDaily. https://www.sciencedaily.com/releases/2015/06/150611082124.htm

208 *women either overweight or underweight...*Mayo Foundation for Medical Education and Research. (2019, October 5). *How to get pregnant.* Mayo Clinic. https://www.mayoclinic.org/healthy-lifestyle/getting-pregnant/in-depth/how-to-get-pregnant/art-20047611

208 *Excessive testosterone, however, can impede sperm production...*Crosnoe, L. E., Grober, E., Ohl, D., & Kim, E. D. (2013). Exogenous testosterone: A preventable cause of male infertility. *Translational Andrology and Urology, 2*(2), 106–113. https://doi.org/10.3978/j.issn.2223-4683.2013.06.01

208 *Men should also avoid tobacco, marijuana, and other drugs...*Duca, Y., Aversa, A., Condorelli, R. A., Calogero, A. E., & La Vignera, S. (2019). Substance abuse and male hypogonadism. *Journal of Clinical Medicine, 8*(5), 732. https://doi.org/10.3390/jcm8050732

208 *It's also wise for men to curb exposure to radiation...*Kesari, K. K., Agarwal, A., & Henkel, R. (2018). Radiations and male fertility. *Reproductive Biology and Endocrinology, 16*(1). https://doi.org/10.1186/s12958-018-0431-1

Gorpinchenko, I., Nikitin, O., Banyra, O., & Shulyak, A. (2014). The influence of direct mobile phone radiation on sperm quality. *Central European Journal of Urology, 67*(01), 65–71. https://doi.org/10.5173/ceju.2014.01.art14

232 *Dicyanoacetylene burns hot like the sun...*Kirshenbaum, A. D., & Grosse, A. V. (1956). The combustion of carbon subnitride, C_4N_2, and a chemical method for the production of continuous temperatures in the range of 5000-6000°K. *Journal of the American Chemical Society, 78*(9), 2020–2020. https://doi.org/10.1021/ja01590a075

234 *Be more grateful for life by "thinking gratefully"*...Froh, J. J., & Bono, G. (2014). *Making grateful kids: The science of building character.* Templeton Press.

Froh, J. J., Bono, G., Fan, J., Emmons, R. A., Henderson, K., Harris, C., Leggio, H., & Wood, A. M. (2014). Nice thinking! An educational intervention that teaches children to think gratefully. *School Psychology Review,* 43(2), 132–152. https://doi.org/10.1080/02796015.2014.12087440

Commandment X: *Thou Shalt Master Mission*

237 *Though a descendent of royalty, Joseph swung a hammer*...Meschler, M. (2017). *The truth about Saint Joseph: Encountering the most hidden of saints.* Sophia Institute Press.

238 *Another 3.4 lbs. can decrease an athlete's*...Inacio, M., Dipietro, L., Visek, A. J., & Miller, T. A. (2011). Influence of upper-body external loading on anaerobic exercise performance. *Journal of Strength and Conditioning Research,* 25(4), 896–902. https://doi.org/10.1519/jsc.0b013e3182082ae7

238 *Another 2-5 lbs. can decrease a racehorse's*...Wellman, L. (1999, December 19). *The impact of weight on the performance of a racehorse.* http://www. goto4winds.com/horse/weighthorse2.html

239 *about 66% of Americans get their car washed*...Business Wire. (2021, June 17). *United States car wash service market report 2021-2028.* https://www. businesswire.com/news/home/20210617005575/en/United-States-Car-Wash-Service-Market-Report-2021-2028---ResearchAndMarkets.com

239 *within several years, the U.S. Department of Commerce expects*...Cleaning service marketing plan. (n.d.). https://www.mplans.com/cleaning_service_ marketing_plan/marketing_strategy_fc.php.

239 *only 2% of Catholics regularly attend confession*...Castaldo, C. (2020, April 8). *What did the pope really say about confession during COVID-19?* ChristianityToday.com. https://www.christianitytoday.com/ct/2020/april-web-only/pope-coronavirus-francis-confession-take-sorrows-to-god.html

239 *Sin is an offense against God that contradicts reason*...Libreria Editrice Vaticana. (1994). *Catechism of the Catholic Church.*

243 *Assume there was a pond about 165 feet wide*...Greene, B. (2003). *The elegant universe teacher's guide.* https://www.pbs.org/wgbh/nova/teachers/ activities/pdf/3012_elegant.pdf

243 *If two atomic nuclei combine...*Specktor, B. (2020, August 31). *Russia de-classifies footage of 'Tsar BOMBA' - The most powerful nuclear bomb in history.* LiveScience. https://www.livescience.com/tsar-bomba-se-cret-test-footage-declassified.html

247 *Gangs recently roamed Kruger National Park...*CBS News. (2001, July 18). *The delinquents.* CBS News. https://www.cbsnews.com/news/the-delin-quents/

"Weird" Science

269 Read the books from *God's Library* to learn about the *"Weird" Science.*

~~Deleted~~ Scenes

277 *Culture shapes our values...*Roccas, S., & Sagiv, L. (2009). Personal values and behavior: Taking the cultural context into account. *Social and Personality Psychology Compass, 4*(1), 30–41. https://doi.org/10.1111/j.1751-9004.2009.00234.x

277 *Danes, compared to Americans, also work less hours per week...*Sauter, M. B. (2020, January 28). *Working for a living: What countries have shorter, or longer, work weeks than the US?* USA Today. https://www.usatoday.com/story/money/2020/01/28/the-length-of-a-typical-work-week-around-the-world/41060709/

277 *and have more (government-funded) vacation weeks (5 vs. 0)...*Harrington, J. (2019, July 23). *Wouldn't you like 30 mandated days off? Here are the countries with the most vacation days.* USA Today. https://www.usatoday.com/story/money/2019/07/23/paid-time-off-countries-with-the-most-va-cation-days-brazil-france/39702323/

277 *Compared to America, Bhutan is...*Belic, R. (2012). *Happy* [Film; DVD]. Passion River.

     Knaster, M. (2008, December 1). *Bhutan at a crossroads.* Greater Good. https://greatergood.berkeley.edu/article/item/bhutan_crossroads

278 *Eating disorders, for example, are sometimes called...*Markey, C. N. (2004). Culture and the development of eating disorders: A tri-partite model. *Eating Disorders, 12*(2), 139-156. https://doi.org/10.1080/10640260490445041

278 *Females aged 15-24 are the most at-risk group*...Smink, F. R., van Hoeken, D., & Hoek, H. W. (2012). Epidemiology of eating disorders: Incidence, prevalence and mortality rates. *Current Psychiatry Reports, 14*(4), 406–414. https://doi.org/10.1007/s11920-012-0282-y

278 *an ongoing study of adolescent and emerging adult females*...Lai, K. Y. (2000). Anorexia nervosa in Chinese adolescents—does culture make a difference? *Journal of Adolescence, 23*(5), 561–568. https://doi.org/10.1006/jado.2000.0343

278 *Even by 3rd grade, girls often believe*...American Psychological Association, Task Force on the Sexualization of Girls. (2007). *Report of the APA task force on the sexualization of girls.* Washington, DC: American Psychological Association. Retrieved from http://www.apa.org/pi/wpo/sexualization.html

Girlguiding response to the Women and Equalities Committee inquiry 'Changing the perfect picture: an inquiry into body image.' girlguiding.org.UK. (2020, July). https://www.girlguiding.org.uk/globalassets/docs-and-resources/research-and-campaigns/girlguiding-response-to-the-inquiry-on-body-image-july-2020.pdf

Girls' attitudes survey. Girlguiding. (n.d.). https://www.girlguiding.org.uk/girlsattitudes/

279 *approximately 10 million American boys and men*...Hudson, J. I., Hiripi, E., Pope, Jr., H. G., & Kessler, R. C. (2007). The prevalence and correlates of eating disorders in the National Comorbidity Survey Replication. *Biological Psychiatry, 61*(3), 348-358. https://pubmed.ncbi.nlm.nih.gov/16815322/

279 *men are excessively exercising*...Anawalt, B. D. (2019). Diagnosis and management of anabolic androgenic steroid use. *The Journal of Clinical Endocrinology & Metabolism, 104*(7), 2490–2500. https://doi.org/10.1210/jc.2018-01882

Pope, H. G., Khalsa, J. H., & Bhasin, S. (2017). Body image disorders and abuse of anabolic-androgenic steroids among men. *JAMA, 317*(1), 23. https://doi.org/10.1001/jama.2016.17441

281 *Developed by clinical psychologists*...Tedeschi, R. G., & Calhoun, L. G. (2004). Posttraumatic growth: Conceptual foundations and empirical evidence. *Psychological Inquiry, 15*(1), 1–18. https://doi.org/10.1207/s15327965pli1501_01

285 *A recent poll conducted by YouGov...*Ballard, J. (2019, July 30). *Millennials are the loneliest generation.* YouGov. https://today.yougov.com/topics/lifestyle/articles-reports/2019/07/30/loneliness-friendship-new-friends-poll-survey

285 *Loneliness increases our risk of heart disease and stroke...*Holt-Lunstad, J., Smith, T. B., Baker, M., Harris, T., & Stephenson, D. (2015). Loneliness and social isolation as risk factors for mortality: A meta-analytic review. *Perspectives on Psychological Science, 10*(2), 227-237. https://doi.org/10.1177/1745691614568352

286 *Per the New York Daily News...*Pesce, N. L. (2018, April 12). *'Selfish,' Kim Kardashian's book with 300 Selfies, is bound for a coffee table near you.* nydailynews.com. https://www.nydailynews.com/entertainment/theater-arts/selfish-kim-kardashian-selfie-book-bound-thrill-fans-article-1.2185387

286 *18-24 year-olds send and receive 110 texts...*Smith, A. (2011, September 19). *How Americans use text messaging.* Pew Research Center: Internet, Science & Tech. https://www.pewresearch.org/internet/2011/09/19/how-americans-use-text-messaging/

This article, however, indicates that on a typical day 18-24 year-olds send and receive about 128 texts, and 25-34 year-olds send and receive about 75 texts: Burke, K. (2016, May 18). *How many texts do people send every day (2018)?* https://www.textrequest.com/blog/how-many-texts-people-send-per-day/

286 *only 53% of Americans report...*New Cigna study reveals loneliness at epidemic levels in America. Multivu. (2018). https://www.cigna.com/assets/docs/newsroom/loneliness-survey-2018-fact-sheet.pdf

286 *it also decreases your biological capacity for connection...*Fredrickson, B. L. (2013, March 23). *Your phone vs. your heart.* The New York Times. https://www.nytimes.com/2013/03/24/opinion/sunday/your-phone-vs-your-heart.html

Fredrickson, B. L., Cohn, M. A., Coffey, K. A., Pek, J., & Finkel, S. M. (2008). Open hearts build lives: Positive emotions, induced through loving-kindness meditation, build consequential personal resources. *Journal of Personality and Social Psychology, 95*(5), 1045–1062. https://doi.org/10.1037/a0013262

286 *Gatebox developed an Anime-inspired VR companion...*Jozuka, E., Chan, A., & Mulholland, T. (2018, December 29). *Beyond dimensions: The man who married a hologram.* CNN. https://www.cnn.com/2018/12/28/health/rise-of-digisexuals-intl/index.html

286 *Softbank Robotics invented the Pepper robot...Pepper the humanoid and programmable robot: SoftBank Robotics.* SoftBank Robotics. (n.d.). https://www.softbankrobotics.com/emea/en/pepper

286 *there's always Sony's robot dogs...*Neuman, S. (2018, May 1). *In Japan, old robot dogs get a Buddhist send-off.* NPR. https://www.npr.org/sections/thetwo-way/2018/05/01/607295346/in-japan-old-robot-dogs-get-a-buddhist-send-off

287 *According to the 2018 U.S. Census Bureau...Percent married among 18-to 34-year-olds: 1978 and 2018.* The United States Census Bureau. (2018, November 14). https://www.census.gov/library/visualizations/2018/comm/percent-married.html

291 *Two millennia later, 31% of people now follow Jesus...The changing global religious landscape.* Pew Research Center's Religion & Public Life Project. (2017, April 5). https://www.pewforum.org/2017/04/05/the-changing-global-religious-landscape/

9 781737 556725